Philosophers Speak f

From Aristotle to Plotinus

Edited by

T. V. SMITH

Phoenix Books

THE UNIVERSITY OF CHICAGO PRESS

CHICAGO & LONDON

This book, together with
FROM THALES TO PLATO (Phoenix Book P 8),
is also available in a one-volume, clothbound edition from
THE UNIVERSITY OF CHICAGO PRESS

THE UNIVERSITY OF CHICAGO PRESS, CHICAGO 60637
The University of Chicago Press, Ltd., London

International Standard Book Number: 0-226-76479-6
Library of Congress Catalog Card Number: 56-4949

PHILOSOPHIC OVERTONES

A PHILOSOPHER'S FAITH

That we shall be better and braver and less helpless if we think that we ought to enquire, than we should have been if we indulged in the idle fancy that there was no knowing and no use in seeking to know what we do not know;—that is a theme upon which I am ready to fight, in word and deed, to the utmost of my power.—PLATO.

A PHILOSOPHER'S CAUTION

It is the mark of an educated man to look for precision in each class of things just so far as the nature of the subject admits; it is evidently equally foolish to accept probable reasoning from a mathematician and to demand from a rhetorician scientific proofs.—ARISTOTLE.

A PHILOSOPHER'S PRAYER

Beloved Pan, and all ye other gods who haunt this place, give me beauty in the inward soul; and may the outward and inward man be at one. May I reckon the wise to be the wealthy, and may I have such a quantity of gold as a temperate man and he only can bear and carry.—SOCRATES.

A PHILOSOPHER'S ADVICE

Absorb not all that you wish, but all that you can hold. Only be of sound mind, and then you will be able to hold all that you wish. For the more the mind receives, the more does it expand.

"What then?" you say, "do we not know certain men who have sat for many years at the feet of a philosopher and yet have not acquired the slightest tinge of wisdom?" Of course I know such men. There are indeed persevering gentlemen who stick at it; I do not call them pupils of the wise, but merely "squatters." . . . . This class, as you will see, constitutes a large part of the listeners,—who regard the philosopher's lecture-room merely as a sort of lounging-place for their leisure. They do not set about to lay aside any faults there, or to receive a rule of life, by which they may test their characters; they merely wish to enjoy to the full the delights of the ear. . . . . But the true hearer is ravished and stirred by the beauty of the subject matter, not by the jingle of empty words. When a bold word has been uttered in defiance of death, or a saucy fling in defiance of Fortune, we take delight in acting straightway upon that which we have heard. Men are impressed by such words, and become what they are bidden to be. . . . . It is easy to rouse a listener so that he will crave righteousness; for Nature has laid the foundations and planted the seeds of virtue in us all.—Seneca.

ACKNOWLEDGMENTS

TO PERSONS

To colleagues, Charles W. Morris, Charles Hartshorne, Charner M. Perry, and Clifford P. Osborne—thanks, all. To the latter two special acknowledgments: to Professor Perry for proofreading, an onerous job done at home at a difficult time while I dreamed in modern Athens of the scenes and thoughts which this book commemorates, and to Dr. Osborne for critical aid on the introductions throughout, particularly on Aristotle; for translating into English the intricate turns of Gorgias' skepticism as reported by Sextus Empiricus; and for aid on the proof.

TO PUBLISHERS

To Kegan Paul, Trench, Trubner and Company and Charles Scribner's Sons, respectively, the English and the American publishers of Fairbanks' *The First Philosophers of Greece*, from which all selections from the pre-Socratics are taken, save as otherwise indicated. To the latter, also, for the material on Democritus. To the Open Court Publishing Company for A. E. Taylor's translation of the first book of Aristotle's *Metaphysics*. To the Macmillan Company for Welldon's translation of Aristotle's *Ethics*, and the few excerpts, indicated in the text, from the Davies and Vaughan translation of Plato's *Republic*.

But most of all to Professor Edward Capps, the American editor of the "Loeb Classical Library" series, from which the majority of my selections are taken. Acknowledgment is made in each several case and at the proper place. But neither that nor this can begin to indicate my debt to this magnificent library. The editor has not only done the handsome thing, which exact justice would not have required, of letting me use a large body of material without charge, but has made it possible in this way for me to call attention in fashion exemplary to the greatest storehouse in English of classic wisdom from Greece and Rome. Every student who uses this book will, I hope, treasure for present and later use the knowledge of where he can get more, much more, of such mellow reflection as he has here sampled from this ever growing Loeb series.

TABLE OF CONTENTS

A PANORAMA

In our earlier volume, *From Thales to Plato*, we came a long way: from Greek animism and superstition to Platonic sophistication. But there is a journey yet before us, an expanse to be negotiated between speculation and knowledge, between theory and practice. In this volume we are to see the major insights of Plato corrected, consolidated, and turned to imperial account in the governance of men.

The Romans were Greeks in cultural aspiration, but they were moderns in converting know-*why* into know-*how*. Aristotle is the key figure between the old speculative bent of Plato and the new practicalism of Rome.

In seeking, like Plato, the good life for men, Aristotle appropriated a distinction which Plato had thought invidious. The Stagirite had discerned that what we have come to call "the pursuit of happiness" must normally be the happiness of *pursuit;* for men are active animals, even before they are social animals and long before they are rational. But there is an activity of the vegetable, an activity of the animal, and then an activity which is above osmosis and more than locomotion. This is contemplation; and it is peculiarly human, representing man at his highest and best. Such an eventuation is Plato still alive in his reluctant student; but man is both vegetable and animal and so partakes of their forms of activity. By stretching the concept of "activity" and rendering all forms of it respectable, Aristotle made it possible for the Romans to remain cultural Greeks without changing their categories.

Man can, then, be rational in following rules which he has not made, and this is honorable. He can be rational in making rules to be followed, and this is honorable. He can be rational in discerning the reasonableness of rules which he follows or makes, and this is honorable—and spiritual as well.

To make reason to run like a thread through the whole of man's activity is to give integrity to culture and continuity to integrity. So to see is to achieve a preview of Aristotle's emendation of classic Greek theory and his contribution to the Roman, indeed to the Christian, way.

CHAPTER I
ARISTOTLE
HIS SYNTHESIS IN ITS HISTORICAL SETTING

<small>ARISTOTLE ON HIS PREDECESSORS (*Metaphysics*)</small>

After a childhood in the atmosphere of the court of the King of Macedon, where his father was physician; after some twenty years as a student and special worker in Plato's Academy at Athens; after being tutor to Alexander the Great—after enough experience to have made a complete life for an ordinary man, Aristotle (384–322) settled down to his vocation in Athens at the head of his own school, the Lyceum. He directed what we should call research and wrote voluminously. Estimates of his output range from four hundred to one thousand manuscripts. What he published during his lifetime was literary dialogues after the manner of Plato. What we have as his work is lecture notes and plans for, and results of, his teaching. He inherited Plato's major problem of the changing versus the changeless, which problem he saw to be still unsolved. Upon it he brought to bear all speculation down to his time. The changeable yields, as with Plato, only opinion; knowledge requires unchanging objects. But Plato's statement of the continuity between the two (i.e., the doctrine of ideas) Aristotle believed to widen rather than to close the gap between the two realms. His criticisms of this doctrine are classic. A theory of development became his own positive reliance. This theory he not only proclaimed, as we shall see in his doctrine of the potential becoming actual through form, but he also illustrated it by showing, as we are at once to see, how his philosophy grew out of and actualized the doctrines of his predecessors. Moreover, his study of the constitutions of Greek city-states, especially the one of Athens, now available, is genuinely genetic in tone. The formal outline of Aristotle's lifework comprises three main kinds of science—theoretical, practical, and poetical. The first is subdivided into physics, mathematics, and first philosophy (metaphysics) or theology. The second falls under two headings, politics and ethics, although for Aristotle ethics is really a subdivision of politics. The third includes the useful and the fine arts. Underlying all of these sciences is logic, which may be defined as a scientific methodology prerequisite to the study of any of the special sciences.

.   .   .

ARISTOTLE ON HIS PREDECESSORS

Being the first book of the *Metaphysics* (A. E. Taylor's trans.). With permission from and acknowledgments to the Open Court Publishing Company, Chicago.

I. All mankind have an instinctive desire of knowledge. This is illustrated by our enjoyment of our sense-perceptions. Even apart from their utility they are enjoyed for their own sake, and above all the others the perceptions of the eye. For we prize sight, speaking roughly, above everything else, not merely as a guide to action, but even when we are not contemplating any action. The reason of this is that of all the senses sight gives us most information and reveals many specific qualities. Now, all animals, when they come into the world, are provided by nature with sensation, but in some of them memory does not result from their sensations, while in others it does. Hence the latter are both more intelligent and more able to learn than those which are incapable of memory. Creatures like the bee, and any other similar species which there may be, which cannot hear sounds, are intelligent without the power to learn; those which, in addition to memory, possess this sense *learn*.

Now, all the animals live by the guidance of their presentations and memories, but only partake to a trifling degree of *experience*, but the human species lives also by the guidance of rules of art and reflective inferences. In man memory gives rise to *experience*, since repeated memories of the same thing acquire the character of a single experience. [Experience, in fact, seems to be very similar to science and art.] And science and art in man are a product of experience. For "experience has created art," as Polus correctly remarks, "but inexperience chance." Art comes into being when many observations of experience give rise to a single universal conviction about a class of similar cases. Thus to be convinced that such and such a treatment was good for Callias when suffering from such and such an ailment, and again for Socrates, and similarly in each of many individual cases, is a result of *experience*, but the conviction that it was found beneficial to *all* persons of a specific constitution, whom we have placed together as a definite class, when suffering from a specific ailment—e.g., sufferers from catarrh, or bile, or fever—is an affair of *art*. Now, for purposes of practice experience is recognized to be not inferior to art; indeed, we observe that persons of experience are actually more successful than those who possess theory without experience. The reason of this is that experience is acquaintance with individual facts, but art with general rules, and all action and production is concerned with the individual. Thus the physician does not cure *man*, except in an accidental sense, but Callias or Socrates or some other individual person of whom it is an *accident* to be a man. Hence, if one possesses the theory without the experience, and is acquainted with the universal concept, but not with the individual fact contained under it, he will often go wrong in his treatment; for what has to be treated is the individual.

In spite of this, however, we ascribe *knowledge* and *understanding* to art rather than to *experience*, and regard artists as *wiser* than persons of mere experience, thus implying that *wisdom* is rather to be ascribed to men in all cases in proportion to their *knowledge*. This is because the former class know the *reason* for the thing; the latter not. Persons of mere experience know the *that*, but not the *why*; the others recognize the *why* and the reason. Hence, too, in every department master workmen are held in higher esteem and thought to know more and to be wiser than manual workers, because they know the reasons for what is done, while manual workers, it is held, are like some inanimate things which produce a result (e.g., fire *burns*), but produce it without any knowledge of it. Thus we estimate superiority in wisdom not by skill in practice, but by the possession of theory and the comprehension of reasons. In general, too, it is an indication of wisdom to be able to teach others, and on this ground, also, we regard art as more truly knowledge than experience; the artist can teach, the man of mere experience cannot. Again, we hold that none of our sense-perceptions is wisdom, though it is they which give us the most assured knowledge of indi-

vidual facts. Still, they do not tell us the *reason why* about anything; e.g., they do not tell us *why* fire is hot, but merely the fact
that it is hot. Hence it was natural that in the earliest times the inventor of any art which goes beyond the common sense-perceptions
of mankind should be universally admired, not merely for any
utility to be found in his inventions, but for the wisdom by which
he was distinguished from other men. But when a variety of arts
had been invented, some of them being concerned with the necessities and others with the social refinements of life, the inventors of
the latter were naturally always considered wiser than those of the
former because their knowledge was not directed to immediate
utility. Hence when everything of these kinds had been already
provided, those sciences were discovered which deal neither with
the necessities nor with the enjoyments of life, and this took place
earliest in regions where men had leisure. This is why the mathematical arts were first put together in Egypt, for in that country
the priestly caste were indulged with leisure.[1] (The difference between art and science and the other kindred concepts has been explained in our course on Ethics; the purpose of the present observations is simply to show that it is universally agreed that the object
of what is called *wisdom* is first causes and principles.) So, as we
have already said, the possessor of experience is recognized as wiser
than the possessor of any form of sense-perception, the artist as
wiser than the mere possessor of experience, the master craftsman
than the manual worker, the speculative sciences than the productive. Thus it is manifest that wisdom is a form of science which is
concerned with some kind of causes and principles.

II. Since we are in quest of this science, we have to ask what
kind of causes and principles are treated of by the science which is
wisdom? Well, the matter will perhaps become clearer if we enumerate the convictions which we currently hold about the wise man.
Well, we currently hold, first, that the wise man, so far as possible,
knows everything, but without possessing scientific knowledge of
the individual details. Secondly, that he is one who is capable of apprehending difficult things and matters which it is not easy for man
to apprehend; (for sense-perception is the common possession of all,

---

[1] Contrast the more historical remark of Herodotus, that Egyptian geometry
arose from the necessity of resurveying the land after the periodical inundations of
the Nile.

and hence easy, and is nothing wise). Again, that in every science he who is more exact and more competent to teach is the wiser man. Also that, among the various sciences, that which is pursued for its own sake and with a view to knowledge has a better claim to be considered wisdom than that which is pursued for its applications, and the more commanding science a better claim than the subsidiary. For the wise man, it is held, has not to be directed by others, but to direct them; it is not for him to take instructions from another, but for those who are less wise to take them from him.

Here, then, is an enumeration of our current convictions about wisdom and the wise. Now, of these marks that of *universality* of knowledge necessarily belongs to him whose knowledge has the highest generality, for in a sense he knows all that is subsumed under it. These most universal truths are also in general those which it is *hardest* for men to recognize, since they are most remote from sense-perception. And the most *exact* of the sciences are those which are most directly concerned with ultimate truths. For the sciences which depend on fewer principles are more exact than those in which additional assumptions are made; e.g., Arithmetic than Geometry. And, again, that science is more competent *to teach* which is more concerned with speculation on the causes of things, for in every case he who states the causes of a thing teaches. And knowledge and science *for their own sake* are found most of all in the science of that which is in the highest sense the object of knowledge. For he who chooses science for its own sake will give the highest preference to the highest science, and this is the science of that which is in the highest sense the object of knowledge. But the highest objects of knowledge are the ultimates and causes. For it is through them and as consequences of them that other truths are apprehended, not they through what is subordinate to them. And the most commanding among the sciences, more truly commanding than the subsidiary sciences, is that which apprehends the end for which each act must be done; this end is, in each individual case, the corresponding *good*, and universally the *highest* good in the universe. All these considerations indicate that the title in question is appropriate to one and the same science. For this science must be one which contemplates ultimate principles and causes; for the good or end is itself one type of cause. That it is not a *productive* science is clear, even from consideration of the earliest philosophies.

For men were first led to study philosophy, as indeed they are to-day, by *wonder*.[2] At first they felt wonder about the more super-ficial problems; afterward they advanced gradually by perplexing themselves over greater difficulties; e.g., the behavior of the moon, the phenomena of the sun [and stars], and the origination of the universe. Now, he who is perplexed and wonders believes himself to be ignorant. (Hence even the lover of myths is, in a sense, a phi-losopher, for a myth is a tissue of wonders.) Thus if they took to philosophy to escape ignorance, it is patent that they were pursuing science for the sake of knowledge itself, and not for any utilitarian applications. This is confirmed by the course of the historical de-velopment itself. For nearly all the requisites both of comfort and social refinement had been secured before the quest for this form of enlightenment began. So it is clear that we do not seek it for the sake of any ulterior application. Just as we call a man *free* who exists for his own ends, and not for those of another, so it is with this, which is the only *liberal* science; it alone of the sciences exists for its own sake.

Hence there would be justice in regarding the enjoyment of it as superhuman. For human nature is in many respects unfree. So, in the words of Simonides, "this meed belongs to God alone; for man, 'tis meet" to seek a science conformable to his estate. Indeed, if there is anything in what the poets say, and Deity is of an envious temper, it would be most natural that it should be shown here, and that all the preeminently gifted should be unlucky. But Deity can-not by any possibility be envious; rather, as the proverb has it, "Many are the lies of the bards," nor is it right to prize any other knowledge more highly than this. For the divinest of sciences is to be prized most highly; and this is the only science which de-serves that name, for two reasons. For that science is divine which it would be most fitting for God to possess, and also that science, if there is one, which deals with divine things. And this is the only science which has both these attributes. For it is universally ad-mitted that God is a cause and a first principle;[3] and, again, God

---

[2] An allusion to Plato, *Theaetetus*, 155d: "This emotion of wonder is very proper to a philosopher; for there is no other starting-point for philosophy."

[3] Hence Aristotle's own name for what his commentators called "metaphysics" is indifferently "first Philosophy" or "Theology." His doctrine of God as the su-preme efficient cause is more particularly contained in book Λ (12) of the present work.

must be thought to possess this science, either alone or in a superlative degree. To be sure, all the sciences are more indispensable, but none is nobler.

However, the acquisition of this science must in a sense lead to a condition which is the opposite of our original state of search. For, as has been said, all begin by *wondering* whether something is so, just as those who have not yet examined the explanation wonder at automatic marionettes. So men wonder about the solstices or the incommensurability of the diagonal. It seems, in fact, a wonderful thing to everybody that something should not be measurable by any measure, even the smallest. But this wonder must end in an opposite, and, as the proverb says, a better state, as it does in these cases when knowledge has been gained. A geometer would wonder at nothing so much as he would if the diagonal were to be found commensurable.

We have explained, then, the nature of the science of which we are in quest, and the character of the end at which this inquiry and this whole branch of knowledge should aim.

III. Since we manifestly must acquire scientific knowledge of ultimate causes (for in an individual case we only claim to *know* a thing when we believe ourselves to have apprehended its primary cause), and since the term "cause" is used in four senses, to signify (1) the *essence* or *essential nature* of things (for the *why* is reducible in the last instance to the *concept* of the thing, but the ultimate *why* is a cause and principle), (2) the *material* or *substrate*, (3) the *source of movement*, (4) cause in a sense opposed to this last, viz., the *purpose* or *good* (for that is the end of all processes of becoming and movement), though we have already treated this subject at length in our discourses on Physics, we may seek further light from the consideration of our predecessors in the investigation of Being and the philosophical examination of Reality. For they, also, obviously speak of certain principles and causes. Hence it will be of service to our present inquiry to review these principles, as we shall thus either discover some further class of causes, or be confirmed in our confidence in the present enumeration.

Now, most of the earliest philosophers regarded principles of a *material* kind as the only principles of all things. That of which all things consist, from which they are originally generated, and into which they are finally dissolved, its substance persisting though its attributes change, this, they affirm, is an element and first principle of Being. Hence, too, they hold that nothing is ever generated or annihilated, since this primary entity[4] always persists. Similarly, we do not say of Socrates that he comes into being, in an absolute sense, when he becomes handsome or cultivated, nor that he is annihilated when he loses these qualifications, because their *substrate*, viz., Socrates himself, persists. In the same way, they held, nothing else absolutely comes into being or perishes. For there must be one or more entities[5] which persist, and out of which all other things are generated. They do not, however, all agree as to the number and character of these principles. Thales, the founder of this type of philosophy, says it is *water*. Hence, he also put forward the view that the earth floats on the water. Perhaps he was led to this conviction by observing that the nutriment of all things is moist, and that even heat is generated from moisture, and lives upon it. (Now, that from which anything is generated is in every case a first principle of it.) He based his conviction, then, on this, and on the fact that the germs of all things are of a moist nature, while water is the first principle of the nature of moist things.[6] There are also some who think that even the men of remote antiquity who first speculated about the gods, long before our own era, held this same view about the primary entity. For they represented Oceanus and Tethys as the progenitors of creation, and the oath of the gods as being by water, or, as they [the poets] call it, Styx. Now, the most ancient of things is most venerable, while the most venerable thing is taken to swear by. Whether this opinion about the primary entity is really so original and ancient is very possibly uncertain; in any case, Thales is said to have put forward this doctrine about the first cause. (Hippo, indeed, from the poverty of his ideas,

---

[4] φύσις; lit., "nature." In the mouths of the early Physicists, of whom Aristotle is here speaking, the word means the supposed primary body or bodies of which all others are special modifications or transformations. (Burnet, *Early Greek Philosophy*, pp. 10–12.)

[5] φύσις; i.e., primary form of body.

[6] Aristotle does not prefer to *know* the reason of Thales for his doctrines, and the biological character of the reasons he conjecturally ascribes to him makes it improbable, as Burnet says (*op. cit.*, p. 43), that they are really those of Thales. Possibly, as Burnet suggests, Aristotle has, in the absence of positive information about the arguments of Thales, credited him with arguments actually employed by Hippo of Samos, who revived his doctrine in the fifth century.

can hardly be thought fit to be ranked with such men as these.) Anaximenes and Diogenes, however, regard *air* as more primitive than water, and as most properly the first principle among the elementary bodies. Hippasus of Metapontium and Heraclitus of Ephesus think it is *fire;* Empedocles, all four elements, *earth* being added as a fourth to the previous three. For they always persist and never come into being, except in respect of multitude and paucity, according as they are combined into a unity or separated out from the unity.[7] But Anaxagoras of Clazomenæ, who, though prior to Empedocles in age, was posterior to him in his achievements, maintains that the number of principles is infinite. For he alleges that pretty nearly all *homœomerous*[8] things come into being and are destroyed in this sense [just like water and fire], viz., only by combination and dissolution. In an absolute sense, they neither come into being nor perish, he thinks, but persist eternally.

According to all this, one might regard the "material" cause, as it is called, as the only kind of cause. But as they progressed further on these lines, the very nature of the problem pointed out the way and necessitated further investigation. For, however true it may be that there is underlying the production and destruction of anything something *out of* which it is produced (whether this be one thing or several), why does the process occur, and what is its cause? For the substrate, surely, is not the agent which effects its own transformation. I mean, e.g., that wood and brass are not the causes of their respective transformations; the wood is not the agent that makes the bed, nor the brass the agent that makes the statue, but something else is the cause of the transformation. To inquire into this cause is to inquire into the second of our principles, in my own terminology, the *source of motion.* Now, those who were the very first to attach themselves to these studies, and who maintained that the substratum was one,[9] gave themselves no trouble over

[7] Cf. Empedocles: "There is no coming into being of any perishable thing, nor any end in baneful death, but only mingling and separation of what has been mingled."

[8] "Homœomerous" things is not an expression of Anaxagoras, but a technical term of Aristotle's own biology, denoting the forms of organic matter (bone, flesh, etc.) which can be divided into parts of the same character as themselves. It is here appropriately applied to the infinity of qualitatively different molecules which Anaxagoras regarded as the primary form of matter. (Burnet, *op. cit.*, p. 289.) The words in brackets are probably a gloss.

[9] I.e., the Ionian Monists of the sixth century.

this point. Still, some[10] at least of those who asserted its unity were, so to say, baffled by this problem, and maintained that the one and the universe as a whole are immutable, not merely as regards generation and destruction (for *that* was a primitive belief in which they all concurred), but in every other sense of the term "change"; and this view was peculiar to them. So none of those who said that the universe is one single thing had an inkling of the kind of causation we are now considering, except possibly Parmenides, and he only recognized its existence so far as to assume not merely one cause, but, in a sense, two.[11] To be sure, those who assume a plurality of causes are in a better position to say something on the subject; e.g., those who assume as causes heat and cold, or fire and earth, for they treat fire as having the nature of an *agent*, but such things as water and earth in the opposite fashion.

After these philosophers and such first principles, since these principles were found inadequate to account for the production of the universe, men were once more compelled, as I have said, by facts themselves to investigate the principle which naturally follows next in order. For it is, perhaps, equally improbable that the reason why there are goodness and beauty both in Being and in Becoming should be fire or earth or anything else of that kind, and that these philosophers should have had such an opinion. Nor, again, would it have been reasonable to ascribe so important a result to accident and chance. So when some one said that it is the presence of *Mind* which is the cause of all order and arrangement in the universe at large, just as it is in the animal organism, he seemed, by contrast with his predecessors, like a sober man compared with idle babblers.[12] Now, we know for certain that Anaxagoras had conceived this idea, but Hermotimus of Clazomenæ is alleged to have given still earlier expression to it. Those who framed this conception, then, assumed the cause of Beauty as a principle in things and, at the same time, as being a principle of the kind by which motion is communicated to things.

[10] Parmenides and his successors of the Eleatic School.

[11] The reference is to the dualistic cosmology of the second part of Parmenides' poem, the "Way of Opinion."

[12] Cf. Plato's account of the effect produced upon Socrates by the famous statement of Anaxagoras about Mind, *Phaedo*, 97b ff. Aristotle probably intends an allusion to this passage.

IV. One might even fancy that this point was first investigated by Hesiod, or any other of the poets who assumed sexual Love or Desire as a principle in things—Parmenides, for instance, who says, in his description of the formation of the universe: "So Love she devised as earliest-born of all the gods." So Hesiod writes, "First of all things was the Abyss, and next broad-breasted Earth, and Love conspicuous above all the immortal ones," implying that there must be in the world some cause to set things in motion and bring them together. (How the question of priority is to be settled between these authors is a point of which we may be allowed to postpone the consideration.) But, further, since it was patent that there is also present in the universe the opposite of good, and not only Order and Beauty, but also Disorder and Ugliness, and that the evil and unseemly things are more numerous than the good and beautiful, another poet introduced the concepts of Love and Strife as the respective causes of each class. For if one follows out the statements of Empedocles with attention to his meaning, and not to its lisping expression in words, it will be found that he treats Love as the cause of good things, Strife as the cause of evil. Hence, if one said that in a sense Empedocles designated, and was the first to designate, Good and Evil as principles, the remark would probably be just, since that which is the cause of all good things is the *Good* itself [and that which is the cause of all evil things is *Evil* itself].

As I have said, then, the writers just referred to manifestly had formed the conception, to the degree already indicated, of two of the senses of Cause which have been distinguished in my discourses on Physics—the Matter and the Source of Motion. Their exposition, however, was obscure and confused, and might be likened to the conduct of untrained recruits in battle. In the general mêlée such recruits often deal admirable blows, but they do not deal them with science. Similarly, these philosophers do not seem to understand the significance of their own statements, for it is patent that, speaking generally, they make little or no application of them. Anaxagoras, for instance, uses his "Mind" as a mechanical device for the production of order in Nature, and when he is at a loss to say by what cause some result is necessitated, then he drags in Mind as a last resource, but in all other cases he assigns anything and everything rather than Mind as the cause of what occurs. Empedocles, again, though he makes more use of his causes than the other, does not make adequate use of them, nor does he succeed in attaining consistency where he does employ them. At least, he frequently treats Love as a separating and Strife as a combining agency. Thus, when the Universe is resolved into its rudiments by Strife, fire and each of the other four are combined into one, but when they coalesce again into the One, under the influence of Love, the parts of each are necessarily separated again. Empedocles, then, differed from his predecessors in being the first to introduce this cause in a *double* form; he assumes, not a single source of motion, but a pair which are opposed to one another. He was also the first to assert that the number of the so-called material elements is four. Yet, he does not employ them as four, but as if they were only two, treating fire on the one side by itself, and the elements opposed to it—earth, air, and water—on the other, as if they were a single nature. One can discover this from his verses by careful reflection. Such, then, were the nature and number of the principles assumed by Empedocles.

But Leucippus and his follower, Democritus, say that the elements are the Full and the Void, calling the one Being and the other Non-being. The full and solid they call Being, the void and rare Non-being. (This, too, is why they say that Non-being is just as real as Being, for the Void is as real as Body.) These are, they declare, the *material* causes of things. And just as those who regard the underlying nature of things as one derive everything else from the modifications of this substrate, assuming density and rarity as the fundamental distinction between these modifications, so Leucippus and Democritus assert that the *differences*[13] are the causes of everything else. Now, of these they say there are three—shape, order, and position. For Being, they say, differs only in *contour, arrangement, situation*. Of these terms, *contour* means shape, *arrangement* means order, and *situation* means position. Thus, e.g., A differs from N in shape, ΛN from NA in order, Z from N in position. Like the rest of the philosophers, they also indolently neglected the question whence or how motion is communicated to things. This, then, is the point to which the investigation of these

[13] I.e., the differences between the atoms of which according to this school Being, or Body, is composed.

two kinds of cause seems to have been carried by the earlier thinkers.

V. At the same time, and even earlier, the so-called Pythagoreans attached themselves to the mathematics and were the first to advance that science by their education, in which they were led to suppose that the principles of mathematics are the principles of all things. So as *numbers* are logically first among these principles, and as they fancied they could perceive in numbers many analogues of what is and what comes into being, much more readily than in fire and earth and water (such and such a property of number being *justice*, such and such another *soul* or *mind*, another *opportunity*, and so on, speaking generally, with all the other individual cases), and since they further observed that the properties and determining ratios of *harmonies* depend on numbers—since, in fact, everything else manifestly appeared to be modelled in its entire character on numbers, and numbers to be the ultimate things in the whole Universe, they became convinced that the elements of numbers are the elements of everything, and that the whole "Heaven" is harmony and number. So, all the admitted analogies they could show between numbers and harmonies and the properties or parts of the "Heaven" and the whole order of the universe, they collected and accommodated to the facts; if any gaps were left in the analogy, they eagerly caught at some additional notion, so as to introduce connection into their system as a whole. I mean, e.g., that since the number 10 is thought to be perfect, and to embrace the whole essential nature of the numerical system, they declare also that the number of revolving heavenly bodies is ten, and as there are only nine[14] visible, they invent the Antichthon as a tenth. But I have discussed this subject more in detail elsewhere.[15] I only enter on it here for the purpose of discovering from these philosophers as well as from the others what principles they assume, and how those principles fit into our previous classification of causes. Well, they, too, manifestly regard number as a principle, both in the sense that it is the *material* of things, and in the sense that it constitutes their *properties* and *states*. The elements of number are, they think, the

[14] Viz., Earth, Moon, Sun, Mercury, Venus, Mars, Jupiter, Saturn, circle of Fixed Stars.

[15] In a now lost work, *On the Pythagoreans*.

Even and the Odd, the former being unlimited, the latter limited. Unity is composed of both factors, for, they say, it is both even and odd. Number is derived from unity, and numbers, as I have said, constitute the whole "Heaven."

Other members of the same school say that the principles are ten, which they arrange in a series of corresponding pairs:

Limit—the Unlimited.	Rest—Motion.
Odd—Even.	Straight—Curved.
Unity—Multitude.	Light—Darkness.
Right—Left.	Good—Evil.
Male—Female.	Square—Oblong.

Alcmæon of Crotona appears to have followed the same line of thought, and must either have borrowed the doctrine from them or they from him, since Alcmæon was contemporary with the old age of Pythagoras. His views were very similar to theirs. He says, in fact, that most things human form pairs, meaning pairs of opposites. He does not, however, like the Pythagoreans, give a precise list of these, but mentions at random any that occur to him, e.g., White-Black, Sweet-Bitter, Good-Bad, Great-Small. Thus in other cases he merely threw out indefinite suggestions, but the Pythagoreans further undertook to explain how many and what the opposites are. From both, then, we can learn this much: that the opposites are the principles of things, but only from the latter how many, and what these are. They have not clearly explained in detail how these opposites are to be reduced to our previous classification of causes, but they appear to treat their elements as the *material* of things; for they say that Being is composed and fashioned out of them as inherent constituent factors. The meaning, then, of those ancients who asserted that the elements of the universe are a plurality can be sufficiently perceived from the foregoing exposition. But there are some[16] who expressed the view that the all is one single entity, though they differed among themselves both in respect of the merits of their doctrine, and in respect of its logical character. Now, a discussion of their views is not strictly relevant to our present inquiry into causation, for, unlike some of the physicists[17] who postulate the unity of Being, and yet treat of its deriva-

---

[16] Viz., the Eleatics.

[17] I.e., the Ionian Monists, from Thales to Heraclitus.

tion from the one substance as its material cause, they maintain the doctrine in a different sense. Those physicists assume, also of course, the existence of *motion*, since they treat of the *derivation* of the All, but this school declares that the All is motionless. Still, one observation at least is relevant to our present inquiry. Parmenides appears to conceive of the One in a formal sense, Melissus in a material. Hence the former calls it limited, the latter unlimited. Xenophanes, who was the first of them to teach the doctrine of unity (for they say that Parmenides had been his disciple), did not make any definite pronouncement, and seems to have formed the notion of neither of these entities, but gazing up at the whole Heaven, declared that the One is God. As I said, then, for the purposes of the present investigation this school may be disregarded. Two of them we may disregard altogether as a little too naïve, viz., Xenophanes and Melissus, but Parmenides appears, perhaps, to speak with greater insight. For, since he claims that Non-being, as contrasted with Being, is nothing, he is forced to hold that Being is one, and that nothing else exists—a doctrine on which we have spoken more fully and clearly in our course on Physics. But, as he is obliged to adapt his views to sensible appearances, he assumes that things are one from the point of view of reason, but many from that of sensation, and thus reintroduces a duality of principles and causes, the Hot and Cold, by which he means, e.g., fire and earth. Of these he co-ordinates the Hot with Being, its counterpart with Non-being.

Now, from the account we have just given, and by a comparison of the thinkers who have previously concerned themselves with the subject, we have arrived at the following result. From the earliest philosophers we have learned of a bodily principle (for water, fire, and the like, are bodies), which some of them[18] regard as a single principle, others[19] as a plurality, though both schools treat these principles as bodily. From others we have learned, in addition to this principle, of a source of motion, and this also is regarded by some[20] of them as one, but by others[21] as twofold. They all, down to the Italian[22] school and exclusive of them, treated the subject in a

---

[18] The Milesians, Heraclitus, Diogenes.

[19] Empedocles, Anaxagoras, the Atomists. [21] I.e., Empedocles.

[20] I.e., Anaxagoras. [22] I.e., the Pythagoreans of Magna Græcia.

rather ordinary way. As I have said, they only employed two kinds of cause, and the second of these, the source of motion, some of them regarded as one, others as two. The Pythagoreans likewise maintained a duality of principles, but they added, and this is peculiar to them, the notion that the limited, the unlimited, the one are not predicates of some other entity, such as fire, or earth, or something else of that kind, but that the Unlimited and the One themselves are the *substance* of the things of which they are predicated. This is why, according to them, number is the *substance* of everything.

This was the doctrine they proclaimed on these points. They also began to discuss the *what* of things, and to give definitions of it, but their method of procedure was extraordinarily crude. Their definitions were superficial, and they regarded anything to which a term under examination first applied as the essential nature of the object in question, as if one were to think that "double of" and "the number 2" are the same thing, on the ground that 2 is the first number which is double of another. But, methinks, it is not the same thing to be double of something as it is to be the number 2. If it were, then one thing would be many,[23] a consequence which actually followed in their system.[24] So much, then, is what may be learned from the earlier thinkers and their successors.

VI. The said philosophies were succeeded by the system of Plato, which was for the most part in harmony with them, but had also some distinctive peculiarities by which it was discriminated from the philosophy of the Italians.[25] In his youth Plato had been familiar with Cratylus and with the Heraclitean doctrines, according to which all things perceived by the senses are in incessant flux, and there is no such thing as scientific knowledge of them, and to this part of the doctrine he remained true through life. Socrates, however, though confining his examination to questions of moral conduct, and giving no study to the nature of the universe as a whole, sought within the moral sphere for the universal, and was the

[23] For, if every number which is double of another *is* the number 2 the single number 2 must be identical with an infinity of other even numbers, 4, 6, 8. . . . .

[24] The way in which this occurred was that the same number was identified, on the strength of different fanciful analogies, with a variety of different objects. Thus 1 was "the point," but it was also "the soul."

[25] I.e., the Pythagoreans.

first to concentrate his attention on definitions. Hence Plato, who succeeded him, conceived for the reason immediately to be mentioned that the objects thus defined cannot be any sensible things, but are of some different kind, since it is impossible that there should be a general definition of a sensible thing, as such things are incessantly changing. Hence he called this kind of things "Ideas," and held that all sensible things exist by the side of them and are named after them; for the multiplicity of things called by the same names as the Ideas exist, he holds, in consequence of their "participation" in them.[26]

In this theory of participation the only innovation lay in the name, for the Pythagoreans say that things exist by "imitation" of the numbers, and Plato by "participation" [a mere change of a word]. But what this "participation in" or "imitation of" the Ideas may be, they left for their successors to inquire.

Further, he teaches that the objects of mathematics exist as an intermediate class beside the Ideas and sensible things. They differ from sensible things in being eternal and immutable, and from the Ideas in this, that there is a multiplicity of similar mathematical objects, but each Idea is a single, self-subsisting entity.[27]

[26] Cf. the fuller parallel passage, *Metaphysics*, M, 1078a 9 ff.: "The theory of Ideas arose in the minds of its originators from their persuasion of the truth of the Heraclitean doctrine, that all sensible things are always in flux. Hence, they inferred, if there is to be scientific knowledge and rational comprehension of anything, there must be other entities distinct from those of sense, and they must be permanent. Now, Socrates confined his studies to the moral virtues, and was the first to attempt universal definition in connection with them. Among the physicists, Democritus had indeed just touched the fringe of the problem, and had given a sort of definition of heat and cold, and the Pythagoreans even earlier had discussed the definition of a few concepts, connecting them with their theory of numbers. They asked, e.g., what is opportunity, or justice, or marriage? But Socrates had a good reason for inquiring into the *what* of things. He was attempting to construct syllogisms, and the 'what is it' is the starting-point of the syllogism. . . . . There are, in fact, two things which must in justice be assigned to Socrates, inductive arguments and universal definition. For both of these have to do with the foundation of science. Socrates, however, did not regard his universals, or definitions, as separable from things; his successors made the separation, and called this class of objects 'Ideas.' "

[27] From the polemic against Plato, which occupies books M and N of the *Metaphysics*, particularly from M 2, 1076b, it appears that Aristotle understood Plato to distinguish between three kinds of entity, each of which is in its ultimate constitution a number, or ratio of numbers: (1) The *sensible* object, e.g., a visible round disc; (2) the "mathematical object," e.g., our visual imagination of a perfectly circular disc; (3) the *Idea*, e.g., *the* circle in the sense in which it is studied by the analytical geometer, and defined by its equation. (2) differs from (3) as "circles" from "*the* circle."

And since the Ideas are the causes of everything else, he thought that their constituent elements are the elements of everything. Their material principle, then, is the "Great and Small," but their formal principle the One. For the numbers [which are the Ideas] are derived from the former principle by participation in the One. In regarding the One as a substance, and not as a predicate of some other entity, his doctrine resembles Pythagoreanism, and also in holding that the numbers are the causes of Being in everything else. But it is peculiar to him to set up a duality instead of the single Unlimited, and to make the Unlimited consist of the Great and Small.[28] It is a peculiarity, also, that he regards the Numbers as distinct from sensible things, whereas the Pythagoreans say that things themselves *are* number, and do not assert the existence of an intermediate class of mathematical objects. This treatment of the One and the Numbers as distinct from things, in which he differed from the Pythagoreans, and also the introduction of the "Ideas," were due to his logical[29] studies (for his predecessors knew nothing of Dialectic); his conception of the second principle as a Duality, to the ease with which numbers other than primes can be generated from such a Duality as a matrix. Yet, the actual process is the reverse of this, and his suggested derivation has no logical foundation. According to his followers, the existence of a multiplicity of things is a consequence of matter, whereas each Form is only productive once for all. Yet, it is notorious that only one table can be fashioned from one and the same piece of timber, whereas he who impresses the form on it, though but a single workman, can make many tables. So with the relation of the male to the female; the latter is impregnated by a single coition, but one male can impregnate many females. And yet these relations are "copies" of those principles!

---

[28] This "Great and Small," or principle of indefinite, variability, is regularly spoken of by Aristotle in the sequel as "the indeterminate Dyad" or "Duality." It corresponds exactly to the notion of "the variable" in modern Logic and Mathematics. The nearest equivalent phrase in the writings of Plato himself occurs at *Philebus*, 24e, where the ἄπειρον or indeterminate is characterized as "all things which appear to us to exist in a greater and a less degree, and admit the qualifications 'intensely,' 'gently,' 'excessively' and the like." According to the ancient commentators, the foregoing account of the composition of the Ideas, which is not to be found explicitly in any of the Platonic writings, was given orally by Plato in lectures which were posthumously edited by Aristotle and others of his disciples.

[29] "His inquiries in the domain of concepts," i.e., his study of the nature of logical definition and division.

This, then, is the account which Plato gave of the questions we are now investigating. From our statement it is clear that he only employed two kinds of cause, the principle of the *what* and the material cause. (The Ideas, in fact, are the cause of the *what* in everything else, and the One in the Ideas themselves.) He also tells us what is the material substratum of which the Ideas are predicated in the case of sensible things, the One in the case of the Ideas, viz., that it is the duality of the "Great and Small." He further identified these two elements with the causes of good and evil, respectively, a line of research which, as we have said, had already been followed by some of his philosophical predecessors, e.g., Empedocles and Anaxagoras.

VII. We have now summarily and in outline answered the questions, what thinkers have treated of principles and of reality, and what doctrines they have taught. This much, however, can be gathered from our sketch of them, viz., that of all who have discussed principles and causes none has spoken of any kind except those which have been distinguished in our discourses on Physics. They are all unmistakably, though obscurely, trying to formulate these. Some of them understand their principle in the sense of a *material* cause, whether this be regarded as one or as several, as a body or as something incorporeal. E.g., Plato, with his Great and Small; the Italians, with their Unlimited; Empedocles, with his fire, earth, water, and air; Anaxagoras, with the infinity of his homœomerous bodies. All these, then, have formed the concept of cause in this sense, as likewise all those who make a first principle of air,[30] or fire,[31] or water,[32] or a body denser than fire but finer than air;[33] for, in fact, some have identified the prime element with such a body. These thinkers, then, apprehended only this form of cause; others had apprehended cause, also, in the sense of the source of motion, e.g., those who make a principle of Love and Strife, or Mind, or sexual Love. The *what* or essential nature has not been explicitly assigned by any of them, but the authors of the theory of Ideas have come nearest to recognizing it. For they neither conceive the Ideas as the *material* of sensible things and the One as that of the Ideas, nor

[30] Anaximenes, Diogenes.
[31] Heraclitus.
[32] Thales (Hippo).
[33] I hold with Burnet . . . . that the allusion is to Anaximander.

do they regard them as providing the source of motion (indeed, they say that they are rather causes of motionlessness and rest), but the *what* is supplied to everything else by the Ideas, and to the Ideas by the One. The end *for the sake of which* actions, changes, and movements take place they do, in a sense, introduce as a cause, but not in this form, nor in one corresponding to its real character. For those who speak of Mind or Love assume these causes, indeed, as something good, but not in the sense that anything is or comes to be *for the sake of them*, but only in the sense that motions are initiated by them. Similarly, those[34] who assert that Being, or the One, are entities of this kind[35] assert, indeed, that they are a cause of existence, but not that anything is or comes to be *for the sake of them*. Consequently they, in a sense, both assert and deny that the Good is a cause, for they treat it as such, not absolutely but *per accidens*.[36] They all thus appear to supply evidence that our own determination of the number and kind of the senses of cause is correct, since they have all failed to conceive of any further sense of cause. Further, it is clear that we must investigate these principles either as they stand in their entirety or a selection of them. We will next, however, examine possible difficulties in the doctrines of the individual thinkers, and their views about principles.

VIII. It is clear, then, that all who regard the universe as one and assume a single entity as its material, and that a bodily and extended entity, have fallen into error in several respects. They only assume constituent elements for bodies, but not for incorporeal entities, though incorporeal entities also really exist, and though they attempt to provide causes for generation and dissolution, and to discuss the nature of all things, they do away with the cause of motion. A further fault is that they do not assume the essential nature, or *what*, as a cause of anything. Another is the levity with which they call any one of the simple bodies except earth a principle, without reflection on the process of their reciprocal generation from each other. [I am speaking of fire, water, earth, and air.]

[34] I.e., Plato and his followers.

[35] I.e., sources of motion.

[36] I.e., they treat "the Good" as being a cause only in a relative and derivative sense, because it happens also to be something which *mechanically* initiates movement.

Some of them are generated from one another by composition, others by separation, and this difference is of the highest importance in deciding the question of priority and posteriority. From one point of view, one might hold that the most elementary of things is that out of which they are all ultimately generated by composition, and such would be the body which is finest in texture and has the minutest parts. Hence those who assume fire as their principle would be most fully in accord with this line of thought, and even each of the others admits that the *element* of bodies must be of this kind; at least, none of the later thinkers who asserted a single principle has ventured to say that this element is earth—the reason clearly being the great size of its parts—though each of the three other elements has found an advocate. For some identify the primary element with fire, others with water, others with air. And yet why do they not say the same thing about earth, too, just as the mass of mankind do? And Hesiod, too, says that earth was the first of bodies, so primitive and popular is this belief found to be.

According to this line of thought, then, whether a man says that the primary body is any one of these other than fire or assumes that it is denser than air but finer than water, he cannot be right in either case. But if what is sequent in the order of production is logically anterior,[37] then, since the compacted and composite comes later in the order of production, we should have an opposite conclusion to the above: water would be prior to air; earth, to water.

So much, then, may be said about those who postulate a single cause of this kind. The same criticisms are pertinent, even if one assumes a plurality of them, like Empedocles, who says that the material of things is four bodies. The same consequences must follow in his system, as well as others peculiar to it. For we see these bodies produced from one another, and this implies that fire and earth do not always remain the same body, a point which has been discussed in our discourses on Physics. And, further, he cannot be thought to have spoken with entire correctness or consistency on the question whether the cause of motion is to be assumed to be single or double. And universally those who teach this doctrine are

---

[37] "Prior in the order of *nature*," it being a doctrine of Aristotle, ultimately based upon his biological studies, that the completed result of a process of development is presupposed by, and therefore logically, and in the end temporally also, prior to its incomplete stages.

forced to deny the reality of qualitative alteration. Nothing will become cold after being hot, or hot after being cold. For there would need to be something to be the subject of these contrasted states. And thus there would be a numerically single entity which becomes successively fire and water; but this *he* denies.

As for Anaxagoras, he would be most rationally interpreted if we understood him to recognize two elements. He did not, indeed, develop this notion himself, but would necessarily have followed another's guidance in this direction. That all things were at first a mixture[38] is indeed a paradoxical view on various grounds, particularly because it follows that they would first have to exist in an unmixed state, and also because it is not the nature of anything and everything to admit of mixture with everything else. Besides, the attributes and accidents of things would be separable from their substances (since things which can mix can also be separated). Still, if one followed up his doctrine and developed his meaning, he would perhaps be found to be asserting a view more akin to that of later thinkers. For when nothing had been separated off, clearly nothing could be truly predicated of the supposed substance. I mean, e.g., that it could not be truly called white, black, buff [nor of any other color], but must necessarily have been colorless, since otherwise it would have had one or the other of these tints. Similarly, for the same reason it could have no taste, nor any other such quality. It could neither have been a quality, nor a quantity, nor a thing. If it had been, it would have had the form of some definite particular thing. But this is impossible, on the assumption that all things were mixed together, for it would be equivalent to being already separated out. But he says that all things were mixed together except Mind, which alone was unmixed and pure. It follows, then, from all this that his theory amounts to assigning as his principles the One (for that is simple and unmixed), and the Other, as we[39] call the Indeterminate before it has been rendered determinate and received a form. Thus what he says is neither correct nor clear; still, what he means is something similar to later theories and more conformable to apparent facts.

[38] The reference is to Anaxagoras.

[39] "We"—i.e., the school of Plato. Throughout the present discussion Aristotle affects to speak as a critic of Plato from within the Platonic circle, a point of which we shall see further illustration in ch. IX.

These thinkers, however, confine themselves exclusively to the study of generation, dissolution, and motion, for in general they inquire exclusively about the causes and principles of that kind of Being. As for those who study all forms of Being, and distinguish between sensible and non-sensible objects, they clearly devote their attention to both classes. Hence, in their case, we may dwell at rather greater length on the question what satisfactory or unsatisfactory contributions they have made to the solution of the problems at present before us.

The so-called Pythagoreans, then, employ less obvious principles and elements than the physicists (the reason being that they did not derive them from *sensible* things; for mathematical objects, with the exception of those with which astronomy is concerned, are devoid of motion). Still, all their discussions and investigations are concerned with physical Nature. For they describe the formation of the "Heaven," and observe what befalls its parts [attributes and activities], and use up their causes and principles upon this task, which implies that they agree with the other physicists, that *what is* is just so much as is perceptible by our senses and comprised by the so-called "Heaven." Yet, as I have said, the causes and principles they assign are adequate for the ascent to the higher classes of entities,[40] and, indeed, more appropriate to these than to the science of Physics. But they fail to explain how there can be motion if all that we presuppose in our premises is merely Limit, the Unlimited, the Odd and the Even, or how without Motion and Change there can be Generation, and Dissolution, or the actions of the bodies that traverse the "Heaven."[41]

Again, even if it were granted them or proved that *magnitude* is composed of these factors, how does this account for the existence of *bodies*, light and heavy? For they reason from the principles they assume just as much about sensible as about mathematical bodies. Hence they have not taught us anything about fire or earth or other such bodies, and naturally not, as they had no special doctrine about sensible objects as such. Again, how can we under-

[40] "higher"—i.e., requiring a greater degree of generalising abstraction for their comprehension; in Aristotle's favorite phrase, "farther removed from sense."

[41] Aristotle's point is, that just because the Pythagoreans (like Descartes after them) conceived of Body in purely geometrical terms they could give no explanation of its sensible physical properties.

stand the view that Number and its properties are the causes of
all that is and that comes to be in the "Heaven," both at the beginning and now, and yet that there is no other kind of number
than this Number of which the universe is composed? For when,
according to them, there is in this region of the universe Opinion
and Opportunity, and a little higher or lower Injustice and Separation or Mixture, and when they say as a proof of this that each of
these is a number, and when it also comes about that there is already in this region a collection of composite[42] magnitudes, because
these properties are attached each to a particular region—is it the
same number as that in the "Heaven," which we are to suppose
to be each of these things, or some other kind of number? Plato, to
be sure, says it is a different kind, though he, too, thinks that both
these things[43] and their causes are numbers, but believes that the
causative numbers are perceived by thought, the other kind by
sense.

IX. For the present, then, we may dismiss the subject of the
Pythagoreans; the foregoing brief mention of them will be found
adequate. As for those who assume the Ideas as causes, in the first
place, in the attempt to discover the causes of the entities of the
actual world they introduced the notion of a second class of entities
equally numerous with them.[44] This is just as if one who wished to
count certain things should fancy that while they remain fewer he
will not succeed, but should first multiply them and then count.
For the Ideas are pretty nearly as numerous as, or not fewer than,
the things by inquiring into whose causes they advanced from
actual objects to Ideas. For there is something synonymous corresponding to every group not only of substances but of all other
things in which there is a One over the Many, both in this world of
actual things and in that of eternal things.

[42] I.e., extended figures or bodies (the Pythagoreans did not distinguish the two),
which, according to them, are "composed" of the numerical factors, Limit, the Unlimited.

[43] "These things" appears now not to mean, as in the last sentence, opportunity,
etc., but the extended figures and bodies previously referred to.

[44] The rest of the critique of Plato down to 991b 7, "of which we Platonists say
there are not Ideas," appears again in *Metaphysics*, M, chs. 4, 5, in a form which is
almost verbally identical with the present chapter, except that there Aristotle does
not, as here, affect by the use of the pronoun of the first person plural to be speaking as a critic from within the Platonic circle itself. This repetition is one of many
indications that the *Metaphysics* is in no sense a literary "work," prepared by its
author for circulation.

Again, none of the methods of argument by which we try to prove the existence of the Ideas really establishes the conclusion. From some of them no necessary conclusion follows; from others, it follows that there would also be Ideas in cases where we do not believe in them. According to the arguments drawn from the sciences, there will be Ideas of all things of which there are sciences. According to that based on the One over the Many, there must be Ideas also of negatives, and according to that based on our ability to conceive of what has perished, Ideas of perishable things; for there is a memory-image of them. Besides, his most exact arguments partly lead to Ideas of relatives, of which there is, according to us, no self-existing class, and partly bring the "third man"[45] into the argument. And, speaking generally, the arguments for the Ideas lead to the denial of things[46] whose reality we Platonists are even

[45] The "third man" is the difficulty known in modern logic as the "indefinite regress." We learn from Alexander that it had been originally raised by the sophist, Polyxenus. Plato himself alludes to it in *Republic*, 597, and explicitly states it in *Parmenides*, 132, though without formally indicating his answer to it. It runs thus: If the likeness between Socrates, Plato, and other persons proves that they are all "copies" of a common archetype, the "Idea of Man," then the likeness between this Idea and Socrates must also prove that both Socrates and the Idea are "copies" of another common archetype, which will be a second and more ultimate Idea of Man; and the likeness between the first and second Ideas of Man proves the existence of a third Idea, which is *their* common archetype, and so on in *indefinitum*. (The real solution of the puzzle is that the relation between Socrates and "man" is not the same as the relation between Socrates and Plato. Socrates and Plato are both members of the class *men;* "man" is not a member of the class "men." Hence the argument of Polyxenus and Aristotle is a sophism, and the difficulty about the "regress" does not arise except in the case of those classes which can be members of themselves.

[46] The "things" in question, Alexander explains, are the constituent elements of the Ideas themselves, the One and the Dyad of the Great and Small. Aristotle contends that the theory of Ideas leads to consequences which are incompatible with the initial assumption as to these elements. E.g., if the Great and Small is one of the two constituents of every Idea, it must be a simpler notion presupposed in every Idea and thus logically prior to all the Ideas. Therefore it must, of course, be prior to the Idea of Number. But, since you can say, e.g., "The Great and Small are a *pair of* entities" or "are *two* entities," and two is *a* number, number should be the class, or universal, of which the Dyad is one instance, and it ought to follow that number is logically prior to what Plato regards as one of its simple constituents. (The reader will readily perceive that this, again, is a sophism, turning on the identification of the Indeterminate Dyad or "Variable" with the *number* 2. The repeated instances of this identification which occur both in this chapter and throughout book *M* afford a striking illustration of Aristotle's deficiency in exact mathematical thought.) He further goes on to object that Plato's theory makes the "relative" prior to the "absolute." This is because the fundamental concepts of that theory, "number" and "archetype," are relative terms. (Every number or archetype is a number or archetype *of* something.)

more concerned to maintain than that of the Ideas. For it follows from them that it is not the Dyad but number which is logically primary, that the relative is prior to the absolute, and all the other inconsistencies between the consequences which have been drawn from the theory of Ideas and its principles. Further, according to the conviction on which our Ideal theory is based, there will be Ideas not only of substances, but of much else (for there are common concepts not only in the case of substances but in other cases, and sciences not only of substances but of other entities, and there is a host of similar consequences). But according to rigid logic, and the accepted theory of the Ideas, if things are related to the Ideas by "participation" there can be Ideas only of substances. For things do not "partake" of them *per accidens;* they only partake of each Idea in so far as it is not predicated of something else as a substitute. What I mean is, e.g., that if anything partakes of the Idea of "double" it also partakes of something eternal, but only *per accidens,* for it is an accident of the Idea of "double" to be eternal.[47] Hence the Ideas must be of substances. But the same terms which denote substance *here* denote it also *there;* or what else can be meant by saying that there is besides the actual things here something which is the unity corresponding to their multiplicity? And if the Ideas and the things which partake of them are members of the same class, they will have something in common. For why should duality be one and the same thing in the case of the perishable pairs and that of the pairs which though many are eternal, and not equally so in the case of the Idea of duality and a particular pair of things?[48] But if they are not members of the same class, they

[47] The point is this: You can say, e.g., "a right-hand glove and a left-hand glove are *two* gloves"; thus in Platonic phrase, the gloves "partake of the Idea of" *two.* But though the Idea of *two,* like all Ideas, is eternal, you cannot say "these two gloves are eternal," for gloves, as we know, wear out. In the terminology of Aristotelian logic the relation of "participation," if it exists, must be between the sensible thing and the *substance* of the corresponding Idea, not between the thing and the *accidents* of the Idea.

[48] The many pairs of things which are eternal are, of course, the instances of couples which occur in pure Mathematics (e.g., pairs of conjugate diameters, pairs of asymptotes). The argument is our old friend, the "third man." "To be a couple," he contends, is predicable alike of the Idea of "two" and of a sensible couple. You can say: "The Idea of 'two' and this pair of gloves are *two couples.*" Therefore, on Platonic principles, there must be a second more ultimate Idea of "two," in which both the first Idea of "two" and the gloves "participate." The sophistical character of the reasoning becomes obvious when we reflect that the Idea of "two" is *not* itself two things, but one thing. Do not confuse this Idea of "two" with the *Indeterminate* Dyad.

can have nothing but their name in common, and it is much as if one called both Callias and a wooden image *men*, without reference to any community of character in them.[49]

Above all, it would be difficult to explain what the Ideas contribute to sensible things, whether to those which are eternal[50] or those which undergo generation and dissolution. For they are not the causes of any movement or change in them. But, once more, they are also of no assistance for the *knowledge* of other things (for the Ideas are not the substance of things; if they were, they would be *in* the things); nor do they contribute to their *Being*, since they are not *present in* the things which partake of them.[51] If they were, they might perhaps be thought to be causes in the sense in which an admixture of white is the cause that something is white. But this line of thought, which was first enunciated by Anaxagoras, and repeated later by Eudoxus and others, is easily refutable, for it is an easy task to collect many impossible consequences in opposition to such a doctrine.[52]

[49] At this point the parallel passage of book *M* (1079b 3) adds the following paragraph:
But if we assume that in general the universal concept coincides with the Idea (e.g., the qualification "plane figure" and the other constituents of the definition with the "Idea of the circle"), but that, in the case of the Idea, it must be further specified of *what* this Idea is the archetype, one has to consider whether this addition is not purely empty. To which constituent of the definition is it to be added? To "center," to "plane," or to all alike? For all the constituents of the essence are Ideas, e.g., "animal" and "biped." [I.e., in the definition of man as a two-footed animal. Tr.] Besides, clearly it [i.e., the proposed extra qualification by which the Idea is to be distinguished from a mere universal generic concept, viz., that it is "the archetype of a class of sensible things." Tr.] must itself be an entity, just as "plane" is an entity which must be present as a genus in all the species. [i.e., he argues that the same grounds which lead the Platonists to say that there is an Idea of "plane" of which circles, ellipses, and all the other plane figures "partake" would equally lead to the view that there is an Idea of "archetype" of which all the other Ideas "partake"—a fresh application of the "third man." Tr.]

[50] I.e., the heavenly bodies, which, according to Aristotle, are ungenerated and incorruptible.

[51] This is the essence of Aristotle's most telling objection to the Platonic doctrine, viz., that Plato regarded the Ideas as "separable" from the sensible things which, nevertheless, depend on them for their Being. In modern terminology the point is, that Plato holds that what we mean to assert in a typical proposition of the form "X is a Y" (e.g., "Socrates is a man") is a *relation* between X (Socrates) and a *second* entity Y ("humanity," the "Idea of Man"). Aristotle regards this as an impossible analysis.

[52] Plato's friend, Eudoxus of Cnidus, the astronomer, had attempted to meet the objection just mentioned by saying that things are a "mixture" in which the Idea is one ingredient. Aristotle regards this as analogous to the doctrine of Anaxagoras,

Once more, other things are not derived from the Ideas in any of the established senses of the term "derivation"; to call them "archetypes" and to say that other things "partake" of them is to employ empty words and poetical metaphors. For what is the agency which actually constructs things with the Idea as its model? A thing may both be and become like something else without being imitated from it. Thus whether Socrates exists or not, there may equally be some one like Socrates, and it is clear that the case would not be altered even if Socrates were eternal. Also, there will be many archetypes, and consequently many Ideas, for the same thing; e.g., "animal" and "biped" will be archetypes in the case of man, as well as the "Idea of Man." Further, the Ideas will be archetypes not only of sensible things, but of Ideas themselves, e.g., the genus will be the archetype of the species contained in it. So one and the same thing will be both archetype and copy.[53] Besides, it may surely be regarded as an impossibility that the substance of a thing and the thing of which it is the substance should be separated. So, how can the Ideas, if they are the substances of things, be separate from them?

In the *Phædo*[54] we are told that the Ideas are causes both of Being and of Becoming. And yet, even if the Ideas exist, the things which partake of them do not come into being unless there is something to set the process in motion; and many other things come into being, e.g., a house, a ring, of which we Platonists say there are not Ideas. Hence, clearly, it is possible for other things as well both to

---

according to which every thing contains some degree of all the contrasted qualities of matter, but exhibits to our senses only those of which it has most. The "consequences" are, no doubt, of the same kind as those urged in ch. 8, against Anaxagoras. Alexander says that Aristotle had developed them more at length in his lost work, *On Ideas*.

[53] He means that if from "Socrates is a man" you can infer the existence of an "Idea of Man" of which Socrates "partakes," you ought equally from "Man is an animal" to infer an "Idea of Animal" of which "the Idea of Man" partakes.

[54] *Phædo*, 100d: "When I am told that anything is beautiful because it has a goodly colour or shape, or anything else of the kind, I pay no attention to such talk, for it only confuses me. I cling simply, plainly, perhaps foolishly, to my own inner conviction that nothing makes a thing beautiful but the presence, or communication, whatever its nature may be, of that Ideal Beauty. Without any further assertion as to the nature of this relation, I assert merely that it is through Beauty that all beautiful things are beautiful."

exist and come into being through the agency of causes of the same kind as those of the objects just referred to.[55]

Further, if the Ideas are *numbers*, how can they be causes? Perhaps, because things are a second set of numbers; e.g., this number is Man, that Socrates, that again Callias. But why, then, are the first set of numbers considered the *causes* of the others? For it will make no difference that the one are eternal and the others not. But if the explanation is that things *here* are *ratios* between numbers— e.g., a musical concord—plainly, there is some one thing *of* which they are ratios. Now, if there is such a thing, viz., matter, manifestly the numbers themselves must be ratios of one thing to a second. I mean that, e.g., if Callias is a numerical ratio of fire, earth, water, and air, the Idea, too, must be a number of some other things which are its substrate, and the "Ideal Man," whether a number or not, still will be a numerical ratio *of* certain things, and not simply a number, nor does it follow on these grounds that he will be a number.[56]

Again, one number can be composed of many other numbers, but how can one Idea be formed of many Ideas? If you say it is not composed of the numbers themselves, but of the units contained in them, e.g., those of the number 10,000, what is the relation between

[55] The argument has two branches. (1) The mere existence of the Idea is not enough to guarantee that of a corresponding group of sensible things. (E.g., the existence of an "Idea of Man" does not secure the existence of Socrates. Socrates must have had parents, and his existence depends on certain *acts* of those parents.) (2) And artificial products, on the other hand, certainly come into being. Yet the Platonists, according to Aristotle, say that there are no Ideas of such products. Why then, if houses and rings can come into being, though there are no Ideas of them, may the same not be true of everything else?

[56] The paragraph develops further the contention that numbers are *relative* terms. The argument is as follows: He suggests that Plato may have reconciled the assertions that the Ideas are Numbers and that they are the causes of things by the view that a sensible thing (e.g., the organism of Callias) is a combination of certain materials in accordance with a definite numerical law. This law would be, in Aristotelian phrase, the "form" or "formal" *cause* of the thing in question. Only, in that case, the thing in question (the body of Callias) is not merely a numerical law, but a law of the combination of certain specific material. Consequently, if the sensible thing (the body of Callias) is a copy of a certain archetype (the "Idea of Man"), this archetype also must contain something corresponding to the material factor in the thing, and thus even on Plato's own principles, the Idea will not be merely a "number" but a numerical law of the combination *of* certain material. There seems to be an allusion to the formation of the human organism out of materials which are definite compounds of the four "elements," as described in the *Timæus*.

these units? If they are all homogeneous, many paradoxical consequences must follow; if they are not homogeneous, neither those
of the same number with one another nor all with all, what can
make the difference between them, seeing that they have no qualities?[57] Such thinking is neither rational nor consistent.

Again, it becomes necessary to construct a second kind of number which is the object of Arithmetic and all the studies which have
been called "intermediate." How or out of what principles can this
be constructed? And on what grounds must it be regarded as
"intermediate" between things *here* and the ideal numbers? Again,
each of the units in the Dyad[58] must be derived from a prior
Dyad; but this is impossible. Again, why is a number of units
when formed into a collection one thing?[59] Again, in addition to

[57] Aristotle's point is, that any two numbers can be added together and their
sum will be a third number of the same kind. But Ideas, or class-concepts, he thinks,
cannot be added. If they are numbers, they must be numbers composed of units
which, unlike those of Arithmetic, are not all of the same kind, and therefore cannot
always be added so as to produce a resultant of the same kind as the factors. He
thinks that you may then suppose either that each of the units which compose one
and the same "Ideal number" may be of the same kind as all the other units of *that*
number, but different in kind from any of the units of a different "Ideal number,"
or that even the units of one and the same "Ideal number" may be all different in
kind from one another, the former being the more natural hypothesis. The two forms
of the supposition, which are here curtly dismissed, are discussed at length in *M*,
ch. 7, 8, 1081a 1–1083a 20. The reader will see that Aristotle's philosophy of
number is doubly defective, since (1) he has no conception of the dependence of
arithmetical addition on the more fundamental process of *logical* addition (for which
see Russell, *Principles of Mathematics*, I., ch. xii); (2) and he has, also, no conception of any class of numbers except the integers.

[58] I.e., the Indeterminate Dyad of the Great and Small. The argument is, that
since this is a dyad or "pair," it must consist of two members; whence, then, are these
derived? (You must not say that they are repetitions of the other element, the One,
because in the Platonic system the "Great and Small" is regarded as being logically
no less ultimate and elementary than the One.) Here, again, we have, as Bonitz observes, an unfair identification of the "Indeterminate Dyad" with the *number* 2. It
is only the latter, not the former, which can be said to consist of two units. And even
in the case of the latter such an expression is a loose and inaccurate way of saying
that 2 is the number determined by the addition of 1 to 1, or the number of the
terms of a class formed by uniting in one class the terms of the classes *a* and *b*, when
a and *b* each have only one term and their terms are not identical.

[59] I.e., each Idea is one thing or unit, an entity corresponding to one determinate
class or type. How then, can it also be a *number*, which is a collection of units? Cf.
H, 1044a 2, where the same complaint is made that the Platonists cannot explain
what it is that makes a number *one* thing, and *M*, 1082a 15, where he asks, "how can
the number 2 be an entity distinct from its two units?" This and many other passages of *M* show how very literally and naïvely Aristotle conceives of integers as
formed by addition. What he does not see is, that "addition is not primarily a

all this, if the units differ, the Platonists have followed the example of those who maintain four or two elements. Each of these thinkers gives the name of *element* not to their common substrate, e.g., body—but to fire and earth, whether they have a common substrate, viz., body, or not. But the One is in fact spoken of as if it were as homogeneous as fire or water. But if it is homogeneous in this sense, the numbers cannot be substances; rather, it is manifest that if there is a self-existing One and this One is a first principle, "one" is an equivocal term.[60] In any other case it is an impossibility.

When we[61] wish to refer our substances to their principles we derive length from the Short and Long, a special case of the Small and Great, the plane from the Broad and Narrow, body from the High and Low. Yet, how can the line be contained in the plane, or the line and plane in the solid? The Broad and Narrow is a different genus from the High and Low. So, just as numbers are not contained in these classes, because the Many and Few is a different class from them, clearly no other of the higher genera will be contained in the lower.[62] Nor, again, is the Broad the genus of which the High is a species, for if it were so, body would be a kind of plane.

---

method of forming numbers, but of forming classes or collections. If we add B to A we do not obtain the number 2, but we obtain A and B, which is a collection of two terms, or a couple." (Russell, *op. cit.*, p. 135.)

[60] I.e., the kind of number meant by the Platonists when they speak of their Ideas as numbers must be something quite different from what the arithmetician means by number.

[61] I.e., "we Platonists."

[62] The argument is aimed at the Platonic application of the principles of the One and the Great and Small to define geometrical extension in one, two, three dimensions. The point is, that whereas, according to Aristotle, a solid contains surfaces, a surface lines, and a line points, this could not be the case on the Platonic principles, according to which each of the three dimensions consists of magnitudes of a different *kind*. (Cf. M, 9, 1085a 7–31.) Hence, he holds, a Platonist ought not to be able to define a plane in terms of the definition of a straight line, nor a solid in terms of the definition of a plane, or vice versa. Now, Aristotle holds that you can do the latter. A plane is, e.g., the *boundary* of a solid; a straight line is the *boundary* of a plane (as we should say, the intersection of two planes). This is what he means by planes being "in" solids, and lines "in" planes. He does not, of course, mean that, as the Pythagoreans had thought, a solid is actually made up of superposed laminæ, or a plane of juxtaposed strips. The argument is, however, fallacious; since, e.g., a plane may quite well be, as the Platonists held, a different kind of magnitude from a straight line and yet be definable in terms of the definition of a straight line. Aristotle has, in fact, been led astray by his inadequate theory of definition as being exclusively by genus and difference. "Higher" genera means, of course, those which require for their conception a higher degree of abstraction and analysis.

Again, how will it be possible for *points* to "be in" figures? Plato, in fact, rejected this class of entities as a mere fiction of the geometers. He used to speak of them as the "beginning of the line," for which he often employed the expression "indivisible line." But even these lines must have a limit, so that the same argument which proves the existence of the line proves, also, that of the point.[63]

To speak generally, though it is the business of wisdom to discover the cause of visible things, we have neglected that task (for we have nothing to say about the cause by which change is initiated), but in the fancy that we are describing their substance we assert the existence of a second class of substances, though our explanation of the way in which they are substances *of* the former set is empty verbiage, for "participation," as I have said, is nothing at all. Nor do the Ideas stand in any connection with the kind of cause which we observe in the practical sciences, the cause *for the sake of* which all Mind and all Nature act, and which we have included among our first principles. Mathematics has been turned by our present-day thinkers into the whole of Philosophy, in spite of their declaration that it ought to be studied for the sake of something further.[64]

[63] Aristotle is referring to a view, known from the commentators to have been held by Xenocrates, and here attributed by him to Plato himself, that there are really no such entities as points, what we call a point being, in fact, not a magnitude but the "starting point" or "beginning" of a magnitude, viz., of the line. There is no trace of this doctrine in the dialogues of Plato, and the imperfect tense shows that Aristotle is referring not to any Platonic passage, but to verbal statements made by Plato in his lectures. Since the view in question was adopted by Xenocrates, the actual president of the Academy during Aristotle's activity in Athens as a teacher, it is natural that he should have treated it to special criticism; among the extant works ascribed to him there is, in fact, a special tract, "On Indivisible Lines." Plato's difficulty, no doubt, was that the point has *no* dimensions; it is a *zero* magnitude. The error of refusing to admit the point, or zero dimension, is exactly analogous to the universal error of Greek arithmeticians in regarding 1, not 0, as the first of the integers. Though, since the definition of a point, often cited by Aristotle as a "unit having position," seems to come from Pythagorean and Platonic sources (Cf. *M*, 8, 1084b 26, 33), it seems possible that Aristotle (and Xenocrates?) may have misunderstood what Plato meant by calling the point an "indivisible line," as is maintained by Milhaud, *op. cit.*, p. 341–2. The reader will note that, though Aristotle's conclusion that Geometry requires the point is sound, his argument is a *petitio principii*, since it *assumes* the existence of the limit.

[64] The reference is specially to the place assigned to Mathematics as a propædeutic to the study of the Ideas in *Republic*, VII., particularly to 531d: "All these are mere preludes to the hymn which has to be learned. For you surely do not consider those who are proficients in them as dialecticians."

Besides, we may fairly regard the entity which they assume as matter as being more properly of a mathematical kind, and as being rather a predicate and a specific difference of substance and matter than identical with matter itself. I mean the Great and the Small; just as the physicists, when speaking of rarity and density, say that these are the primary specific differences of the material substrate, for they are a kind of excess and defect. And as to motion, if these elements[65] are to constitute motion, plainly the ideas will be in motion;[66] if they are not to constitute it, whence has it come? Thus the whole study of physical Nature is abolished. And even the proof, which is fancied to be so easy, that all things are one, does not follow. Their method of "exposition,"[67] even if one grants all their assumptions, does not prove that all things are one, but only that there *is* a self-existing One, and does not even prove this unless it is granted that the universal is a genus; but in some cases that is impossible. And as for the objects they consider logically posterior to the numbers, viz., lines and planes and solids, no rational grounds can be produced to show how they exist or can exist, nor what character they possess. They cannot be Ideas (for they are not numbers), nor the "intermediate" class of objects (for these are mathematical figures), nor yet can they be identical with perishable things. Manifestly, we have here, again, a fresh and a fourth class of objects.[68]

[65] Viz., the Great and Small.

[66] Because the Great and Small is a constituent of every Idea. That the Ideas should "be in motion" is impossible, on Platonic principles, because one chief characteristic of them is their immutability.

[67] The method here and elsewhere called by Aristotle "exposition" is the familiar Platonic procedure of inferring from the existence of many individual things possessing some common predicate the existence of a *single* supersensible entity, the Idea, which is their common archetype. He objects (1) that the argument, in any case, does not prove that all the individual things *are* one thing, but only that, beside them, there is one ideal archetype of which they are all copies; (2) it does not even prove this unless the common predicate is the name of a "real kind" or genus. This is a corollary from his previous conclusion that if there are Ideas they can only be Ideas of substances.

[68] The point is this: The Platonists hold that the many lines, planes, solids, of Geometry are *copies* of certain single archetypal entities—*the* line, *the* plane, *the* solid. These are the "objects" posterior to the "Numbers" here spoken of. But what *are* these objects? Not Ideas (since they are not numbers, and every Idea is a number); not geometrical figures (since geometrical figures are copies of *them*); not physical things, since they are immutable. Thus they must be a fourth class of objects, not provided for in the Platonic classification of objects into Ideas, mathematical objects, and sensible things.

In general, it is impossible to discover the elements of existing things if one does not first distinguish the different "senses of existence," especially when the inquiry is directed towards the problem of what elements existing things are composed. For one certainly cannot discover what are the elements of which activity or passivity or straightness is composed. If the problem is soluble at all, it is only soluble in the case of substances.[69] So it is an error to ask after, or to think one has found, the elements of everything. How, indeed, could one possibly learn the elements of everything? For it is clear that one could not possibly have been in previous possession of any information at all. Just as he who is learning geometry may very well have previous knowledge about other things, but has no previous acquaintance with the truths which be-

[69] He concludes his polemic by an attack on the general theory of the nature of science which is tacitly implied in the Platonic doctrine, viz., that the objects of all the sciences are composed of the same constituent elements. He has already explained that Plato thought that the elements of the Ideas are the elements of everything. It follows that there is ultimately only one science, viz., Dialectic, which, as we learn from *Republic*, VI., 511, cognizes the ultimate axioms from which *all* scientific truth can be deduced. Aristotle holds that there is no such supreme science of first principles; every science has its own special subject-matter, and consequently its own special axioms (*Analytica Posteriora*, I., 76a 16). In this passage he urges two objections to the Platonic view. (1) Analysis into constituent elements is only possible in the case of substances. In a substance you have always the two constituent logical elements of *matter* and *form* (which appear in its definition as *genus* and *difference*), but these elements cannot be found in a quality, an action, or a state. Cf. *H.* 1044b 8: "Things which exist in nature, but are not substances, have no matter, but their substrate is their substance. E.g., what is the cause of an *eclipse?* What is its matter? There is none, but the *moon* is the thing affected." He means, then, that Plato thinks that in the end all objects of knowledge are *made of* the same ingredients, and therefore there is only one science of them all; but Aristotle says there is no sense in asking what qualities or activities are *made* of. (2) The second objection depends on the principle that all learning of anything depends on and requires previous knowledge. To learn the truth by *demonstration*, you must previously know the *premises* of the proof; to learn it from a *definition*, you must know the meaning of the *terms* employed; to learn it by *induction*, i.e., comparison of instances, you must previously be acquainted with the individual instances. Hence if all truths constituted a single science, before learning that science you would know no truths at all, and therefore the process of learning itself would be impossible. To meet the retort which a Platonist, who held with Plato that all knowledge is really recollection, would be sure to make, viz., that the knowledge of the ultimate axioms is "innate," and not acquired at all (Cf. Plato, *Meno*, 81c, etc.), he argues that if we had such innate cognitions we could not be unconscious of having them—the same argument afterward employed by Locke.

As an argument against the doctrine of an all-embracing science the reasoning seems a pure *petitio principii*, since it merely goes to prove the necessity of some self-evident truths.

long to that science, and which he is about to learn, so it is in all other cases. So, if there is, as some assert, a universal science of everything, he who learns it must have no previous acquaintance with anything. And yet all learning is effected through previous acquaintance with some or all of the matters concerned. This is true both of learning from demonstration and of learning from definitions. The parts which compose the definition must be previously known and familiar. The same is true, also, of learning from induction. But if it be suggested that this knowledge is really innate, it is surely a mystery how we can possess the most excellent of sciences and yet be unconscious of the fact. Besides, how are we to *recognize* what existence consists of? How can the result be *established?* There is a difficulty implied here, since the same doubt might be suggested as about certain syllables. Some say that the syllable ZA consists of Σ, Δ, and A, others that it is a distinct sound, different from those·already familiar. Besides, how could one become acquainted with the objects of sense-perception, without possessing the corresponding form of sense-perception? Yet, this ought to be possible if all things are composed of the same constituent elements,[70] as composite articulate sounds are composed of their own special elements.

X. It is clear, then, even from the preceding review, that all philosophers seem to be investigating the forms of cause enumerated in our discourses on Physics, and that we can specify no further form of cause besides these. But their treatment of them was obscure, and though in one sense all the causes had been previously recognized, in another sense this had not been done at all. For at first, and in its beginnings, owing to its youth, the earliest philosophy resembled in its utterances on all topics the lisping speech of an infant. Thus even Empedocles says that the existence of *bone* depends on a ratio,[71] but this ratio is, in fact, the essen-

[70] I.e., if, for instance, a visible object, such as a shade or color, is ultimately constituted by a combination of purely logical categories, like the One and the Great and Small (as must be the case if the "elements of the Ideas are the elements of all things"), a Platonic philosopher, even though blind from birth, ought to be able to have "pure anticipated cognitions" of all the colors of the spectrum.

[71] The reference is to Empedocles, where bone is said to consist of fixed proportions of the elementary bodies. The point is, simply, that Empedocles is recognizing that what a thing is depends primarily on its *form* or *formal cause*, or, as we should say, the *law* of its composition, and not merely on the nature of the *stuff* of which it is made.

tial nature or *essence* of the object. But it follows with equal necessity that there must also be a ratio for flesh, and every other individual thing, or for none at all. This, then, and not the matter, of which Empedocles speaks, viz., fire, and earth and water and air, will be the true ground of the existence of flesh and bone and everything else. If another had explained this he would have had no alternative but to admit it, but he did not express it clearly himself. These and similar points, then, have been explained above, but we may now return to the consideration of the difficulties which might be raised about these same topics. Perhaps a study of them may pave the way for an answer to our subsequent difficulties.

PHILOSOPHY OF NATURE
How We Are To Conceive Nature and Cause (*Physics*)

*Aristotle's natural philosophy deals chiefly with the problem
of motion. It is concerned with natural bodies, namely, bodies
that are capable of motion or rest. Aristotle's general conception
of change as actualization of potentiality ("Motion is the
actuality of that which is in potentiality in so far as it is in
potentiality") holds good for all the special types of change.
He distinguishes four kinds, in our ensuing selection from the
"Metaphysics": (1) substantial—coming into being and passing away, (2) quantitative—increase and decrease in size, (3)
qualitative—transformation of one thing into another, (4) local
—change of place. Substantial change applies only to particular
objects; there can be no origination and destruction in the absolute sense. The last three types of change correspond respectively
to organic, chemical, and mechanical processes. Aristotle, in
general, divides the universe into two parts—celestial and
terrestrial. The former is characterized by the perfect circular
motions of the heavenly bodies, and the latter by the rectilinear
motions of the four elements—earth, air, fire, and water. These
elemental bodies have natural tendencies to move in certain
directions. Earth, for example, tends to move toward the center
of the universe and fire toward the circumference. In the construction of the four elements Aristotle uses the fundamental
opposites of pre-Socratic philosophy—hot and cold, dry and
moist. Hot and dry combine to form fire, hot and moist, air; cold
and moist, water; cold and dry, earth. These original elements
combine in various proportions to form composite bodies, and
these combinations are not transpositions but transformations,
thoroughgoing qualitative changes. But nothing is to be understood without analysis; and when analysis is finished it is not
easy to tell the objects of physics from those of metaphysics, as
comparison of the next two selections disclose. The four causes
do continuous service in physics and in metaphysics.*

. . .

HOW WE ARE TO CONCEIVE NATURE AND CAUSE

Physics. Wicksteed and Cornford translation ("Loeb Classical Library" series). This selection is from Book ii, comprising most of chaps. 1, 2, 3. Precisely it runs continuously from 193a to 195a. It is of course but a very small fraction of the long treatise as a whole.—T. V. S.

I. . . . . Some hold that the nature and substantive existence of natural products resides in their material on the analogy of the wood of a bedstead or the bronze of a statue. (Antiphon took it as an indication of this that if a man buried a bedstead and the sap in it took force and threw out a shoot it would be tree and not bedstead that came up, since the artificial arrangement of the material by the craftsman is merely an incident that has occurred to it, whereas its essential and natural quality is to be found in that which persists continuously throughout such experiences.) And in like manner, it is thought, if the materials themselves bear to yet other substances the same relation which the manufactured articles bear to them—if, for instance, water is the material of bronze or gold, or earth of bone or timber, and so forth—then it is in the water or earth that we must look for the 'nature' and essential being of the gold and so forth. And this is why some have said that it was earth that constituted the nature of things, some fire, some air, some water, and some several and some all of these elemental substances. For whichever substance or substances each thinker assumed to be primary he regarded as constituting the substantive existence of all things in general, all else being mere modifications, states, and dispositions of them. Any such ultimate substance they regarded as eternal (for they did not admit the transformation of elementary substances into each other), while they held that all else passed into existence and out of it endlessly.

This then is one way of regarding 'nature'—as the ultimately underlying material of all things that have in themselves the principle of movement and change. But from another point of view we may think of the nature of a thing as residing in its form, that is to say in the 'kind' of thing it is by definition. For as we give the name of 'art' to a thing which is the product of art and is itself artistic, so we give the name of 'nature' to the products of nature which themselves are 'natural.' And as, in the case of art, we should not allow that what was only potentially a bedstead and had not yet received the form of bed had in it as yet any art-formed element, or could be called 'art,' so in the case of natural products; what is potentially flesh or bone has not yet the 'nature' of flesh until it actually assumes the form indicated by the definition that constitutes it the thing in question, nor is this potential flesh or bone as yet a product of nature. These considerations would lead us to revise our definition of nature as follows: Nature is the distinctive form or quality of such things as have within themselves a principle of motion, such form or characteristic property not being separable from the things themselves, save conceptually. (The *compositum*—a man, for example—which material and form combine to constitute, is not itself a 'nature,' but a thing that comes to be by natural process.) And this view of where to look for the nature of things is preferable to that which finds it in the material; for when we speak of the thing into the nature of which we are inquiring, we mean by its name an actuality not a potentiality merely.

Again men propagate men, but bedsteads do not propagate bedsteads; and that is why they say that the natural factor in a bedstead is not its shape but the wood—to wit, because wood and not bedstead would come up if it germinated. If, then, it is this incapacity of reproduction that makes a thing art and not nature, then the form of natural things will be their nature, as in the parallel case of art; for man is generated by man, whereas a bedstead is not generated from a bedstead.

Again, *na-ture* is etymologically equivalent to *gene-sis* and (in Greek) is actually used as a synonym for it; nature, then, *qua* genesis proclaims itself as the path to nature *qua* goal. Now, it is true that healing is so called, not because it is the path to the healing art, but because it is the path to health, for of necessity healing proceeds from the healing art, not to the healing art itself; but this is not the relation of nature to nature, for that which is born starts as something and advances or grows towards something else. Towards what, then, does it grow? Not towards its original state at birth, but towards its final state or goal. It is, then, the form that is nature; but, since 'form' and 'nature' are ambiguous terms, inasmuch as shortage is a kind of form, we shall leave to future investigation whether shortage is, or is not, a sort of contrasted term (opposed to positive form) in absolute generation.[72]

[72] The question is frequently discussed in other works of Aristotle, notably in *Physics* V and in the *De gen. et cor.* A3. The answer in substance is that there is really

II. Now that we have determined the different senses in which "nature" may be understood (as signifying either 'material' or 'form'), we have next to consider how the mathematician differs from the physicist or natural philosopher; for nature bodies have surfaces and occupy spaces, have lengths and present points, all which are subjects of mathematical study. And then there is the connected question whether astronomy is a separate science from physics or only a special branch of it; for if the student of Nature is concerned to know what the sun and moon are, it were strange if he could avoid inquiry into their essential properties; especially as we find that writers on Nature have, as a fact, discoursed on the shape of the moon and sun and raised the question whether the earth, or the cosmos, is spherical or otherwise.

Physicists, astronomers, and mathematicians, then, all have to deal with lines, figures and the rest. But the mathematician is not concerned with these concepts *qua* boundaries of natural bodies, nor with their properties as manifested in such bodies. Therefore he abstracts them from physical conditions; for they are capable of being considered in the mind in separation from the motions of the bodies to which they pertain, and such abstraction does not affect the validity of the reasoning or lead to any false conclusions.

Now the exponents of the philosophy of 'Ideas' also make abstractions, but in doing so they fall unawares into error; for they abstract physical entities, which are not really susceptible to the process as mathematical entities are. And this would become obvious if one should undertake to define, respectively, the mathematical and the 'ideal' entities, together with their properties; for the concepts 'odd,' 'even,' 'straight,' 'curved,' will be found to be independent of movement; and so too with 'number,' 'line,' and 'figure.' But of 'flesh' and 'bone' and 'man' this is no longer true, for these are in the same case as a 'turned-up-nose,' not in the same case as 'curved.' The point is further illustrated by those sciences which are rather physical than mathematical, though combining both disciplines, such as optics, harmonics, and astronomy; for the relations between them and geometry are, so to speak, recip-

---

no such thing as absolute genesis and therefore no contrast to concrete entity. But we say that a concrete entity has perished when the indestructible matter which lies at the core of it has assumed forms which evade our ability to recognize its identity any longer.

rocal; since the geometer deals with physical lines, but not *qua* physical, whereas optics deals with mathematical lines, but *qua* physical not *qua* mathematical.

Since 'nature' is used ambiguously, either for the form or for the matter, Nature, as we have seen, can be regarded from two points of view, and therefore our speculations about it may be likened to an inquiry as to what 'snubnosed-ness' is; that is to say, it can neither be isolated from the material subject in which it exists, nor is it constituted by it.

At this point, in fact, we may again raise two questions. Which of the two aspects of Nature is it that claims the attention of the physicist? Or is his subject the *compositum* that combines the two? In that case—if he is concerned with the *compositum*—he must also inquire into its two factors; and then we must ask further whether this inquiry is the same for both factors or different for each.

In reading the ancients one might well suppose that the physicist's only concern was with the material; for Empedocles and Democritus have remarkably little to say about kinds of things and what is the constituent essence of them. But if art imitates Nature, and if in the arts and crafts it pertains to the same branch of knowledge both to study its own distinctive aspect of things and likewise (up to a point) the material in which the same is manifested (as the physician, for instance, must study health and also bile and phlegm, the state of which constitutes health; and the builder must know what the house is to be like and also that it is built of bricks and timber; and so in all other cases), it seems to follow that physics must take cognizance both of the formal and of the material aspect of Nature.

And further the same inquiry must embrace both the purpose or end and the means to that end [i.e., both the form and the matter]. And the 'nature' is the goal for the sake of which the rest exist; for if any systematic and continuous movement is directed to a goal, this goal is an end in the sense of the purpose to which the movement is a means. (A confusion on this point betrayed the poet into the unintentionally comic phrase in reference to a man's death: 'He has reached his end, for the sake of which he was born.' For the 'goal' does not mean any kind of termination, but only the best.) For in the arts, too, it is in view of the end that the materials are either made or suitably prepared, and we make use of all things that we have at our command as though they existed for our sake; for we too are, in some sort, a goal ourselves. For the expression 'that for the sake of which' a thing exists or is done has two senses (as we have explained in our treatise On Philosophy). Accordingly, the arts which control the material and possess the necessary knowledge are two: the art which uses the product and the art of the master-craftsman who directs the manufacture. Hence the art of the user also may in a sense be called the master-art; the difference is that this art is concerned with knowing the form, the other, which is supreme as controlling the manufacture, with knowing the material. Thus, the helmsman knows what are the distinctive characteristics of the helm as such—that is to say, its form—and gives his orders accordingly; while what the other knows is out of what wood and by what manipulations the helm is produced. In the crafts, then, it is we that prepare the material for the sake of the function it is to fulfil, but in natural products Nature herself has provided the material. In both cases, however, the preparation of the material is commanded by the end to which it is directed.

And again, the conception of 'material' is relative, for it is different material that is suited to receive the several forms.

How far then, is the physicist concerned with the form and identifying essence of things and how far with their material? With the form primarily and essentially, as the physician is with health; with the material up to a certain point, as the physician with sinew and the smith with bronze. For his main concern is with the goal, which is formal; but he deals only with such forms as are conceptually, but not factually, detachable from the material in which they occur. In Nature man generates man; but the process presupposes and takes place in natural material already organized by the solar heat and so forth. But how we are to take the sejunct and what it is, is a question for First Philosophy to determine.[73]

III. We have next to consider in how many senses 'because' may answer the question 'why.' For we aim at understanding, and since we never reckon that we understand a thing till we can give an account of its 'how and why,' it is clear that we must look into the

---

[73] *Met.* E I, Physics deals with natural bodies, which have separate existence and can change; Mathematics, with unchanging entities, which exist not separately but only as qualifying substances; Theology, with pure forms, unchanging and separately existing.

'how and why' of things coming into existence and passing out of it, or more generally into the essential constituents of physical change, in order to trace back any object of our study to the principles so ascertained.

Well then, (1) the existence of *material* for the generating process to start from (whether specifically or generically considered) is one of the essential factors we are looking for. Such is the bronze for the statue, or the silver for the phial (Material). Then, naturally, (2) the thing in question cannot be there unless the material has actually received the *form* or characteristics of the type, conformity to which brings it within the definition of the thing we say it is, whether specifically or generically.[74] Thus the interval between two notes is not an octave unless the notes are in the ratio of 2 to 1; nor do they stand at a musical interval at all unless they conform to one or other of the recognized ratios (Formal). Then again (3), there must be something to initiate the process of the change or its cessation when the process is completed, such as the act of a voluntary agent (of the smith, for instance), or the father who begets a child; or more generally the prime, conscious or unconscious, *agent* that produces the effect and starts the material on its way to the product, changing it from what it was to what it is to be (Efficient). And lastly, (4) there is the *end* or purpose, for the sake of which the process is initiated, as when a man takes exercise for the sake of his health. 'Why does he take exercise?' we ask. And the answer 'Because he thinks it good for his health' satisfies us (Final). Then there are all the intermediary agents which are set in motion by the prime agent and make for the goal, as means to the end. Such are the reduction of superfluous flesh and purgation, or drugs and surgical instruments, as means to health. For both actions and tools may be means, or '*media*,' through which the efficient cause reaches the end aimed at.

This is a rough classification of the causal determinants of things; but it often happens that, when we specify them, we find a number of them coalescing as joint factors in the production of a single effect, and that not merely incidentally; for it is *qua* statue that the statue depends for its existence alike on the bronze and on the statuary. The two, however, do not stand on the same foot-

[74] That is to say, it must have actually 'arrived' and realized its 'being-what-it-had-to-be.'

ing, for one is required as the material and the other as initiating the change.

Also, it can be said of certain things indifferently that either of them is the cause or the effect of the other. Thus we may say that a man is in fine condition 'because' he has been in training 'because' of the good condition he expected as the result. But one is the cause as aim (final) and the other as initiating the process (efficient).

Again, the same cause is often alleged for precisely opposite effects. For if its presence causes one thing, we lay the opposite to its account if it is absent. Thus, if the pilot's presence would have brought the ship safe to harbour, we say that he caused its wreck by his absence.

But in all cases the essential and causal determinants we have enumerated fall into four main classes. For letters are the causes of syllables, and the material is the cause of manufactured articles, and fire and the like are causes of physical bodies, and the parts are causes of the whole, and the premises are causes of the conclusion,[75] in the sense of that out of which these respectively are made; but of these things some are causes in the sense of the *substratum* (e.g. the parts stand in this relation to the whole), others in the sense of the *essence*—the whole or the synthesis or the form. And again, the fertilizing sperm, or the physician, or briefly the voluntary or involuntary *agent* sets going or arrests the transformation or movement. And finally, there is the goal or *end* in view, which animates all the other determinant factors as the best they can attain to; for the attainment of that 'for the sake of which' anything exists or is done is its final and best possible achievement (though of course 'best' in this connection means no more than 'taken to be the best').

[75] The technical term for the propositions of a syllogism apart from their logical connexion is 'material,' so that the propositions 'mammals are animals,' 'squirrels are animals,' 'squirrels are mammals,' are the 'material' of the syllogism: 'mammals are animals, squirrels are animals, therefore squirrels are mammals.' Here all three propositions, major, minor, and conclusion, are true. Therefore the conclusion is materially sound, but formally the syllogism is not sound; for the conclusion does not follow from the premises, though they are all true. Aristotle frequently points out that the conclusion of a syllogism is materially true, but not formally proved.

PHILOSOPHY OF FIRST PRINCIPLES
DEVELOPMENT AS MATTER TAKING ON FORM (*Metaphysics*)
THE FINAL CAUSE OF DEVELOPMENT FROM THE POTENTIAL
TO ACTUALITY (*ibid.*)

Aristotle, as we have frequently seen, objected to the sharp gap that Plato had left between the world of forms and the world of things. He retained the forms in order to explain the phenomenal world, but for this very reason he rejected their transcendence and made them immanent as the true essences of things. The forms are the sole objects of genuine knowledge and the veritable causes of all change. But in addition to their formal aspect individual things have also a material aspect. Matter is the substrate which underlies all change. As a sort of permanent possibility of becoming, matter is to be regarded as potentiality; when it realizes its form it has taken on actuality. Change, then, is a process of development in which potentiality is being actualized. In the field of technology, Aristotle, as we have observed, mentions four causes of change, material, efficient, formal and final; but in the field of biology the last three merge into one, leaving only the material and the formal. In the Aristotelian synthesis, the material cause represents the mechanical principle of Democritus, and the formal cause represents the teleological principle of Plato. Matter acts as an obstruction and balks the perfect realization of the form. When the relation between matter and form is applied to different individual things, the result is a hierarchy of things in which the same object may be form for what lies below it and matter for what stands above it. The lower limit of this scale is pure matter, which has no separate existence; and the upper limit is pure form, the unmoved mover, which ought not to exist by itself, but which does exist to serve as deity for contemplation and as final cause of motion, by being a worthy object for the appetition of all things.

. . .

DEVELOPMENT AS MATTER TAKING ON FORM

Metaphysics, Book viii, with irrelevant matter excluded at the beginning. Tre-
dennick translation ("Loeb Classical Library" series). This is less than one-tenth
of the treatise.—T. V. S.

I. . . . . Now let us proceed to discuss those substances which
are generally accepted as such.

Now these are the sensible substances, and all sensible substances contain matter. And the substrate is substance; in one
sense matter (by matter I mean that which is not actually, but is
potentially, an individual thing); and in another the formula and
the specific shape (which is an individual thing and is theoretically
separable); and thirdly there is the combination of the two, which
alone admits of generation and destruction, and is separable in an
unqualified sense—for of substances in the sense of formula some
are separable[76] and some are not.

That matter is also substance is evident; for in all opposite processes of change there is something that underlies those processes;
e.g., if the change is of *place*, that which is now in one place and
subsequently in another; and if the change is of *magnitude*, that
which is now of such-and-such a size, and subsequently smaller or
greater; and if the change is of *quality*, that which is now healthy
and subsequently diseased. Similarly, if the change is in respect of
being, there is something which is now in course of generation, and
subsequently in course of destruction, and which is the underlying
substrate, now as *this* individual thing, and subsequently as deprived of its individuality. In this last process of change the others
are involved, but in either one or two of the others it is not involved;
for it does not necessarily follow that if a thing contains matter
that admits of change of place, it also contains matter that is generable and destructible. The difference between absolute and qualified generation has been explained in the *Physics*.

II. Since substance in the sense of substrate or matter is admittedly substance, and this is potential substance, it remains to explain the nature of the actual substance of sensible things. Now
Democritus apparently assumes three differences in substance; for
he says that the underlying body is one and the same in material,
but differs in figure, i.e. shape; or inclination, i.e. position; or inter-

[76] In point of fact the only form which is absolutely separable is Mind or Reason.

contact, i.e. arrangement. But evidently there are many differences; e.g. some things are defined by the way in which their materials are combined, as, for example, things which are unified by mixture, as honey-water; or by ligature, as a faggot; or by glue, as a book; or by clamping, as a chest; or by more than one of these methods. Other things are defined by their position, e.g. threshold and lintel (for these differ in being situated in a particular way); and others by time, e.g. dinner and breakfast; and others by the attributes peculiar to sensible things, e.g. hardness and softness, density and rarity, dryness and humidity. Some are distinguished by some of these differences, and others by all of them; and in general some by excess and some by defect.

Hence it is clear that "is" has the same number of senses; for a thing "is" a threshold because it is situated in a particular way, and "to be a threshold" means to be situated in this particular way; and "to be ice" means to be condensed in this particular way. Some things have their being defined in all these ways: by being partly mixed, partly blended, partly bound, partly condensed, and partly subjected to all the other different processes; as, for example, a hand or a foot. We must therefore comprehend the various kinds of differences—for these will be principles of being—i.e. the differences in degree, or in density and rarity, and in other such modifications; for they are all instances of excess and defect. And if anything differs in shape or in smoothness or roughness, all these are differences in straightness and curvature. For some things mixture will constitute being, and the opposite state not-being.

From this it is evident that if substance is the cause of the existence of each thing, we must look among these "differences" for the cause of the being of each thing. No one of them, nor the combination of any two of them, is substance, but nevertheless each one of them contains something analogous to substance. And just as in the case of substances that which is predicated of the matter is the actuality itself, so in the other kinds of definition it is the nearest approximation to actuality. E.g., if we have to define a threshold, we shall call it "a piece of wood or stone placed in such-and-such a way"; and we shall define a house as "bricks and timber arranged in such-and-such a way"; or again in some cases there is the final cause as well. And if we are defining ice, we shall describe it as "water congealed or condensed in such-and-such a way"; and a harmony is "such-and-such a combination of high and low"; and similarly in the other cases.

From this it is evident that the actuality or formula is different in the case of different matter; for in some cases it is a combination, in others a mixture, and in others some other of the modes which we have described. Hence in defining the nature of a house, those who describe it as stones, bricks and wood, describe the potential house, since these things are its matter; those who describe it as "a receptacle for containing goods and bodies," or something else to the same effect, describe its actuality; but those who combine these two definitions describe the third kind of substance, that which is composed of matter and form. For it would seem that the formula which involves the differentiae is that of the form and the actuality, while that which involves the constituent parts is rather that of the matter. The same is true of the kind of definitions which Archytas[77] used to accept; for they are definitions of the combined matter and form. E.g., what is "windlessness?" Stillness in a large extent of air; for the air is the matter, and the stillness is the actuality and substance. What is a calm? Levelness of sea. The sea is the material substrate, and the levelness is the actuality or form.

From the foregoing account it is clear what sensible substance is, and in what sense it exists; either as matter, or as form and actuality, or thirdly as the combination of the two.

III. We must not fail to realize that sometimes it is doubtful whether a name denotes the composite substance or the actuality and the form—e.g. whether "house" denotes the composite thing, "a covering made of bricks and stone arranged in such-and-such a way," or the actuality and form, "a covering"; and whether "line" means "duality in length" or "duality"; and whether "animal" means "a soul in a body" or "a soul"; for the soul is the substance and actuality of some body. The term "animal" would be applicable to both cases; not as being defined by one formula, but as relating to one concept. These distinctions are of importance from another point of view, but unimportant for the investigation of sensible substance; because the essence belongs to the form and the actualization. Soul and essence of soul are the same, but man and essence of man are not, unless the soul is also to be called man; and although this is so in one sense, it is not so in another.

It appears, then, when we inquire into the matter, that a syllable

77 A celebrated Pythagorean, contemporary with Plato.

is not derived from the phonetic elements *plus* combination, nor is a house bricks *plus* combination. And this is true; for the combination or mixture is not derived from the things of which it is a combination or mixture, nor, similarly, is any other of the "differences." E.g., if the threshold is defined by its position, the position is not derived from the threshold, but rather *vice versa*. Nor, indeed, is man "animal" *plus* "two-footed"; there must be something which exists besides these, if they are matter; but it is neither an element nor derived from an element, but the substance; and those who offer the definition given above are omitting this and describing the matter. If, then, this something else is the cause of a man's being, and this is his substance, they will not be stating his actual substance.

Now the substance must be either eternal or perishable without ever being in process of perishing, and generated without ever being in process of generation. It has been clearly demonstrated elsewhere that no one generates or creates the form; it is the individual thing that is created, and the compound that is generated. But whether the substances of perishable things are separable or not is not yet at all clear; only it is clear that this is impossible in some cases, i.e. in the case of all things which cannot exist apart from the particular instances; e.g. house or implement. Probably, then, neither these things themselves, nor anything else which is not naturally composed, are substances; for their nature is the only substance which one can assume in the case of perishable things. Hence the difficulty which perplexed the followers of Antisthenes and others similarly unlearned has a certain application; I mean the difficulty that it is impossible to define *what* a thing is (for the definition, they say, is a lengthy formula), but it *is* possible actually to teach others what a thing is *like;* e.g., we cannot say *what* silver is, but we can say that it is like tin. Hence there can be definition and formula of one kind of substance, i.e. the composite, whether it is sensible or intelligible; but not of its primary constituents, since the defining formula denotes something predicated of something, and this must be partly of the nature of matter and partly of the nature of form.

It is also obvious why, if numbers are in any sense substances, they are such in this sense, and not, as some[78] describe them, aggre-

[78] Aristotle is referring to the Pythagoreans and Platonists, but seems as usual to misrepresent their views. His object in this section is to show that the relation of number to substance is only one of analogy.

gates of units. For (a) the definition is a kind of number, since it is divisible, and divisible into indivisible parts (for formulae are not infinite); and number is of this nature. And (b) just as when any element which composes the number is subtracted or added, it is no longer the same number but a different one, however small the subtraction or addition is; so neither the definition nor the essence will continue to exist if something is subtracted from or added to it. And (c) a number must be something in virtue of which it is a unity (whereas our opponents cannot say what makes it one); that is, if it is a unity. For either it is not a unity but a kind of aggregate, or if it is a unity, we must explain what makes a unity out of a plurality. And the definition is a unit; but similarly they cannot explain the definition either. This is a natural consequence, for the same reason applies to both, and substance is a unity in the way which we have explained, and not as some thinkers say: e.g. because it is a kind of unit or point; but each substance is a kind of actuality and nature. And (d) just as a number does not admit of variation in degree, so neither does substance in the sense of form; if any substance does admit of this, it is substance in combination with matter.

Let this suffice as a detailed account of the generation and destruction of so-called substances, in what sense they are possible and in what sense they are not; and of the references of things to number.

IV. As regards material substance, we must not fail to realize that even if all things are derived from the same primary cause, or from the same things as primary causes;[79] i.e. even if all things that are generated have the same matter for their first principle, nevertheless each thing has some matter peculiar to it; e.g., "the sweet" or "the viscous" is the proximate matter of mucus, and "the bitter" or some such things is that of bile—although probably mucus and bile are derived from the same ultimate matter. The result is that there is more than one matter of the same thing, when one thing is the matter of the other; e.g., mucus is derived from "the viscous"; and from "the sweet," if "the viscous" is derived from "the sweet"; and from bile, by the analysis of bile into its ultimate matter. For there are two senses in which X comes from Y; either because X

[79] I.e. from prime matter or the four elements.

will be found further on than Y in the process of development, or because X is produced when Y is analysed into its original constituents. And different things can be generated by the moving cause when the matter is one and the same, e.g., a chest and a bed from wood. But some different things must necessarily have different matter; e.g., a saw cannot be generated from wood, nor does this lie in the power of the moving cause, for it cannot make a saw of wool or wood.

If, then, it is possible to make the same thing from different matter, clearly the art, i.e. the moving principle, is the same; for if both the matter and the mover are different, so too is the product.

So whenever we inquire what the cause is, since there are causes in several senses, we must state all the possible causes. E.g., what is the material cause of a man? The menses. What is the moving cause? The semen. What is the formal cause? The essence. What is the final cause? The end. (But perhaps both the latter are the same.) We must, however, state the most proximate causes. What is the matter? Not fire or earth, but the matter proper to man.

Thus as regards generable natural substances we must proceed in this manner, if we are to proceed correctly; that is, if the causes are these and of this number, and it is necessary to know the causes. But in the case of substances which though natural are eternal the principle is different. For presumably some of them have no matter, or no matter of this kind, but only such as is spatially mobile. Moreover, things which exist by nature but are not substances have no matter; their substrate is their substance. E.g., what is the cause of an eclipse; what is its matter? It has none; it is the moon which is affected. What is the moving cause which destroys the light? The earth. There is probably no final cause. The formal cause is the formula; but this is obscure unless it includes the efficient cause. E.g., what is an eclipse? A privation of light; and if we add "caused by the earth's intervention," this is the definition which includes the «efficient» cause. In the case of sleep it is not clear what it is that is proximately affected. Is it the animal? Yes; but in respect of what, and of what proximately? The heart, or some other part. Again, by what is it affected? Again, what is the affection which affects that part, and not the whole animal? A particular kind of immobility? Yes; but in virtue of what affection of the proximate subject is it this?

V. Since some things both are and are not, without being liable
to generation and destruction—e.g. points, if they exist at all; and
in general the forms and shapes of things (because white does not
come to be, but the wood becomes white, since everything which
comes into being comes from something and becomes something)—
not all the contraries can be generated from each other. White is
not generated from black in the same way as a white man is generated from a black man; nor does everything contain matter, but
only such things as admit of generation and transformation into
each other. And such things as, without undergoing a process of
change, both are and are not, have no matter.

There is a difficulty in the question how the matter of the individual is related to the contraries. E.g., if the body is potentially
healthy, and the contrary of health is disease, is the body potentially both healthy and diseased? Probably in the one case it is
the matter in respect of the positive state and form, and in the
other case in respect of privation and degeneration which is contrary to its proper nature.

There is also a difficulty as to why wine is not the matter of vinegar, nor potentially vinegar (though vinegar comes from it), and
why the living man is not potentially dead. In point of fact they are
not; their degeneration is accidental, and the actual matter of the
living body becomes by degeneration the potentiality and matter of
the dead body, and water the matter of vinegar; for the one becomes
the other just as day becomes night. All things which change recip-
rocally in this way must return into the matter; e.g., if a living
thing is generated from a dead one, it must first become the matter,
and then a living thing; and vinegar must first become water, and
then wine.

VI. With regard to the difficulty which we have described in connexion with definitions and numbers, what is the cause of the unification? In all things which have a plurality of parts, and which are
not a total aggregate but a whole of some sort distinct from the
parts, there is some *cause;* inasmuch as even in bodies sometimes
contact is the cause of their unity, and sometimes viscosity or some
other such quality. But a definition is *one* account, not by connexion, like the *Iliad*, but because it is a definition of one thing.

What is it, then, that makes "man" one thing, and why does it
make him one thing and not many, e.g. "animal" and "two-footed,"

especially if, as some say, there is an Idea of "animal" and an Idea of "two-footed?" Why are not these Ideas "man," and why should not man exist by participation, not in any "man," but in two Ideas, those of "animal" and "two-footed"? And in general "man" will be not one, but two things—"animal" and "two-footed." Evidently if we proceed in this way, as it is usual to define and explain, it will be impossible to answer and solve the difficulty. But if, as we maintain, man is part matter and part form—the matter being potentially, and the form actually man—, the point which we are investigating will no longer seem to be a difficulty. For this difficulty is just the same as we should have if the definition of X were "round bronze"; for this name would give a clue to the formula, so that the question becomes "what is the cause of the unification of 'round' and 'bronze'?" The difficulty is no longer apparent, because the one is matter and the other form. What then is it (apart from the active cause) which causes that which exists potentially to exist actually in things which admit of generation? There *is* no other cause of the potential sphere's being an actual sphere; this was the essence of each.[80]

Some matter is intelligible and some sensible, and part of the formula is always matter and part actuality; e.g., the circle is a plane figure.[81] But such things[82] as have no matter, neither intelligible nor sensible, are *ipso facto* each one of them essentially something one; just as they are essentially something existent: an individual substance, a quality, or a quantity. Hence neither "existent" nor "one" is present in something one, just as it is something existent. Hence also there is no other cause of the unity of any of these things, or of their existence; for each one of them is "one" and "existent" not because it is contained in the genus "being" or "unity," nor because these genera exist separately apart from their particulars, but *ipso facto*.

It is because of this difficulty that some thinkers[83] speak of "participation," and raise the question of what is the cause of par-

---

[80] I.e., it was the essence of the potential sphere to become the actual sphere, and of the actual sphere to be generated from the potential sphere.

[81] Even formulae contain matter in a sense ("intelligible matter"); i.e. the generic element in the species. "Plane figure" is the generic element of "circle."

[82] The highest genera, or categories.

[83] The Platonists.

ticipation, and what participation means; and others speak of "communion"; e.g., Lycophron[84] says that knowledge is a communion of the soul with "knowing"; and others call life a combination or connexion of soul with body. The same argument, however, applies in every case; for "being healthy" will be the "communion" or "connexion" or "combination" of soul and health; and "being a bronze triangle" a "combination" of bronze and triangle; and "being white" a "combination" of surface and whiteness. The reason for this is that people look for a unifying formula, and a difference, between potentiality and actuality. But, as we have said, the proximate matter and the shape are one and the same; the one existing potentially, and the other actually. Therefore to ask the cause of their unity is like asking the cause of unity in general; for each individual thing is one, and the potential and the actual are in a sense one. Thus there is no cause other than whatever initiates the development from potentiality to actuality. And such things as have no matter are all, without qualification, essential unities.

THE FINAL CAUSE OF DEVELOPMENT FROM THE POTENTIAL TO ACTUALITY

A few excerpts are here added from *Metaphysics*, Book xi, chap. 7, to show how Aristotle concludes his discussion of substance with the suprasensual as divine host of all excellence and instigator of all motion. The translation is John H. M'Mahon's ("Bohn's Classical Library" series).—T. V. S.

. . . . Something always would there be that is being moved with a motion that is incessant, but this is that which is circular; and this is evident not merely from reason, but from the fact itself. Wherefore, the first heaven would be eternal. There is, therefore, also something that imparts motion. Since, however, that which has motion impressed upon it, and which imparts motion, subsists as a medium, there is, therefore, something which, not having motion impressed upon it, yet imparts motion, which is a thing that is eternal, being both substance and energy. But in this way it imparts motion—I mean, that which is desirable and that which is intelligible impart motion, whereas they are not moved themselves. . . . .

[84] A disciple of Gorgias.

For the final cause of anything resides in those things of which the one is in existence and the other is not. Now, that which first imparts motion does so as a thing that is loved; and that which has motion impressed upon it imparts motion to other things. If, indeed, therefore, anything is being moved, it is admissible, also, that it should subsist in a different manner. Wherefore, if the primary motion constitute energy also, so far forth as the thing is moved, in this way is it likewise possible that it should subsist after a different mode in place though not in substance. Since, however, there is something that imparts motion, itself being immovable, and subsisting in energy, this does not by any means admit of subsisting in a different manner; for the primary motion belongs to the changes, and of this that which is circular; but this First Mover imparts motion to that.

Of necessity, in this case, must this Immovable First Mover constitute an entity; and so far forth as it subsists necessarily, so far forth does it subsist after an excellent manner; and in this way constitutes a first principle. . . . . From a first principle, then, of this kind—I mean, one that is involved in the assumption of a First Mover—hath depended the Heaven and Nature.

Now, the course of life of this First Mover—in like manner with our own, for a limited period of time—is such, also, as is the most excellent; for, in the present instance, doth that First Mover continue in the enjoyment of the principle of life forever; for with us, certainly, such a thing as this would be impossible; but not so with the First Mover, since even doth the energy or activity of this First Mover give rise unto pleasure or satisfaction on the part of such; and on this account vigilance, exercise of the senses, and perception in general, are what is most productive of pleasure or satisfaction; and with hopes and recollections is the case the same for these reasons. Now, essential perception is the perception of that which is essentially the most excellent; and that which is most essential perception is the perception of that which is most essential. The mind, however, is cognisant of itself by participation in that which falls within the province of the mind as its object; for it becomes an object of perception by contact, and by an act of intellectual apprehension. So that the mind and that which is an object of perception for the mind are the same; for that which is receptive of impressions from what is an object of perception, and is substance, constitutes mind: and when in possession of these impressions it energizes, or subsists in a condition of activity. Wherefore, that seems to belong to the First Mover rather than to the mind of man. . . . . In this way, however, is the Deity disposed as to existence, and the principle of life is, at any rate, inherent in the Deity; for the energy or active exercise of Mind constitutes life, and God—as above delineated—constitutes this energy; and essential energy belongs to God as his best and everlasting life. Now, our statement is this,—that the Deity is an animal that is everlasting and most excellent in nature; so that with the Deity life and duration are uninterrupted and eternal: for this constitutes the very essence of God.

THE FUNCTION OF MAN AND THE TECHNIQUE OF INTELLIGENCE

THE THEORY OF THE GOOD LIFE (*Ethics*)
EDUCATION FOR CITIZENSHIP (*Politics*)

Man shares the teleological yearnings of the whole of nature, but in him alone the quest for the good becomes self-conscious. He seeks not only his good, but his unique good. He shares the form of good that both vegetable and animal life seeks, since he has both a vegetative and an animal nature. But, besides, he seeks a rational good. His highest good is happiness; but happiness means many things. At its best it means the activity of man's highest capacity, his reason operating as contemplation. But man is not only rational; he is social as well. His happiness may therefore take the form of reason realizing itself in the life of citizenship. Man's reason comes to birth in a social environment and may well find fulfilment in meeting the expectations of the state. So conceived, the creation of friendship, its enjoyment, and its perpetuation stand for the duties and opportunities of the human station. Ethics is the principles of politics, and politics the goal of the rational man at his best. Ethics will discover the golden mean and politics will organize it into social justice and individual happiness. Only a beast or a god would welcome a solitary life. Civic life lifts man above the beasts; it raises him to a contemplation of God. But God is the head of the whole hierarchy of nature, self-satisfied in his moving immobility. To contemplate God is to desire to become like him. And this aspiration gives man as rational a new orientation, one that makes citizenship second rate as material for happiness. For God is solitary; and so self-sufficiency rather than social participation becomes the norm of the very highest good. Moreover, God thinks only about himself, or about the rational structure of true being; and so the contemplation of the species and genera of nature rather than knowledge of political ways and means becomes the mark of the very wisest man. Where ethics and politics leave off, logic begins. Logic may be socially useful, but its highest function is to reveal the morphology of being, the contemplation of which leaves man nearest God. This dilemma marks the culmination, if not also the frustration, of Aristotle. Moreover, it bodied forth an alternative (soon after Aristotle to become dominant) to the common Greek identification of a good man and a good citizen. While he collected constitutions and laid the basis for legislation, his eyes roved now and then in the direction his successors were to take: toward the self-sufficient sage with contemplation, if not worship, as compensation.

. . .

THE THEORY OF THE GOOD LIFE

Ethics. From J. E. C. Welldon's translation. Being Books i and x complete with an excerpt on the golden mean from Book ii of the *Nichomachean Ethics* of Aristotle. By permission of the Macmillan Co. (publishers).—T. V. S.

BOOK I

I. Every art and every scientific inquiry, and similarly every action and purpose, may be said to aim at some good. Hence the good has been well defined as that at which all things aim. But it is clear that there is a difference in the ends; for the ends are sometimes activities, and sometimes results beyond the mere activities. Also, where there are certain ends beyond the actions, the results are naturally superior to the activities.

As there are various actions, arts, and sciences, it follows that the ends are also various. Thus health is the end of medicine, a vessel of shipbuilding, victory of strategy, and wealth of domestic economy. It often happens that there are a number of such arts or sciences which fall under a single faculty, as the art of making bridles, and all such other arts as make the instruments of horsemanship, under horsemanship, and this again as well as every military action under strategy, and in the same way other arts or sciences under other faculties. But in all these cases the ends of the architectonic arts or sciences, whatever they may be, are more desirable than those of the subordinate arts or sciences, as it is for the sake of the former that the latter are themselves sought after. It makes no difference to the argument whether the activities themselves are the ends of the actions, or something else beyond the activities as in the above mentioned sciences.

If it is true that in the sphere of action there is an end which we wish for its own sake, and for the sake of which we wish everything else, and that we do not desire all things for the sake of something else (for, if that is so, the process will go on *ad infinitum*, and our desire will be idle and futile) it is clear that this will be the good or the supreme good. Does it not follow then that the knowledge of this supreme good is of great importance for the conduct of life, and that, *if we know it*, we shall be like archers who have a mark at which to aim, we shall have a better chance of attaining what we want? But, if this is the case, we must endeavour to comprehend, at least in outline, its nature, and the science or faculty to which it belongs.

It would seem that this is the most authoritative or architectonic science or faculty, and such is evidently the political; for it is the political science or faculty which determines what sciences are necessary in states, and what kind of sciences should be learnt, and how far they should be learnt by particular people. We perceive too that the faculties which are held in the highest esteem, e.g. strategy, domestic economy, and rhetoric, are subordinate to it. But as it makes use of the other practical sciences, and also legislates upon the things to be done and the things to be left undone, it follows that its end will comprehend the ends of all the other sciences, and will therefore be the true good of mankind. For although the good of an individual is identical with the good of a state, yet the good of the state, whether in attainment or in preservation, is evidently greater and more perfect. For while in an individual by himself it is something to be thankful for, it is nobler and more divine in a nation or state.

These then are the objects at which the present inquiry aims, and it is in a sense a political[85] inquiry. But our statement of the case will be adequate, if it be made with all such clearness as the subject-matter admits; for it would be as wrong to expect the same degree of accuracy in all reasonings as in all manufactures. Things noble and just, which are the subjects of investigation in political science, exhibit so great a diversity and uncertainty that they are

---

[85] It is characteristic of Aristotle's philosophy to treat Ethics as a branch or department of Politics.

sometimes thought to have only a conventional, and not a natural, existence. There is the same sort of uncertainty in regard to good things, as it often happens that injuries result from them; thus there have been cases in which people were ruined by wealth, or again by courage. As our subjects then and our premises are of this nature, we must be content to indicate the truth roughly and in outline; and as our subjects and premises are true generally *but not universally*, we must be content to arrive at conclusions which are only generally true. It is right to receive the particular statements which are made in the same spirit; for an educated person will expect accuracy in each subject only so far as the nature of the subject allows; he might as well accept probable reasoning from a mathematician as require demonstrative proofs from a rhetorician. But everybody is competent to judge the subjects which he understands, and is a good judge of them. It follows that in particular subjects it is a person of *special* education, and in general a person of universal education, who is a good judge. Hence the young[86] are not proper students of political science, as they have no experience of the actions of life which form the premises and subjects of the reasonings. Also it may be added that from their tendency to follow their emotions they will not study the subject to any purpose or profit, as its end is not knowledge but action. It makes no difference whether a person is young in years or youthful in character; for the defect *of which I speak* is not one of time but is due to the emotional character of his life and pursuits. Knowledge is as useless to such a person as it is to an intemperate person. But where the desires and actions of people are regulated by reason the knowledge of these subjects will be extremely valuable.

II. But having said so much by way of preface as to the students of political science, the spirit in which it should be studied, and the object which we set before ourselves, let us resume our argument as follows:

As every knowledge and moral purpose aspires to some good, what is in our view the good at which the political science aims, and

[86] This is believed to be the passage which Shakespeare had in mind, though the reference to it is put in Hector's mouth,

> "young men, whom Aristotle thought
> Unfit to hear moral philosophy."
> *Troilus and Cressida*, Act ii. Scene 2.

what is the highest of all practical goods? As to its name there is, I may say, a general agreement. The masses and the cultured classes agree in calling it happiness, and conceive that "to live well" or "to do well" is the same thing as "to be happy." But as to the nature of happiness they do not agree, nor do the masses give the same account of it as the philosophers. The former define it as something visible and palpable, e.g. pleasure, wealth, or honour; different people give different definitions of it, and often the same person gives different definitions at different times; for when a person has been ill, it is health, when he is poor, it is wealth, and, if he is conscious of his own ignorance, he envies people who use grand language above his own comprehension. Some *philosophers*[87] on the other hand have held that, besides these various goods, there is an absolute good which is the cause of goodness in them all. It would perhaps be a waste of time to examine all these opinions, it will be enough to examine such as are most popular or as seem to be more or less reasonable.

But we must not fail to observe the distinction between the reasonings which proceed from first principles and the reasonings which lead up to first principles. For Plato[88] was right in raising the difficult question whether the *true* way was from first principles or to first principles, as in the race-course from the judges to the goal, or *vice versa*. We must begin then with such facts as are known. But facts may be known in two ways, i.e. either relatively to ourselves or absolutely. It is probable then that *we* must begin with such facts as are known to us, *i.e. relatively*. It is necessary therefore, if a person is to be a competent student of what is noble and just and of politics in general, that he should have received a good moral training. For the fact that a thing is so is a first principle or starting-point,[89] and, if the fact is sufficiently clear, it will not be necessary to go on to ask the reason of it. But a person who has received a good moral training either possesses first principles, or will have no difficulty in acquiring them. But if he does not

[87] Aristotle is thinking of the Platonic "ideas."

[88] The reference is probably not to any special passage in the dialogues of Plato, but to the general drift or scope of the Socratic dialectics.

[89] Aristotle's reasoning depends in part on the double meaning of ἀρχή viz. (1) starting-point or beginning, (2) first principle or axiomatic truth.

possess them, and cannot acquire them, he had better lay to heart
Hesiod's lines:

> Far best is he who is himself all-wise,
> And he, too, good who listens to wise words;
> But whoso is not wise nor lays to heart
> Another's wisdom is a useless man.

III. But to return from our digression: It seems not unreasonable that people should derive their conception of the good or of
happiness from men's lives. Thus ordinary or vulgar people conceive it to be pleasure, and accordingly approve a life of enjoyment.
For there are practically three prominent lives, the sensual, the
political, and, thirdly, the speculative. Now the mass of men present an absolutely slavish appearance, as choosing the life of brute
beasts, but they meet with consideration because so many persons
in authority share the tastes of Sardanapalus.[90] Cultivated and
practical people, on the other hand, identify happiness with honour,
as honour is the general end of political life. But this appears too
superficial for our present purpose; for honour seems to depend
more upon the people who pay it than upon the person to whom it
is paid, and we have an intuitive feeling that the good is something,
which is proper to a man himself and cannot easily be taken away
from him. It seems too that the reason why men seek honour is that
they may be confident of their own goodness. Accordingly they
seek it at the hands of the wise and of those who know them well,
and they seek it on the ground of virtue; hence it is clear that in
their judgment at any rate virtue is superior to honour. It would
perhaps be right then to look upon virtue rather than honour as
being the end of the political life. Yet virtue again, it appears, lacks
completeness; for it seems that a man may possess virtue and yet
be asleep or inactive throughout life, and, not only so but he may
experience the greatest calamities and misfortunes. But nobody
would call such a life a life of happiness, unless he were maintaining
a paradox. It is not necessary to dwell further on this subject, as it
is sufficiently discussed in the popular philosophical treatises.
The third life is the speculative which we will investigate here-
after.[91]

[90] The most luxurious, and the last, Assyrian monarch.

[91] The investigation of the speculative life occurs in Book x.

The life of money-making is in a sense a life of constraint, and it is clear that wealth is not the good of which we are in quest; for it is useful in part as a means to something else. It would be a more reasonable view therefore that the things mentioned before, viz. *sensual pleasure, honour and virtue*, are ends than that wealth is, as they are things which are desired on their own account. Yet these too are apparently not ends, although much argument has been employed to show that they are.

IV. We may now dismiss this subject; but it will perhaps be best to consider the universal *good*, and to discuss the meaning in which the phrase is used, although there is this difficulty in such an inquiry, that the *doctrine of* ideas has been introduced by our friends.[92] Yet it will perhaps seem the best, and indeed the right course, at least when the truth is at stake, to go so far as to sacrifice what is near and dear to us, especially as we are philosophers. For friends and truth are both dear to us, but it is a sacred duty to prefer the truth.

Now the authors of this theory did not make ideas of things in which they predicated priority and posteriority. Hence they did not constitute an idea of numbers. But good is predicated equally of substance, quality and relation, and the absolute or essential, *i.e. substance*, is in its nature prior to the relative, as relativity is like an offshoot or accident of existence; hence there cannot be an idea which is common to them both. Again, there are as many ways of predicating good as of predicating existence; for it is predicated of substance as e.g. of God or the mind, or of quality as of the virtues, or of quantity as of the mean, or of relativity as of the useful, or of time as of opportunity, or of place as of a habitation, and so on. It is clear then that it cannot be a common universal idea or a unity; otherwise it would not be predicated in all the categories but only in one. Thirdly, as there is a single science of all such things as fall under a single idea, there would have been a single science of all good things, *if the idea of "good" were single;* but in fact there are many sciences even of such good things as fall under a single category, strategy, e.g. being the science of opportunity in war, and medicine the science of opportunity in disease, medicine again being the science of the mean in respect of

---

[92] In reference, of course, to Plato.

food, and gymnastic the science of the mean in respect of exercise. It would be difficult, too, to say what is meant by the "absolute" in anything, if in "absolute man" and in "man" there is one and the same conception of man. For there will be no difference between them in respect of manhood, and, if so, neither will there be any difference between "absolute good" and "good" in respect of goodness. Nor again will good be more good if it is eternal, since a white thing which lasts for a long time is not whiter than that which lasts for a single day. There seems to be more plausibility in the doctrine of the Pythagoreans[93] who place unity in the catalogue of goods, and Speusippus[94] apparently agrees with them. However these are questions which may be deferred to another occasion; but there is an objection to my arguments which suggests itself, viz. that the *Platonic* theory does not apply to every good, that the things which in themselves are sought after and welcomed are reckoned as one species and the things which tend to produce or in any sense preserve these or to prevent their opposites are reckoned as goods in a secondary sense as being means to these. It is clear then that there will be two kinds of goods, some being absolute goods, and others secondary. Let us then separate goods which are merely serviceable from absolute goods and consider if they are conceived as falling under a single idea. But what kind of things is it that may be defined as absolute goods? Will it be all such as are sought after independently of their consequences, e.g. wisdom, sight, and certain pleasures and honours? For granting that we seek after these sometimes as means to something else, still we may define them as absolute goods. Or is none of these things an absolute good, nor anything else except the idea? But then the type *or idea* will be purposeless, *i.e. it will not comprise any particulars*. If, on the other hand, these things too are absolute goods, the conception of the good will necessarily appear the same in them all, as the conception of whiteness appears the same in snow and in white lead. But the conception of honour, wisdom and pleasure, are distinct and different in respect of goodness. "Good" then is not a common term falling under one idea. But in what

[93] The point is that it is apparently more reasonable to describe unity as a good than to describe good as a unity. The Pythagoreans, or some of them, drew up catalogues of opposites as Aristotle explains *Metaphysics* i. ch. 5.

[94] Plato's nephew and successor in the Academy.

sense is the term used? For it does not seem to be an accidental homonymy.[95] Is it because all goods issue from one source or all tend to one end; or is it rather a case of analogy? for as the sight is to the body, so is the mind to the soul, *i.e. the mind may be called the eye of the soul, and so on.* But it will perhaps be well to leave this subject for the present, as an exact discussion of it would belong rather to a different branch of philosophy. But the same is true of the idea; for even if there is some one good which is predicated of all these things, or some abstract and absolute good, it will plainly not be such as a man finds practicable and attainable, and therefore will not be such a good as we are in search of. It will possibly be held, however, that it is worth while to apprehend this *universal good,* as having a relation to the goods which are attainable and practicable; for if we have this as a model, we shall be better able to know the things which are good relatively to ourselves, and, knowing them, to acquire them. Now although there is a certain plausibility in this theory, it seems not to harmonize with scientific experience; for while all sciences aim at a certain good and seek to supply a deficiency, they omit the knowledge of the universal good. Yet it is not reasonable to suppose that what would be so extremely helpful is ignored, and not sought at all by artists generally. But it is difficult to see what benefit a cobbler or carpenter will get in reference to his art by knowing the absolute good, or how the contemplation of the absolute idea will make a person a better physician or general. For it appears that a physician does not regard health abstractedly, but regards the health of man or rather perhaps of a particular man, as he gives his medicine to individuals.

V. But leaving this subject for the present let us revert to the good of which we are in quest and consider what its nature may be. For it is clearly different in different actions or arts; it is one thing in medicine, another in strategy, and so on. What then is the good in each of these instances? It is presumably that for the sake of which all else is done. This in medicine is health, in strategy, victory, in domestic architecture, a house, and so on. But in every action and purpose it is the end, as it is for the sake of the end that people all do everything else. If then there is a certain end of

[95] What is meant by an "accidental homonymy" or equivocation is easily seen in the various senses of a single English word such as *bull.*

all action, it will be this which is the practicable good, and if there are several such ends it will be these.

Our argument has arrived by a different path at the same conclusion as before; but we must endeavour to elucidate it still further. As it appears that there are more ends than one and some of these, e.g. wealth, flutes, and instruments generally we desire as means to something else, it is evident that they are not all final ends. But the highest good is clearly something final. Hence if there is only one final end, this will be the object of which we are in search, and if there are more than one, it will be the most final of them. We speak of that which is sought after for its own sake as more final than that which is sought after as a means to something else; we speak of that which is never desired as a means to something else as more final than the things which are desired both in themselves and as means to something else; and we speak of a thing as absolutely final, if it is always desired in itself and never as a means to something else.

It seems that happiness preeminently answer to this description, as we always desire happiness for its own sake and never as a means to something else, whereas we desire honour, pleasure, intellect, and every virtue, partly for their own sakes (for we should desire them independently of what might result from them) but partly also as being means to happiness, because we suppose they will prove the instruments of happiness. Happiness, on the other hand, nobody desires for the sake of these things, nor indeed as a means to anything else at all.

We come to the same conclusion if we start from the consideration of self-sufficiency, if it may be assumed that the final good is self-sufficient. But when we speak of self-sufficiency, we do not mean that a person leads a solitary life all by himself, but that he has parents, children, wife, and friends, and fellow-citizens in general, as man is naturally a social being. But here it is necessary to prescribe some limit; for if the circle be extended so as to include parents, descendants, and friends' friends, it will go on indefinitely. Leaving this point, however, for future investigation, we define the self-sufficient as that which, taken by itself, makes life desirable, and wholly free from want, and this is our conception of happiness.

Again, we conceive happiness to be the most desirable of all things, and that not merely as one among other good things. If it were one among other good things, the addition of the smallest good would increase its desirableness; for the accession makes a superiority of goods, and the greater of two goods is always the more desirable. It appears then that happiness is something final and self-sufficient, being the end of all action.

VI. Perhaps, however, it seems a truth which is generally admitted, that happiness is the supreme good; what is wanted is to define its nature a little more clearly. The best way of arriving at such a definition will probably be to ascertain the function of Man. For, as with a flute-player, a statuary, or any artisan, or in fact anybody who has a definite function and action, his goodness, or excellence seems to lie in his function, so it would seem to be with Man, if indeed he has a definite function. Can it be said then that, while a carpenter and a cobbler have definite functions and actions, Man, unlike them, is naturally functionless? The reasonable view is that, as the eye, the hand, the foot, and similarly each several part of the body has a definite function, so Man may be regarded as having a definite function apart from all these. What, then, can this function be? It is not life; for life is apparently something which man shares with the plants; and it is something peculiar to him that we are looking for. We must exclude therefore the life of nutrition and increase. There is next what may be called the life of sensation. But this, too, is apparently shared by Man with horses, cattle, and all other animals. There remains what I may call the practical life of the rational part *of Man's being*. But the rational part is twofold; it is rational partly in the sense of being obedient to reason, and partly in the sense of possessing reason and intelligence. The practical life too may be conceived of in two ways,[96] viz., *either as a moral state, or as a moral activity:* but we must understand by it the life of activity, as this seems to be the truer form of the conception.

The function of Man then is an activity of soul in accordance with reason, or not independently of reason. Again the functions of a person of a certain kind, and of such a person who is good of his kind e.g. of a harpist and a good harpist, are in our view generically the same, and this view is true of people of all kinds with-

[96] In other words life may be taken to mean either the mere possession of certain faculties or their active exercise.

out exception, the superior excellence being only an addition to the function; for it is the function of a harpist to play the harp, and of a good harpist to play the harp well. This being so, if we define the function of Man as a kind of life, and this life as an activity of soul, or a course of action in conformity with reason, if the function of a good man is such activity or action of a good and noble kind, and if everything is successfully performed when it is performed in accordance with its proper excellence, it follows that the good of Man is an activity of soul in accordance with virtue or, if there are more virtues than one, in accordance with the best and most complete virtue. But it is necessary to add the words "in a complete life." For as one swallow or one day does not make a spring, so one day or a short time does not make a fortunate or happy man.

VII. This may be taken as a sufficiently accurate sketch of the good; for it is right, I think, to draw the outlines first and afterwards to fill in the details. It would seem that anybody can carry on and complete what has been satisfactorily sketched in outline, and that time is a good inventor or cooperator in so doing. This is the way in which the arts have made their advances, as anybody can supply a deficiency.

But bearing in mind what has been already said, we must not look for the same degree of accuracy in all subjects; we must be content in each class of subjects with accuracy of such a kind as the subject-matter allows, and to such an extent as is proper to the inquiry. For while a carpenter and a geometrician both want to find a right angle, they do not want to find it in the same sense; the one wants only such an approximation to it as will serve his practical purpose, the other, as being concerned with truth, wants to know its nature or character. We must follow the same course in other subjects, or we shall sacrifice the main points to such as are subordinate. Again, we must not insist with equal emphasis in all subjects upon ascertaining the reason of things. We must sometimes e.g. in dealing with first principles be content with the proper evidence of a fact; the fact itself is a first point or principle. But there are various ways of discovering first principles; some are discovered by induction, others by perception, others by what may be called habituation, and so on. We must try to apprehend them all in the natural *or appropriate* way, and must take pains to define them satisfactorily, as they have a vital influence upon all that follows from them. For it seems that the first principle or beginning is more than half the whole, and is the means of arriving at a clear conception of many points which are under investigation.

VIII. In considering the first principle we must pay regard not only to the conclusion and the premisses of our argument, but also to such views as are popularly held about it. For while all experience harmonizes with the truth, it is never long before truth clashes with falsehood.

Goods have been divided into three classes, viz. external goods as they are called, goods of the soul and goods of the body. Of these three classes we consider the goods of the soul to be goods in the strictest or most literal sense. But it is to the soul that we ascribe psychical actions and activities. Thus our definition is a good one, at least according to this theory, which is not only ancient but is accepted by students of philosophy at the present time. It is right too, inasmuch as certain actions and activities are said to be the end; for thus it appears that the end is some good of the soul and not an external good. It is in harmony with this definition that the happy man should live well and do well, as happiness, it has been said, is in fact a kind of living and doing well.

IX. It appears too that the requisite characteristics of happiness are all contained in the definition; for some people hold that happiness is virtue, others that it is prudence,[97] others that it is wisdom of some kind, others that it is these things or one of them conjoined with pleasure or not dissociated from pleasure, others again include external prosperity. Some of these views are held by many ancient thinkers, others by a few thinkers of high repute. It is probable that neither side is altogether wrong, but that in some one point, if not in most points, they are both right.

Now the definition is in harmony with the view of those who hold that happiness is virtue or excellence of some sort; for activity in accordance with virtue implies virtue. But it would seem that there is a considerable difference between taking the supreme good to consist in acquisition or in use, in a moral state or in an activity. For a moral state, although it exists, may produce nothing good, e.g. if a person is asleep, or has in any other way become inactive.

---

[97] The difference between "prudence" or "practical wisdom" and "speculative" or "theoretical wisdom" is commonly assumed by Aristotle.

But this cannot be the case with an activity, as activity implies action and good action. As in the Olympian games it is not the most beautiful and strongest persons who receive the crown but they who actually enter the lists as combatants—for it is some of these who become victors—so it is they who act rightly that attain to what is noble and good in life. Again, their life is pleasant in itself. For pleasure is a psychical fact, and whatever a man is said to be fond of is pleasant to him, e.g. a horse to one who is fond of horses, a spectacle to one who is fond of spectacles, and similarly just actions to a lover of justice, and virtuous actions in general to a lover of virtue. Now most men find a sense of discord in their pleasures, because their pleasures are not such as are naturally pleasant. But to the lovers of nobleness natural pleasures are pleasant. It is actions in accordance with virtue that are naturally pleasant. Such actions then are pleasant both relatively to these persons and in themselves. Nor does their life need that pleasure should be attached to it as a sort of amulet; it possesses pleasure in itself. For it may be added that a person is not good, if he does not take delight in noble actions, as nobody would call a person just if he did not take delight in just actions, or liberal if he did not take delight in liberal actions, and so on. But if this is so, it follows that actions in accordance with virtue are pleasant in themselves. But they are also good and noble, and good and noble in the highest degree, if the judgment of the virtuous man upon them is right, his judgment being such as we have described. Happiness then is the best and noblest and pleasantest thing in the world, nor is there any such distinction between goodness, nobleness, and pleasure as the epigram at Delos suggests:

> Justice is noblest, Health is best,
> To gain one's end is pleasantest.

For these are all essential characteristics of the best activities, and we hold that happiness consists in these or in one and the noblest of these. Still it is clear that happiness requires the addition of external goods, as we said; for it is impossible, or at least difficult for a person to do what is noble unless he is furnished with external means. For there are many things which can only be done through the instrumentality of friends or wealth or political power, and there are some things the lack of which must mar felicity, e.g. noble birth, a prosperous family, and personal beauty. For a person is incapable of happiness if he is absolutely ugly in appearance, or low born, or solitary and childless, and perhaps still more so, if he has exceedingly bad children or friends, or has had good children or friends and has lost them by death. As we said, then, it seems that prosperity of this kind is an indispensable addition to virtue. It is for this reason that some persons identify good fortune, and others virtue, with happiness.

X. The question is consequently raised whether happiness is something that can be learnt or acquired by habit or discipline of any other kind, or whether it comes by some divine dispensation or even by chance.

Now if there is anything in the world that is a gift of the Gods to men, it is reasonable to suppose that happiness is a divine gift, especially as it is the best of human things. This however is perhaps a point which is more appropriate to another investigation than the present. But even if happiness is not sent by the Gods but is the result of virtue and of learning or discipline of some kind, it is apparently one of the most divine things in the world; for it would appear that that which is the prize and end of virtue is the supreme good and is in its nature divine and blessed. It will also be widely extended; for it will be capable of being produced in all persons, except such as are morally deformed, by a process of study or care. And if it is better that happiness should be produced in this way than by chance, it may reasonably be supposed that it is so produced, as the order of things is the best possible in Nature and so too in art, and in causation generally, and most of all in the highest kind of causation. But it would be altogether inconsistent to leave what is greatest and noblest to chance. But the definition *of happiness* itself helps to clear up the question; for happiness has been defined as a certain kind of activity of the soul in accordance with virtue. Of the other goods, *i.e. of goods besides those of the soul*, some are necessary as antecedent conditions of happiness, others are in their nature co-operative and serviceable as instruments of happiness.

The conclusion at which we have arrived agrees with our original position. For we laid it down that the end of political science is the supreme good; and political science is concerned with nothing so much as with producing a certain character in the citizens, or in other words with making them good, and capable of performing noble actions. It is reasonable then not to speak of an ox, or a horse, or any other animal as happy; for none of them is capable of participating in activity as so defined. For the same reason no child can be happy, as the age of a child makes it impossible for him to display this activity at present, and if a child is ever said to be happy, the ground of the felicitation is his promise, *rather than his actual performance*. For happiness demands, as we said, a complete virtue and a complete life. For there are all sorts of changes and chances in life, and it is possible that the most prosperous of men will, in his old age, fall into extreme calamities as is told of Priam in the heroic legends. But if a person has experienced such chances, and has died a miserable death, nobody calls him happy.

XI. Is it the case then that nobody in the world may be called happy so long as he is alive? Must we adopt Solon's[98] rule of looking to the end? and, if we follow Solon, can it be said that a man is really happy after his death? Surely such a view is wholly absurd, especially for us who define happiness as a species of activity. But if we do not speak of one who is dead as happy, and if Solon's meaning is not this but rather that it is only when a man is dead that it is safe to call him fortunate as being exempt at last from evils and calamities, this again is a view which is open to some objection. For it seems that one who is dead is capable of being affected both by good and by evil in the same way as one who is living but unconscious, e.g. by honours and dishonours and by the successes or reverses of his children and his descendants generally. But here again a difficulty occurs. For if a person has lived a fortunate life up to old age, and has died a fortunate death, it is possible that he may experience many vicissitudes of fortune in the persons of his descendants. Some of them may be good and may enjoy such a life as they deserve; others may be bad and may have a bad life. It is clear, too, that descendants may stand in all sorts of different degrees of relationship to their ancestor. It would be an extraordinary result, if the dead man were to share the vicissitudes of their fortune and to become happy at one time and miserable at another, *as they became either happy or miserable*. But it would be equally

---

[98] Herodotus I. ch. 32 is the authority for the celebrated warning which Solon is said to have addressed to Crœsus.

extraordinary, if the future of descendants should not affect their parents at all or for a certain time. It will be best, however, to revert to the difficulty which was raised before, as it will perhaps afford an answer to the present question. If it is right to look to the end, and when the end comes to felicitate a person not as being fortunate but as having been so before, surely it is an extraordinary thing that at the time when he is happy we should not speak the truth about him, because we do not wish to call the living happy in view of the vicissitudes to which they are liable and because we have formed a conception of happiness as something that is permanent and exempt from the possibility of change and because the same persons are liable to many revolutions of fortune. For it is clear that, if we follow the changes of fortune, we shall often call the same person happy at one time, and miserable at another, representing the happy man as "a[99] sort of chameleon without any stability of position." It cannot be right to follow the changes of fortune. It is not upon these that good or evil depends; they are necessary accessories of human life, as we said; but it is a man's activities in accordance with virtue that constitute his happiness and the opposite activities that constitute his misery. The difficulty which has now been discussed is itself a witness that this is the true view. For there is no human function so constant as the activities in accordance with virtue; they seem to be more permanent than the sciences themselves. Among these activities, too, it is the most honourable which are the most permanent, as it is in them that the life of the fortunate chiefly and most continuously consists. For this is apparently the reason why such activities are not liable to be forgotten.[100]

The element of permanency which is required will be found in the happy man, and he will preserve his character throughout life; for he will constantly or in a preeminent degree pursue such actions and speculations as accord with virtue; nor is there anybody who will bear the chances of life so nobly, with such a perfect and complete harmony, as he who is truly good and "foursquare without

[99] Apparently an Iambic line.

[100] Aristotle means that it is comparatively easy to forget scientific truths, when they have once been learnt, but it is difficult, if not impossible, to lose the habit of virtuous activity. In other words, he means that knowledge is less stable, and therefore less valuable, than character.

a flaw."[101] Now the events of chance are numerous and of different magnitudes. It is clear then that small incidents of good fortune, or the reverse, do not turn the scale of life, but that such incidents as are great and numerous augment the felicity of life, if they are fortunate, as they tend naturally to embellish it and the use of them is noble and virtuous, and on the other hand, if they are of a contrary character, mar and mutilate its felicity by causing pains and hindrances to various activities. Still even in these circumstances nobility shines out, when a person bears the weight of accumulated misfortunes with calmness, not from insensibility but from innate dignity and magnanimity.

But if it is the activities which determine the life, as we said, nobody who is fortunate can become miserable; for he will never do what is hateful and mean. For our conception of the truly good and sensible man is that he bears all the chances of life with decorum and always does what is noblest in the circumstances, as a good general uses the forces at his command to the best advantage in war, a good cobbler makes the best shoe with the leather that is given him, and so on through the whole series of the arts. If this is so, it follows that the happy man can never become miserable; I do not say that he will be fortunate, if he meets such chances of life as Priam. Yet he will not be variable or liable to frequent change, as he will not be moved from his happiness easily or by ordinary misfortunes but only by such misfortunes as are great and numerous; and after them it will not be soon that he will regain his happiness, but, if he regains it at all, it will be only in a long and complete period of time and after attaining in it to great and noble results.

We may safely then define a happy man as one whose activity accords with perfect virtue and who is adequately furnished with external goods, not for a casual period of time but for a complete or perfect lifetime. But perhaps we ought to add, that he will always live so, and will die as he lives; for it is not given us to foresee the

---

[101] The phrase "foursquare without a flaw," is taken from Simonides, as Plato says in his *Protagoras* 339 B, where the passage in which the phrase occurs is quoted at length. Cp. *Rhetoric* III. ch. 11 p. 1411 B$_{27}$. In a similar, but not identical sense a modern poet speaks of the great Duke of Wellington as

"that tower of strength
Which stood foursquare to all the winds that blew."

future, but we take happiness to be an end, and to be altogether perfect and complete, and, this being so, we shall call people fortunate during their lifetime, if they possess and will possess these characteristics, but fortunate only so far as men may be fortunate.

But to leave the discussion of this subject: The idea that the fortunes of one's descendants and of one's friends generally have no influence at all upon oneself seems exceedingly harsh, and contrary to received opinions. But as the events of life are numerous and present all sorts of differences, and some are of more concern to us than others, it would be clearly a long, if not an infinite task, to define them individually; we must, I think, be content to describe them generally and in outline. Now, as in personal misfortunes some have a certain weight and influence upon our life, and others, it seems, are comparatively light, so it is with such misfortunes as affect our friends generally. But as the difference between the experiences of the living or the dead is far greater than the difference between terrible crimes when enacted upon the stage in tragedies and the same crimes when merely assumed to have already occurred, it is necessary to take account of this difference also, and still more perhaps of the serious doubt which has been raised as to the participation of the dead in any good or evil. For it is probable in this view that if anything, whether good or evil, reaches the dead at all, it is feeble and insignificant, either absolutely, or in relation to them, or if not, is of such a magnitude and character as to be incapable of making people happy if they are not happy or of depriving them of their felicity, if they are.

It would seem then that the dead are affected or influenced in some way by the prosperity and the adversity of their friends, but that the influence is of such a kind and degree as not to make people happy, if they are not happy, nor to have any similar effect.

XII. Having determined these points, let us consider whether happiness belongs rather to such things as are objects of praise or to such things as are objects of honour. For it is clearly not a mere potential good.

It appears that whatever is an object of praise is praised as possessing a certain character, and standing in a certain relation to something. For we praise one who is just and manly and good in any way, or we praise virtue, because of their actions and productions. We praise one who is strong and swift and so on, as naturally possessing a certain character and standing in a certain relation to something that is itself good and estimable. The truth of this statement becomes clear, if we take the case of praises bestowed upon the Gods. Such praise appears ridiculous as implying a reference to ourselves, and there must be such a reference, because, as we said, praise invariably implies a reference *to a higher standard*. But if this is the nature of praise, it is clear that it is not praise but something greater and better which is appropriate to all that is best, as indeed is evident; for we speak of the Gods as "blessed" and "happy" *rather than as "praiseworthy"* and we speak of the most godlike men as "blessed." It is the same with goods; for nobody praises happiness as he praises justice, but he calls it blessed, as being in its nature better and more divine. It is sometimes held on these grounds that Eudoxus[102] was right in advocating the supremacy of pleasure; for the fact that pleasure is a good and yet is not praised, indicates, as he thought, that it is higher than the objects of praise, as God and the good are higher, these being the standards to which everything else is referred. For praises are appropriate to virtue, as it is virtue which makes us capable of noble deeds; but panegyrics to accomplished results, whether they be results of the body or of the soul. But it may be said that an exact discussion of these points belongs more properly to the special study of panegyrics. We see clearly, however, from what has been said, that happiness is something honourable and final. And that it is so seems to follow also from the fact that it is a first principle; for it is for the sake of happiness that we all do everything else, and the first principle or the cause of all that is good we regard as something honourable and divine.

XIII. Inasmuch as happiness is an activity of soul in accordance with complete or perfect virtue, it is necessary to consider virtue, as this will perhaps be the best way of studying happiness.

It appears that virtue is the object upon which the true statesman has expended the largest amount of trouble, as it is his wish to make the citizens virtuous and obedient to the laws. We have instances of such statesmen in the legislators of Crete and Lacedaemon and such other legislators as have resembled them. But if this inquiry is proper to political science, it will clearly accord with our

[102] A pupil of Plato, whose personal character is favourably noticed by Aristotle in Book x. ch. 2. He was an astronomer as well as a philosopher.

original purpose to pursue it. But it is clear that it is human virtue which we have to consider; for the good of which we are in search is, as we said, human good, and the happiness, human happiness. By human virtue or excellence we mean not that of the body, but that of the soul, and by happiness we mean an activity of the soul.

If this is so, it is clearly necessary for statesmen to have some knowledge of the nature of the soul in the same way as it is necessary for one who is to treat the eye or any part of the body, to have some knowledge of it, and all the more as political science is better and more honourable than medical science. Clever doctors take a great deal of trouble to understand the body, and similarly the statesman must make a study of the soul. But he must study it with a view to his particular object and so far only as his object requires; for to elaborate the study of it further would, I think, be to aggravate unduly the labour of our present undertaking.

There are some facts concerning the soul which are adequately stated in the popular or exoterical discourses, and these we may rightly adopt. It is stated e.g. that the soul has two parts, one irrational and the other possessing reason. But whether these parts are distinguished like the parts of the body and like everything that is itself divisible, or whether they are theoretically distinct, but in fact inseparable, as convex and concave in the circumference of a circle, is of no importance to the present inquiry.

Again, it seems that of the irrational part of the soul one part is common, *i.e. shared by man with all living things*, and vegetative; I mean the part which is the cause of nutrition and increase. For we may assume such a faculty of the soul to exist in all things that receive nutrition, even in embryos, and the same faculty to exist in things that are full grown, as it is more reasonable to suppose that it is the same faculty than that it is different. It is clear then that the virtue or excellence of this faculty is not distinctively human but is shared by man with all living things; for it seems that this part and this faculty are especially active in sleep, whereas good and bad people are never so little distinguishable as in sleep— whence the saying that there is no difference between the happy and the miserable during half their lifetime. And this is only natural; for sleep is an inactivity of the soul in respect of its virtue or vice, except in so far as certain impulses affect it to a slight extent, and make the visions of the virtuous better than those of ordinary people. But enough has been said on this point, and we must now leave the principle of nutrition, as it possesses no natural share in human virtue.

It seems that there is another natural principle of the soul which is irrational and yet in a sense partakes of reason. For in a continent or incontinent person we praise the reason, and that part of the soul which possesses reason, as it exhorts men rightly and exhorts them to the best conduct. But it is clear that there is in them another principle which is naturally different from reason and fights and contends against reason. For just as the paralysed parts of the body, when we intend to move them to the right, are drawn away in a contrary direction to the left, so it is with the soul; the impulses of incontinent people run counter to reason. But there is this difference, however, that while in the body we see the part which is drawn astray, in the soul we do not see it. But it is probably right to suppose with equal certainty that there is in the soul too something different from reason, which opposes and thwarts it, although the sense in which it is distinct from reason is immaterial. But it appears that this part too partakes of reason, as we said; at all events in a continent person it obeys reason, while in a temperate or courageous person it is probably still more obedient, as being absolutely harmonious with reason.

It appears then that the irrational part of the soul is itself twofold; for the vegetative faculty does not participate at all in reason, but the faculty of desire or general concupiscence participates in it more or less, in so far as it is submissive and obedient to reason. But *it is obedient* in the sense in which we speak of "paying attention to a father" or "to friends," but not in the sense in which we speak of "paying attention to mathematics." All correction, rebuke and exhortation is a witness that the irrational part of the soul is in a sense subject to the influence of reason. But if we are to say that this part too possesses reason, then the part which possesses reason will have two divisions, one possessing reason absolutely and in itself, the other listening to it as a child listens to its father.

Virtue or excellence again, admits of a distinction which depends on this difference. For we speak of some virtues as intellectual and of others as moral, wisdom, intelligence and prudence, being intellectual, liberality and temperance being moral, virtues. For when we describe a person's character, we do not say that he is wise or intelligent but that he is gentle or temperate. Yet we praise a wise man too in respect of his mental state, and such mental states as deserve to be praised we call virtuous.

BOOK II

IV. We have next to consider the nature of virtue.[103]

Now, as the qualities of the soul are three, viz. emotions, faculties and moral states, it follows that virtue must be one of the three. By the emotions I mean desire, anger, fear, courage, envy, joy, love, hatred, regret, emulation, pity, in a word whatever is attended by pleasure or pain. I call those faculties in respect to which we are said to be capable of experiencing these emotions, e.g. capable of getting angry or being pained or feeling pity. And I call those moral states in respect of which we are well or ill disposed towards the emotions, ill-disposed e.g. towards the passion of anger, if our anger be too violent or too feeble, and well-disposed, if it be duly moderated, and similarly towards the other emotions.

Now neither the virtues nor the vices are emotions; for we are not called good or evil in respect of our emotions but in respect of our virtues or vices. Again, we are not praised or blamed in respect of our emotions; a person is not praised for being afraid or being angry, nor blamed for being angry in an absolute sense, but only for being angry in a certain way; but we are praised or blamed in respect of our virtues or vices. Again, whereas we are angry or afraid without deliberate purpose, the virtues are in some sense deliberate purposes, or do not exist in the absence of deliberate purpose. It may be added that while we are said to be moved in respect of our emotions, in respect of our virtues or vices we are not said to be moved but to have a certain disposition.

These reasons also prove that the virtues are not faculties. For we are not called either good or bad, nor are we praised or blamed, as having an abstract capacity for emotion. Also while Nature gives us our faculties, it is not Nature that makes us good or bad, but this is a point which we have already discussed. If then the

[103] Here begins the brief excerpt on the golden mean from Book ii.—T. V. S.

virtues are neither emotions nor faculties, it remains that they must be moral states.

V. The nature of virtue has been now generically described. But it is not enough to state merely that virtue is a moral state, we must also describe the character of that moral state.

It must be laid down then that every virtue or excellence has the effect of producing a good condition of that of which it is a virtue or excellence, and of enabling it to perform its function well. Thus the excellence of the eye makes the eye good and its function good, as it is by the excellence of the eye that we see well. Similarly, the excellence of the horse makes a horse excellent and good at racing, at carrying its rider and at facing the enemy.

If then this is universally true, the virtue or excellence of man will be such a moral state as makes a man good and able to perform his proper function well. We have already explained how this will be the case, but another way of making it clear will be to study the nature or character of this virtue.

Now, in everything, whether it be continuous or discrete,[104] it is possible to take a greater, a smaller, or an equal amount, and this either absolutely or in relation to ourselves, the equal being a mean between excess and deficiency. By the mean in respect of the thing itself, or the absolute mean, I understand that which is equally distinct from both extremes; and this is one and the same thing for everybody. By the mean considered relatively to ourselves I understand that which is neither too much nor too little; but this is not one thing, nor is it the same for everybody. Thus if 10 be too much and 2 too little we take 6 as a mean in respect of the thing itself; for 6 is as much greater than 2 as it is less than 10, and this is a mean in arithmetical proportion. But the mean considered relatively to ourselves must not be ascertained in this way. It does not follow that if 10 pounds *of meat* be too much and 2 be too little for a man to eat, a trainer will order him 6 pounds, as this may itself be too much or too little for the person who is to take it; it will be too little e.g. for Milo,[105] but too much for a beginner in gymnastics. It will be the same with running and wrestling; *the*

---

[104] In Aristotelian language, as Mr. Peters says, a straight line is a "continuous quantity" but a rouleau of sovereigns a "discrete quantity."

[105] The famous Crotoniate wrestler.

right amount will vary with the individual.[106] This being so, everybody who understands his business avoids alike excess and deficiency; he seeks and chooses the mean, not the absolute mean, but the mean considered relatively to ourselves.

Every science then performs its function well, if it regards the mean and refers the works which it produces to the mean. This is the reason why it is usually said of successful works that it is impossible to take anything from them or to add anything to them, which implies that excess or deficiency is fatal to excellence but that the mean state ensures it. Good artists too, as we say, have an eye to the mean in their works. But virtue, like Nature herself, is more accurate and better than any art; virtue therefore will aim at the mean;—I speak of moral virtue, as it is moral virtue which is concerned with emotions and actions, and it is these which admit of excess and deficiency and the mean. Thus it is possible to go too far, or not to go far enough, in respect of fear, courage, desire, anger, pity, and pleasure and pain generally, and the excess and the deficiency are alike wrong; but to experience these emotions at the right times and on the right occasions and towards the right persons and for the right causes and in the right manner is the mean or the supreme good, which is characteristic of virtue. Similarly there may be excess, deficiency, or the mean, in regard to actions. But virtue is concerned with emotions and actions, and here excess is an error and deficiency a fault, whereas the mean is successful and laudable, and success and merit are both characteristics of virtue.

It appears then that virtue is a mean state, so far at least as it aims at the mean.

Again, there are many different ways of going wrong; for evil is in its nature infinite, to use the Pythagorean[107] figure, but good is

[106] That is the reason why it is so hard to be virtuous; for it is always hard work to find the mean in anything, e.g., it is not everybody, but only a man of science, who can find the mean or center of a circle. So too anybody can get angry—that is an easy matter—and anybody can give or spend money, but to give it to the right persons, to give the right amount of it, and to give it at the right time and for the right cause and in the right way, this is not what anybody can do, nor is it easy. (*Ethics* 1108b).—T. V. S.

[107] The Pythagoreans, starting from the mystical significance of number, took the opposite principles of "the finite" and "the infinite" to represent good and evil.

finite. But there is only one possible way of going right. Accordingly the former is easy and the latter difficult; it is easy to miss the mark but difficult to hit it. This again is a reason why excess and deficiency are characteristics of vice and the mean state a characteristic of virtue.

For good is simple, evil manifold.[108]

VI. Virtue then is a state of deliberate moral purpose consisting in a mean that is relative to ourselves, the mean being determined by reason, or as a prudent man would determine it.

It is a mean state *firstly as lying* between two vices, the vice of excess on the one hand, and the vice of deficiency on the other, and secondly because, whereas the vices either fall short of or go beyond what is proper in the emotions and actions, virtue not only discovers but embraces the mean.

Accordingly, virtue, if regarded in its essence or theoretical conception, is a mean state, but, if regarded from the point of view of the highest good, or of excellence, it is an extreme.

BOOK X

I. It is natural, I think, to discuss pleasure next; for it seems that there is, in a preeminent degree, an affinity between pleasure and our human nature, and that is the reason why, in the education of the young, we steer their course by the rudders of pleasure and pain. It seems too that there is no more important element in the formation of a virtuous character than a rightly directed sense of pleasure and dislike; for pleasure and pain are coextensive with life, and they exercise a powerful influence in promoting virtue and happiness of life, as we choose what is pleasant and avoid what is painful.

Considering, then, the importance of these questions, it would seem to be clearly a duty not to pass them over, especially as they admit of much dispute. For some people say that the good[109] is pleasure; others, on the contrary, that pleasure is something utterly bad, whether, as is possible, they are convinced that it really is so, or they think it better in the interest of human life to represent

---

[108] A line—perhaps Pythagorean—of unknown authorship.

[109] Aristotle in this book speaks of "the good" meaning the highest good or *summum bonum*.

pleasure as an evil, even if it is not so, feeling that men are generally inclined to pleasure, and are the slaves of their pleasures, and that it is a duty therefore to lead them in the contrary direction, as they will so arrive at the mean *or proper* state.

But I venture to think that this is not a right statement of the case. For in matters of the emotions and actions theories are not so trustworthy as facts; and thus, when theories disagree with the facts of perception, they fall into contempt, and involve the truth itself in their destruction. For if a person censures pleasure and yet is seen at times to make pleasure his aim, he is thought to incline to pleasure as being entirely desirable; for it is beyond the power of ordinary people to make distinctions. It seems then the true theories are exceedingly useful, not only as the means of knowledge but as guides of life; for as being in harmony with facts, they are believed, and being believed they encourage people who understand them to regulate their lives in accordance with them.

Enough then of such considerations; let us review the various doctrines of pleasure.

II. Eudoxus held that pleasure was the good, because he saw that all things, whether rational or irrational, make pleasure their aim. He argued that in all cases that which is desirable is good, and that which is most desirable is most good; hence the fact of all things being drawn to the same object is an indication that that object is the best for all, as everything discovers what is good for itself in the same way as it discovers food; but that that which is good for all, and is the aim of all, is the good.

His theories were accepted, not so much for their intrinsic value as for the excellence of his moral character; for he was regarded as a person of exemplary temperance. It seemed then that he did not put forward these views as being a votary of pleasure, but that the truth was really as he said. He held that this truth resulted with equal clearness from a consideration of the opposite *of pleasure;* for as pain is something which everybody should avoid, so too its opposite is something which everybody should desire. He argued that a thing is in the highest degree desirable, if we do not desire it for any ulterior reason, or with any ulterior motive, and this is admittedly the case with pleasure; for if a person is pleased, nobody asks the further question, What is his motive in being pleased? a fact which proves that pleasure is desirable in itself. And further that the addition of pleasure to any good, e.g. to just or temperate conduct, renders that good more desirable, and it follows that if the good is augmented by a thing, that thing must itself be a good.

It seems then that this argument proves pleasure to be a good, but not to be a good in a higher sense than anything else; for any good whatever is more desirable with the addition of another good than when it stands alone. It is by a precisely similar argument that Plato tries to prove that pleasure is not the good. Pleasure (he says) is not the chief good, for the pleasant life is more desirable with the addition of prudence than without it; but if the combination is better, pleasure is not the good, as the good itself cannot be made more desirable by any addition.

But it is clear that, *if pleasure is not the good*, neither can anything else be which is made more desirable by the addition of any absolute good. What is it then which is incapable of such addition, but at the same time admits of our participating in it? For it is a good of this kind which is the object of our research.

People who argue on the other hand that that which all things aim at is not a good may be said to talk nonsense; for we accept the universal opinion as true, and one who upsets our trust in the universal opinion will find it hard to put forward any opinion that is more trustworthy. If it were only unintelligent beings that longed for pleasure, there would be something in what he says; but if intelligent beings also long for it, how can it be so? It is probable that even in the lower creatures there is some natural principle which is superior to the creatures themselves, and aims at their proper good.

Nor does it seem that these people fairly meet the argument drawn from the opposite of pleasure. They say it does not follow that, if pain is an evil, pleasure is a good, as not only is one evil opposed to another, but both are opposed to that which is neither one nor the other, *but a neutral state*. This is true enough, but it does not apply to pleasure and pain. For if both pleasure and pain were evil, it would have been a duty to avoid both, and if neither were evil, it would have been a duty not to avoid either, or not to avoid one more than the other; whereas in fact it is clear that people avoid one as an evil, and desire the other as a good. It follows then that pleasure and pain are opposed to each other as good and evil.

Nor again does it follow that, if pleasure is not a quality, neither is it a good, for the activities of virtue are not qualities, nor is happiness.

It is argued too that good is definite, but pleasure is indefinite, as it admits of degrees.

Now if the ground of this opinion is that it is possible to be pleased *in a greater or a less degree*, the same thing is true of justice and the other virtues. For here it is evident that we speak of persons as possessing the several virtues in a greater or less degree; some people are just and courageous in a greater *or less* degree than others, and it is possible to act with a greater or less degree of justice and temperance.

If however the meaning is that the indefiniteness resides in the pleasures, this is, I think, not the true explanation, supposing that some pleasures are mixed and others unmixed.[110]

Again, health is definite, yet it admits of degrees; and why should it not be so with pleasure? For health is not the same symmetry or proportion of elements in all people, nor is it always uniform in the same person; it admits of relaxation up a to certain point, and of different degrees, without ceasing to be health. Something of the same kind then may be also true of pleasure.

Again, *the opponents of pleasure*, looking upon the good as perfect or complete, and the processes of movement and production as imperfect or incomplete, try to prove that pleasure is motion or production. But they are wrong, I think, nor is pleasure a motion at all. For quickness and slowness are characteristic, it seems, of every motion, either absolutely, as of the motion of the universe, or else relatively, but neither of them is a condition inherent in pleasure. It is possible to *become* pleased, as it is to *become* angry, quickly, but not to *be* pleased quickly or relatively, *i.e. in comparison with somebody else*, as it is to walk or to grow quickly and so on. The transition then, to a state of pleasure may be quick or slow, but the active experience of pleasure, i.e. the state of being pleased, cannot be quick.

In what sense, too, can pleasure be a process of production? It is apparently not the case that anything can be produced out of anything; it is the case that a thing is resolved into that out of which

---

[110] Aristotle, following Plato's theory of "mixed" and "unmixed" pleasures, argues that it is only such pleasures as are "mixed" which can be said to possess the character of "indefiniteness." Cf. *Philebus* 52.

it is produced. Also, pain is the destruction of that of which pleasure is the production. It is said too that pain is a deficiency of the natural state, and pleasure its satisfaction. But this deficiency and this satisfaction are emotions of the body. If, then, pleasure is a satisfaction of the natural state, it follows that the part which is the seat of satisfaction will feel pleasure i.e. the body. But this seems not to be the case. We conclude therefore that pleasure is not a satisfaction of the natural state, although one may feel pleasure while the process of satisfaction is going on, as he may feel pain while undergoing an operation.

This view of pleasure, *viz. that it is a process of satisfaction*, seems to have originated in the pleasures and pains of eating and drinking, as in them we first feel a deficiency and an antecedent pain, and then feel pleasure at the satisfaction. But this is not true of all pleasures; the pleasures of mathematics e.g. have no such antecedent pain, nor among the pleasures of the senses have those of the smell, nor again many sounds and sights, memories and hopes. What is there then of which these will be processes of production? For in them there has been no deficiency to be satisfied.

But if the instance of immoral pleasures be adduced *to prove that pleasure is a bad thing*, we may answer that these are not really pleasant. They may be pleasant to people who are in a bad condition, but it must not be inferred that they are pleasant except to such people, any more than that things are healthful or sweet or bitter in themselves, because they are so to invalids, or that things are white, because they appear so to people who are suffering from ophthalmia.

Perhaps the truth may be stated thus: Pleasures are desirable, but not if they are immoral in their origin, just as wealth is pleasant, but not if it be obtained at the cost of turning traitor to one's country, or health, but not at the cost of eating any food, however disagreeable. Or it may be said that pleasures are of different kinds, those which are noble in their origin are different from those which are dishonourable, and it is impossible to enjoy the pleasure of the just man without being just, or that of the musician without being musical, and so on. The distinction drawn between a friend and a flatterer seems to bring out clearly the truth that pleasure is not a good, or that there are pleasures of different kinds; for it seems that while the object of the friend in social intercourse is good, that of the flatterer is pleasure, and while the flatterer is censured, the friend for his disinterestedness is praised.

Again, nobody would choose to live all his life with the mind of a child, although he should enjoy the pleasures of childhood to the utmost, or to delight in doing what is utterly shameful, although he were never to suffer pain for doing it. There are many things too upon which we should set our hearts, even if they brought no pleasure with them, e.g. sight, memory, knowledge, and the possession of the virtues; and if it be true that these are necessarily attended by pleasures, it is immaterial, as we should desire them even if no pleasure resulted from them. It seems to be clear then that pleasure is not the good, nor is every pleasure desirable, and that there are some pleasures which are desirable in themselves, and they differ in kind or in origin from the others.

We may regard this as a sufficient account of such views as are held in regard to pleasure and pain.

III. But the nature or character of pleasure will be more clearly seen, if we resume our argument from the beginning.

It seems that the act of sight is perfect or complete at any time; it does not lack anything which will afterwards be produced, and will make it perfect of its kind. Pleasure appears to resemble sight in this respect; it is a whole, nor is it possible at any time to find a pleasure which will be made perfect of its kind by increased duration.

It follows that pleasure is not a motion; for every motion takes a certain time, and aims at a certain end. Thus the builder's art is perfect or complete when it has accomplished its object. It is complete, either in respect of the whole time which the building took, or in respect of the moment *when it was completed*. But in the various parts of the time the various processes or motions are imperfect and different in kind from the whole and from one another; for the setting of the stones is different from the fluting of the pillar, and both from the building of the temple *as a whole*, and whereas the building of the temple is complete, nothing being wanting to the object proposed, that of the basement and the triglyph is incomplete, as each is only the building of a part of the temple. These processes or motions are therefore different in kind, and it is impossible at any time *when the building is going on* to find a motion which is complete or perfect of its kind. Such a motion, if found at all, will be found only in the whole time.

It is much the same with walking or any other process. For here again, although all locomotion is a motion from one place to another, there are different kinds of locomotion, such as flying, walking, jumping, and the like. And not only so, but walking itself is of different kinds; for the starting-point and the goal are not the same in the whole course, and in a part of it, or in one part of the course and in another; nor is it the same thing to cross one line as to cross another; for it is not only that a person crosses a line, but the line which he crosses is in a certain place, and one line is in a different place from another.

The subject of motion has been accurately discussed in another treatise. Motion is apparently not complete in any and every period of time; on the contrary, most motions are incomplete and different in kind, inasmuch as the starting-point and the goal constitute a difference of kind. Pleasure on the other hand seems to be complete or perfect of its kind in any and every period of time.

It is clear then that motion and pleasure must be distinct from one another, and that pleasure is something which is whole and perfect.

Another reason for holding this view is that motion is impossible except in a period of time, but pleasure is not; for the pleasure of a moment is a whole.

It is clear from these considerations that pleasure is not rightly described as a motion or process of production, for such a description is not appropriate to all things but only to such as are divisible into parts and are not wholes. For there is no process of production in an act of sight or in a mathematical point or in a unit, nor is any one of these things a motion or a process of production. It follows that there is no such process in pleasure, as it is a whole.

IV. Again, every sense exercises its activity upon its own object, and the activity is perfect only when the sense itself is in a sound condition, and the object is the noblest that falls within the domain of that sense; for this seems to be preeminently the character of the perfect activity. We may say that it makes no difference whether we speak of the sense itself or of the organ in which it resides as exercising the activity; in every instance the activity is highest when the part which acts is in the best condition, and the object upon which it acts is the highest of the objects which fall within its domain. Such an activity will not only be the most perfect, but the most pleasant; for there is pleasure in all sensation, and similarly in all thought and speculation, and the activity will be pleasantest when it is most perfect, and it will be most perfect when it is the activity of the part being in a sound condition and acting upon the most excellent of the objects that fall within its domain.

Pleasure perfects the activity, but not in the same way in which the excellence of the sense or of the object of sense perfects it, just as health is the cause of our being in a healthy state in one sense and the doctor is the cause of it in another.

It is clear that every sense has its proper pleasure; for we speak of pleasant sights, pleasant sounds and so on. It is clear too that the pleasure is greatest when the sense is best, and its object is best; but if the sentient subject and the sensible object are at their best, there will always be pleasure so long as there is a subject to act and an object to be acted upon.

When it is said that pleasure perfects the activity, it is not as a state *or quality* inherent in the subject but as a perfection superadded to it, like the bloom of youth to people in the prime of life.

So long then as the object of thought or sensation and the critical or contemplative subject are such as they ought to be, there will be pleasure in the exercise of the activity; for this is the natural result if the agent and the patient remain in the same relation to each other.

It may be asked then, How is it that nobody feels pleasure continuously? It is probably because we grow weary. Human beings are incapable of continuous activity, and as the activity comes to an end, so does the pleasure; for it is a concomitant of the activity. It is for the same reason that some things give pleasure when they are new, but give less pleasure afterwards; for the intelligence is called into play at first, and applies itself to its object with intense activity, as when we look a person full in the face *in order to recognize him*, but afterwards the activity ceases to be so intense and becomes remiss, and consequently the pleasure also fades away.

It may be supposed that everybody desires pleasure, for everybody clings to life. But life is a species of activity and a person's activity displays itself in the sphere and with the means which are after his own heart. Thus a musician exercises his ears in listening to music, a student his intellect in speculation, and so on.

But pleasure perfects the activities; it therefore perfects life, which is the aim of human desire. It is reasonable then to aim at pleasure, as it perfects life in each of us, and life is an object of desire.

V. Whether we desire life for the sake of pleasure or pleasure for the sake of life, is a question which may be dismissed for the moment. For it appears that pleasure and life are yoked together and do not admit of separation, as pleasure is impossible without activity and every activity is perfected by pleasure.

If this be so, it seems to follow that pleasures are of different kinds, as we hold that things which are different in kind are perfected by things which are themselves different in kind. For this is apparently the rule in the works of nature or of art, e.g. animals, trees, pictures, statues, a house, or a piece of furniture. Similarly we hold that energies which are different in kind are perfected by things which are also different in kind.

Now the pleasures of the intellect are different from the pleasures of the senses, and these again are different in kind from one another. It follows that the pleasures which perfect them will also be different.

This conclusion would appear also to result from the intimate connexion of each pleasure with the activity which it perfects. For the activity is increased by its proper pleasure, as if the activity is pleasant, we are more likely to arrive at a true judgment or an accurate result in any matter. It is so e.g. with people who are fond of geometry; they make better geometricians and understand the various problems of geometry better than other people. It is so too with people who are fond of music or architecture or any other subject; their progress in their particular subject is due to the pleasure which they take in it. Pleasure helps to increase activity, and that which helps to increase a thing must be closely connected with it. Where things then are different in kind, the things which are closely connected with them will also be different in kind.

This becomes still clearer when we observe that the pleasures which spring from one activity are impediments to the exercise of another. Thus people who are fond of the flute are incapable of attending to an argument, if they hear somebody playing the flute, as they take a greater pleasure in flute-playing than in the activity which they are called to exercise at the moment; hence the pleasure of the flute-playing destroys their argumentative activity. Much the same result occurs in other cases, when a person exercises his activity on two subjects simultaneously; the pleasanter of the two drives out the other, especially if it be much the pleasanter, until the activity of the other disappears. Accordingly, if we take intense delight in anything, we cannot do anything else at all. It is only when we do not care much for a thing that we do something else as well, just as people who eat sweetmeats in the theatres do so most when the actors are bad.

As the pleasure then which is proper to an activity refines it and gives it greater permanence and excellence, while alien pleasures impair it, it is clear that there is a wide difference between these pleasures. It may almost be said that the pleasures which are alien to it have the same effect as the pains which are proper to it; for the pains which are proper to an activity destroy it, as, when a person finds writing or thinking unpleasant and painful, he does not write or does not think, as the case may be.

The pleasures and pains then which are proper to an activity have opposite effects upon it. I mean by "proper" such as are the consequences of the activity *per se*. But it has been already stated that alien pleasures have much the same effect as pain; they are destructive of the activity, although not destructive of it in the same way.

Again, as the activities differ in goodness and badness, some being desirable, some undesirable, and some neither the one nor the other, so it is with pleasures, as every activity has its proper pleasure. Thus the pleasure which is proper to a virtuous activity is good, and that which is proper to a low activity is vicious. For the desires of what is noble are themselves laudable, the desires of what is disgraceful are censurable; but the pleasures which reside in the activities are more strictly proper to them than the desires, as the latter are distinct[III] from the activities in time and nature, but the former are closely related in time to the activities, and are so diffi-

---

[III] The desire is distinct from the activity in time, as being antecedent to it, and in nature, as being less complete in itself.

cult to distinguish from them that it is a question whether the activity is identical with the pleasure.

It seems however that pleasure is not the same thing as thought or sensation; it would be strange if it were so; but the impossibility of separating them makes some people regard them as the same.

As the activities then are different, so are the pleasures. Sight is different from or superior to touch in purity, hearing and smell are superior to taste; there is a corresponding difference therefore in their pleasures. The pleasures of the intellect too are different from or superior to these, and there are different kinds of pleasures of the senses or of the intellect. It seems that there is a pleasure, as there is a function, which is proper to every living thing, viz. the pleasure inherent in its activity. If we consider individual living things, we see this is so; for the pleasures of a horse, a dog, and a man are different, and as Heraclitus says, "a donkey would choose a bundle of hay in preference to gold; for fodder is pleasanter to donkeys than gold."

As the pleasures then of beings who are different in kind are themselves different in kind, it would be reasonable to suppose that there is no difference between the pleasures of the same beings. But there is a wide difference, at least in the case of men; the same things give pleasure to some people and pain to others, to some they are painful and hateful, to others pleasant and lovable. This is true of sweet things; the same things do not seem sweet to a person in a fever and to a person in good health, nor does the same thing seem hot to an invalid and to a person in a good physical condition. It is much the same with other things as well.

But in all these cases it seems that the thing really is what it appears to the virtuous man to be. But if this is a true statement of the case, as it seems to be, if virtue or the good man *qua* good is the measure of everything, it follows that it is such pleasures as appear pleasures to the good man that are really pleasures, and the things which afford him delight that are really pleasant. It is no wonder if what he finds disagreeable seems pleasant to somebody else, as men are liable to many corruptions and defilements; but such things are not pleasant except to these people, and to them only when they are in this condition.

It is clear then that we must not speak of pleasures which are admitted to be disgraceful as pleasures, except in relation to people who are thoroughly corrupt. But the question remains, Among such pleasures as are seen to be good, what is the character or nature of the pleasures that deserve to be called the *proper* pleasures of Man? It is plain, I think, from a consideration of the activities; for the activities bring pleasures in their train. Whether then there is one activity or there are several belonging to the perfect and fortunate man, it is the pleasures which perfect these activities that would be strictly described as the *proper* pleasures of Man. All other pleasures are only in a secondary or fractional sense the pleasures of Man, as are all other activities.

VI. After this discussion of the kinds of virtue and friendship and pleasure it remains to give a sketch of happiness, since we defined happiness as the end of human things. We shall shorten our account of it if we begin by recapitulating our previous remarks.

We said that happiness is not a moral state; for, if it were, it would be predicable of one who spends his whole life in sleep, living the life of a vegetable, or of one who is utterly miserable. If then we cannot accept this view, if we must rather define happiness as an activity of some kind, as has been said before, and if activities are either necessary and desirable as a means to something else or desirable in themselves, it is clear that we must define happiness as belonging to the class of activities which are desirable in themselves, and not desirable as means to something else; for happiness has no want, it is self-sufficient.

Again activities are desirable in themselves, if nothing is expected from them beyond the activity. This seems to be the case with virtuous actions, as the practice of what is noble and virtuous is a thing desirable in itself. It seems to be the case also with such amusements as are pleasant, we do not desire them as means to other things; for they often do us harm rather than good by making us careless about our persons and our property. Such pastimes are generally the resources of those whom the world calls happy. Accordingly people who are clever at such pastimes are generally popular in the courts of despots, as they make themselves pleasant to the despot in the matters which are the objects of his desire, and what he wants is to pass the time pleasantly.

The reason why these things are regarded as elements of happiness is that people who occupy high positions devote their leisure to them. But such people are not, I think, a criterion. For a high position is no guarantee of virtue or intellect, which are the sources on which virtuous activities depend. And if these people, who have never tasted a pure and liberal pleasure, have recourse to the pleasures of the body, it must not be inferred that these pleasures are preferable; for even children suppose that such things as are valued or honoured among them are best. It is only reasonable then that, as men and children differ in their estimate of what is honourable, so should good and bad people.

As has been frequently said, therefore, it is the things which are honourable and pleasant to the virtuous man that are really honourable and pleasant. But everybody feels the activity which accords with his own moral state to be most desirable, and accordingly the virtuous man regards the activity in accordance with virtue as most desirable.

Happiness then does not consist in amusement. It would be paradoxical to hold that the end of human life is amusement, and that we should toil and suffer all our life for the sake of amusing ourselves. For we may be said to desire all things as means to something else except indeed happiness, as happiness is the end *or perfect state*.

It appears to be foolish and utterly childish to take serious trouble and pains for the sake of amusement. But to amuse oneself with a view to being serious seems to be right, as Anacharsis says; for amusement is a kind of relaxation, and it is because we cannot work for ever that we need relaxation.

Relaxation then is not an end. We enjoy it as a means to activity; but it seems that the happy life is a life of virtue, and such a life is serious, it is not one of mere amusement. We speak of serious things too (*for serious things are virtuous*) as better than things which are ridiculous and amusing, and of the activity of the better part of man's being or of the better man as always the more virtuous. But the activity of that which is better is necessarily higher and happier. Anybody can enjoy bodily pleasures, a slave can enjoy them as much as the best of men; but nobody would allow that a slave is capable of happiness unless he is capable of life;[112] for happiness consists not in such pastimes as I have been speaking of, but in virtuous activities, as has been already said.

---

[112] I.e. the life of a free Athenian citizen.

VII. If happiness consists in virtuous activity, it is only reasonable to suppose that it is the activity of the highest virtue, or in other words, of the best part of our nature. Whether it is the reason or something else which seems to exercise rule and authority by a natural right, and to have a conception of things noble and divine, either as being itself divine or as relatively the most divine part of our being, it is the activity of this part in accordance with its proper virtue which will be the perfect happiness.

It has been already stated that it is a speculative activity, *i.e. an activity which takes the form of contemplation*. This is a conclusion which would seem to agree with our previous arguments and with the truth itself; for the speculative is the highest activity, as the intuitive reason is the highest of our faculties, and the objects with which the intuitive reason is concerned are the highest of things that can be known. It is also the most continuous; for our speculation can more easily be continuous than any kind of action. We consider too that pleasure is an essential element of happiness, and it is admitted that there is no virtuous activity so pleasant as the activity of wisdom or philosophic reflexion; at all events it appears that philosophy possesses pleasures of wonderful purity and certainty, and it is reasonable to suppose that people who possess knowledge pass their time more pleasantly than people who are seekers after truth.

Self-sufficiency too, as it is called, is preeminently a characteristic of the speculative activity; for the wise man, the just man, and all others, need the necessaries of life; but when they are adequately provided with these things, the just man needs people to whom and with whom he may do justice, so do the temperate man, the courageous man and everyone else; but the wise man is capable of speculation by himself, and the wiser he is, the more capable he is of such speculation. It is perhaps better for him in his speculation to have fellow-workers; but nevertheless he is in the highest degree self-sufficient.

It would seem too that the speculative is the only activity which is loved for its own sake as it has no result except speculation, whereas from all moral actions we gain something more or less besides the action itself.

Again, happiness, it seems, requires leisure; for the object of our business is leisure, as the object of war is the enjoyment of peace.

Now the activity of the practical virtues is displayed in politics or war, and actions of this sort seem incompatible with leisure. This is absolutely true of military actions, as nobody desires war, or prepares to go to war, for its own sake. A person would be regarded as absolutely bloodthirsty if he were to make enemies of his friends for the mere sake of fighting and bloodshed. But the activity of the statesman too is incompatible with leisure. It aims at securing something beyond and apart from politics, viz. the power and honour or at least the happiness of the statesman himself and his fellow citizens, which is different from the political activity and is proved to be different by our search for it *as something distinct*.

If then political and military actions are preeminent among virtuous actions in beauty and grandeur, if they are incompatible with leisure and aim at some end, and are not desired for their own sakes, if the activity of the intuitive reason seems to be superior in seriousness as being speculative, and not to aim at any end beyond itself, and to have its proper pleasure, and if this pleasure enhances the activity, it follows that such self-sufficiency and power of leisure and absence of fatigue as are possible to a man and all the other attributes of felicity are found to be realized in this activity. This then will be the perfect happiness of Man, if a perfect length of life is given it, for there is no imperfection in happiness. But such a life will be too good for Man. He will enjoy such a life not in virtue of his humanity but in virtue of some divine element within him, and the superiority of this activity to the activity of any other virtue will be proportionate to the superiority of this divine element in man to his composite *or material* nature.

If then the reason is divine in comparison with *the rest of* Man's nature, the life which accords with reason will be divine in comparison with human life in general. Nor is it right to follow the advice of people who say that the thoughts of men should not be too high for humanity or the thoughts of mortals too high for mortality; for a man, as far as in him lies, should seek immortality and do all that is in his power to live in accordance with the highest part of his nature, as, although that part is insignificant in size, yet in power and honour it is far superior to all the rest.

It would seem too that this is the true self of everyone, if a man's true self is his supreme or better part. It would be absurd then that a man should desire not the life which is properly his own but the life which properly belongs to some other being. The remark already made will be appropriate here. It is what is proper to everyone that is in its nature best and pleasantest for him. It is the life which accords with reason then that will be best and pleasantest for Man, as a man's reason is in the highest sense himself. This will therefore be also the happiest life.

VIII. It is only in a secondary sense that the life which accords with other, *i.e. non-speculative*, virtue can be said to be happy; for the activities of such virtue are human, *they have no divine element*. Our just or courageous actions or our virtuous actions of any kind we perform in relation to one another, when we observe the law of propriety in contracts and mutual services and the various moral actions and in our emotions. But all these actions appear to be human affairs. It seems too that moral virtue is in some respects actually the result of physical organization and is in many respects closely associated with the emotions. Again, prudence is indissolubly linked to moral virtue, and moral virtue to prudence, since the principles of prudence are determined by the moral virtues, and moral rectitude is determined by prudence. But the moral virtues, as being inseparably united with the emotions, must have to do with the composite *or material* part *of our nature*, and the virtues of the composite part *of our nature* are human, *and not divine*, virtues. So too therefore is the life which accords with these virtues; so too is the happiness *which accords with them*.

But the happiness *which consists in the exercise* of the reason is separated *from these emotions*. It must be enough to say so much about it; for to discuss it in detail would take us beyond our present purpose. It would seem too to require external resources only to a small extent or to a less extent than moral virtue. It may be granted that both will require the necessaries of life and will require them equally, even if the politician devotes more trouble to his body and his bodily welfare than the philosopher; for the difference will not be important. But there will be a great difference in respect of their activities. The liberal man will want money for the practice of liberality, and the just man for the requital of services which have been done him; for our wishes, *unless they are manifested in actions*, must always be obscure, and even people who are not just pretend that it is their wish to act justly. The courageous man too will want physical strength if he is to perform any virtuous action, and the temperate man liberty, as otherwise it will be impossible for him or for anybody else to show his character.

But if the question be asked whether it is the purpose or the performance that is the surer determinant of virtue, as virtue implies both, it is clear that both are necessary to perfection. But action requires various conditions, and the greater and nobler the action, the more numerous will the conditions be.

In speculation on the other hand there is no need of such conditions, at least for its activity; it may rather be said that they are actual impediments to speculation. It is as a human being and as living in society that a person chooses to perform virtuous actions. Such conditions then will be requisite if he is to live as a man.

That perfect happiness is a species of speculative activity will appear from the following consideration among others. Our conception of the Gods is that they are preeminently happy and fortunate. But what kind of actions do we properly attribute to them? Are they just actions? But it would make the Gods ridiculous to suppose that they form contracts, restore deposits, and so on. Are they then courageous actions? Do the Gods endure dangers and alarms for the sake of honour? Or liberal actions? But to whom should they give money? It would be absurd to suppose that they have a currency or anything of the kind. Again, what will be the nature of their temperate actions? Surely to praise the Gods for temperance is to degrade them; they are exempt from low desires. We may go through the whole category of virtues, and it will appear that whatever relates to moral action is petty and unworthy of the Gods.

Yet the Gods are universally conceived as living and therefore as displaying activity; they are certainly not conceived as sleeping like Endymion. If then action and still more production is denied to one who is alive, what is left but speculation? It follows that the activity of God being preeminently blissful will be speculative, and if so then the human activity which is most nearly related to it will be most capable of happiness.

It is an evidence of this truth that the other animals, as being perfectly destitute of such activity, do not participate in happiness; for while the whole life of the Gods is fortunate or blessed, the life of men is blessed in so far as it possesses a certain resemblance to their speculative activity. But no other animal is happy, as no other animal participates at all in speculation.

We conclude then that happiness is coextensive with speculation, and that the greater a person's power of speculation, the greater will be his happiness, not as an accidental fact but in virtue of the speculation, as speculation is honourable in itself. Hence happiness must be a kind of speculation.

IX. Man, as being human, will require external prosperity. His nature is not of itself sufficient for speculation, it needs bodily health, food, and care of every kind. It must not however be supposed that, because it is impossible to be fortunate without external goods, a great variety of such goods will be necessary to happiness. For neither self-sufficiency nor moral action consists in excess; it is possible to do noble deeds without being lord of land and sea, as moderate means will enable a person to act in accordance with virtue. We may clearly see that it is so; for it seems that private persons practise virtue not less but actually more than persons in high place. It is enough that such a person should possess as much as is requisite for virtue; his life will be happy if he lives in the active exercise of virtue. Solon was right perhaps in his description of the happy man as one "who is moderately supplied with external goods, and yet has performed the noblest actions,"—such was his opinion—"and had lived a temperate life," for it is possible to do one's duty with only moderate means. It seems too that Anaxagoras did not conceive of the happy man as possessing wealth or power when he said that he should no. be surprised if the happy man proved a puzzle in the eyes of the world; for the world judges by externals alone, it has no perception of anything that is not external.

The opinions of philosophers then seem to agree with our theories. Such opinions, it is true, possess a sort of authority; but it is the facts of life that are the tests of truth in practical matters, as they possess a supreme authority. It is right then to consider the doctrines which have been already advanced in reference to the facts of life, to accept them if they harmonize with those facts, and to regard them as mere theories if they disagree with them.

Again, he whose activity is directed by reason and who cultivates reason, and is in the best, *i.e. the most rational*, state of mind is also, as it seems, the most beloved of the Gods. For if the Gods care at all for human things, as is believed, it will be only reasonable to hold that they delight in what is best and most related to themselves, i.e. in reason, and that they requite with kindness those who love and honour it above all else, as caring for what is dear to themselves and performing right and noble actions.

It is easy to see that these conditions are found preeminently in the wise man. He will therefore be most beloved of the Gods. We may fairly suppose too that he is most happy; and if so, this is another reason for thinking that the wise man is preeminently happy.

X. Supposing then that our sketch of these subjects and of the virtues, and of friendship too, and pleasure, has been adequate, are we to regard our object as achieved? Or are we to say in the old phrase that in practical matters the end is not speculation and knowledge but action? It is not enough to know the nature of virtue; we must endeavour to possess it, and to exercise it, and to use whatever other means are necessary for becoming good.

Now, if theories were sufficient of themselves to make men good, they would deserve to receive any number of handsome rewards, as Theognis said, and it would have been our duty to provide them. But it appears in fact that, although they are strong enough to encourage and stimulate youths who are already liberally minded, although they are capable of bringing a soul which is generous and enamoured of nobleness under the spell of virtue, they are impotent to inspire the mass of men to chivalrous action; for it is not the nature of such men to obey honour but terror, nor to abstain from evil for fear of disgrace but for fear of punishment. For, as their life is one of emotion, they pursue their proper pleasures and the means of gaining these pleasures, and eschew the pains which are opposite to them. But of what is noble and truly pleasant they have not so much as a conception, because they have never tasted it. Where is the theory or argument which can reform such people as these? It is difficult to change by argument the settled features of character. We must be content perhaps if, when we possess all the means by which we are thought to become virtuous, we gain some share of virtue.

Some people think that men are made good by nature, others by habit, others again by teaching.

Now it is clear that the gift of Nature is not in our own power but is bestowed through some divine providence upon those who are truly fortunate. It is probably true also that reason and teaching are not universally efficacious; the soul of the pupil must first have been cultivated by habit to a right spirit of pleasure and aversion, like the earth that is to nourish the seed. For he whose life is governed by emotion would not listen to the dissuasive voice of reason, or even comprehend it, and if this is his state, how is it possible to convert him? Emotion, it seems, never submits to reason but only to force. It is necessary then to presuppose a character which is in a sense akin to virtue, which loves what is noble and dislikes what is dishonourable. But it is difficult for one to receive from his early days a right inclination to virtue, unless he is brought up under virtuous laws; for a life of temperance and steadfastness is not pleasant to most people, least of all to the young. It follows that the nurture and pursuits *of the young* should be regulated by law, as they will not be painful, if he becomes used to them.

But it is not enough, I think, that we should receive a right nurture and control in youth; we must practise what is right and get the habit of doing it when we have come to man's estate. We shall need laws then to teach us what is right, and so to teach us all the duty of life; for most people are moved by necessity rather than by reason, and by the fear of punishment rather than by the love of nobleness.

Accordingly it is sometimes held that legislators should on the one hand invite and exhort men to pursue virtue because it is so noble, as they who have been already trained in virtue will pay heed to them, and on the other hand, if they are disobedient and degenerate, should inflict punishments and chastisements on them and utterly expel them, if they are incurable; for so the good man who lives by the rule of honour will obey reason, and the bad man whose aim is pleasure must be chastened by pain like a beast of burden. Hence too it is said that the pains ought to be such as are most opposed to a person's favourite pleasures.

If then, as has been said, he who is to be a good man should receive a noble nurture and training and then should live accordingly in virtuous pursuits and never voluntarily or involuntarily do evil, this result will only be attained if we live, so to say, in accordance with reason and right order resting upon force.

Now the authority of a father does not possess such force or compulsion, nor indeed does that of any individual, unless he is a king or some such person. But the law has a compulsory power, as being itself in a sense the outcome of prudence and reason; and whereas we hate people who oppose our inclinations, even if they are right in so doing, we do not feel the law to be grievous in its insistence upon virtue.

It is only in the state of Lacedaemon and a few other states that the legislator seems to have undertaken to control the nurture and pursuits of the citizens. In the great majority of states there is an absolute neglect of such matters, and everybody lives as he chooses, "being lawgiver of wife and children" like the Cyclops.[113]

It is best then that the state should undertake the control of these matters and should exercise it rightly and should have the power of giving effect to its control. But if the state altogether neglects it, it would seem to be the duty of every citizen to further the cause of virtue in his own children and friends, or at least to set before himself the purpose of furthering it. It would seem too from what has been said that he will be best able to do this, if he has learnt the principles of legislation; for the control of the state is clearly exercised through the form of laws, and is good if the laws are virtuous. Whether they are written or unwritten laws, and whether they are suited to the education of an individual or of a number of people is apparently a matter of indifference, as it is in music or gymnastic or other studies. For as in a state it is law and custom which are supreme, so in a household it is the paternal precepts and customs, and all the more because of the father's relationship to the members of his family, and of the benefits which he has conferred upon them; for the members of a family are naturally affectionate and obedient to the father from the first.

Again, there is a superiority in the individual as against the general methods of education; it is much the same as in medicine where, although it is the general rule that a feverish patient needs to be kept quiet and to take no food, there may perhaps be some exceptions. Nor does a teacher of boxing teach all his pupils to box in the same style.

It would seem then that a study of individual character is the best way of perfecting the education of the individual, as then everyone has a better chance of receiving such treatment as is

[113] Homer's description of the Cyclopean life (to which Aristotle frequently refers) is found in the *Odyssey* ix. 114, 115.

suitable. Still the individual case may best be treated, whether in medicine or in gymnastic or in any other subject, by one who knows the general rule applicable to all people or to people of a particular kind; for the sciences are said to deal, and do deal, with general laws. At the same time there is no reason why even without scientific knowledge a person should not be successful in treating a particular case if he has made an accurate, although empirical, observation of the results which follow from a particular course of treatment, as there are some doctors who seem to be excellent doctors in their own cases, although they would be unable to relieve anybody else.

Nevertheless if a person wishes to succeed in art or speculation, it is, I think, his duty to proceed to a universal principle and to make himself acquainted with it as far as possible; for sciences, as has been said, deal with universals. Also it is the duty of any one who wishes to elevate people, whether they be few or many, by his treatment, to try to learn the principles of legislation, if it is laws that are the natural means of making us good. So in education it is not everybody—it is at the most only the man of science—who can create a noble disposition in all who come to him as patients, as it is in medicine or in any other art which demands care and prudence.

Is it not then our next step to consider the sources and means of learning the principles of legislation? It may be thought that here as elsewhere we must look *to the persons who practise the principles*, *i.e.* to statesmen; for legislation, as we saw, is apparently a branch of politics. But there is this difference between politics and all other sciences and faculties. In these it is the same people who are found to teach the faculties and to make practical use of them, e.g. doctors and painters; whereas in politics it is the sophists who profess to teach, but it is never they who practise. The practical people are the active statesmen who would seem to be guided in practical life by a kind of faculty or experience rather than by intelligence; for we see that they never write or speak on these subjects, although it is perhaps a nobler task than the composition of forensic or parliamentary speeches, nor have they ever made their own sons or any other people whom they care for into statesmen. Yet it might be expected that they should do so, if it were in their power, for they could not have bequeathed any better legacy to their state, nor is there anything which they would have preferred for themselves or their dearest friends to such a faculty. Still it must be admitted that experience does much good; otherwise people could not be made statesmen by familiarity with politics. It follows that, if people desire to understand politics, they need experience as well as theory.

These sophists however who are lavish in their professions appear to be far from teaching *statesmanship;* in fact they are absolutely ignorant of the sphere or nature of statesmanship. If it were not so they would not have made statesmanship identical with, or inferior to, rhetoric; they would not have thought it easy work to form a legislative code by merely collecting such laws as are held in high repute; they would not have supposed that all they have to do is to make a selection of the best laws, as if the selection itself did not demand intelligence, and as if a right judgment were not a thing of the greatest difficulty in legislation no less than in music. For it is only such persons as possess experience of particular arts who can form a correct judgment of artistic works, and understand the means and manner of executing them, and the harmony of particular combinations. Inexperienced persons on the other hand are only too glad if they are alive to the fact that a work has been well or badly executed, as in painting. But laws are like the artistic works of political science. How then should *a mere collection of* laws make a person capable of legislating, or of deciding upon the best laws? It does not appear that *the study* of medical books makes people good doctors; yet medical books affect not only to state methods of treatment, but to state the way of curing people, and the proper method of treating particular cases by classifying the various states of health. But all this, although it seems useful to the experienced, is useless to those who are ignorant of medical science. It may be supposed then that collections of laws and polities would be useful to those who are capable of considering and deciding what is right or wrong, and what is suitable to particular cases; but if people who examine such questions have not *the proper* frame of mind, they will find it impossible to form a right judgment unless indeed by accident, although they may gain a more intelligent appreciation of them.

As previous writers have failed to investigate the subject of legislation, it will perhaps be better to examine it ourselves, and indeed to examine the whole subject of politics,[114] in order that the philosophy of human life may be made as complete as possible.

Let us try then, first of all, to recount such particular opinions as have been rightly expressed by our predecessors, then, in view of the polities which we have collected, to consider the preservatives and destructives of states and of particular polities, and the reasons why some polities are good and others bad. For when we have considered these, it will perhaps be easier to see what kind of polity is best, and what is the best way of ordering it and what are its laws and customs.

EDUCATION FOR CITIZENSHIP

Politics. This selection is from the Rackham translation ("Loeb Classical Library" series). It is from Book viii, being chaps. 1, 2, and part of 3. Precisely it runs from 1337a to 1338b, and concludes the *Politics* but for a brief further discussion of music.—T. V. S.

I. Now nobody would dispute that the education of the young requires the special attention of the lawgiver. Indeed the neglect of this in states is injurious to their constitutions; for education ought to be adapted to the particular form of constitution, since the particular character belonging to each constitution both guards the constitution generally and originally establishes it—for instance the democratic spirit promotes democracy and the oligarchic spirit oligarchy; and the best spirit always causes a better constitution. Moreover in regard to all the faculties and crafts certain forms of preliminary education and training in their various operations are necessary, so that manifestly this is also requisite in regard to the actions of virtue. And inasmuch as the end for the whole state is one, it is manifest that education also must necessarily be one and the same for all and that the superintendence of this must be public, and not on private lines, in the way in which at present each man superintends the education of his own children, teaching them privately, and whatever special branch of knowledge he thinks fit. But matters of public interest ought to be under public supervision; at the same time also we ought not to think that any of the citizens belongs to himself, but that all belong to the state, for each is a part of the state, and it is natural for the superintendence of

---

[114] Aristotle thus paves the way for his *Politics*, a treatise published later than the *Nicomachean Ethics*.

the several parts to have regard to the superintendence of the whole. And one might praise the Spartans in respect of this, for they pay the greatest attention to the training of their children, and conduct it on a public system.

It is clear then that there should be legislation about education and that it should be conducted on a public system. But consideration must be given to the question, what constitutes education and what is the proper way to be educated. At present there are differences of opinion as to the proper tasks to be set; for all peoples do not agree as to the things that the young ought to learn, either with a view to virtue or with a view to the best life, nor is it clear whether their studies should be regulated more with regard to intellect or with regard to character. And confusing questions arise out of the education that actually prevails, and it is not at all clear whether the pupils should practise pursuits that are practically useful, or morally edifying, or higher accomplishments—for all these views have won the support of some judges; and nothing is agreed as regards the exercise conducive to virtue, for, to start with, all men do not honour the same virtue, so that they naturally hold different opinions in regard to training in virtue.

II. It is therefore not difficult to see that the young must be taught those useful arts that are indispensably necessary; but it is clear that they should not be taught all the useful arts, those pursuits that are liberal being kept distinct from those that are illiberal, and that they must participate in such among the useful arts as will not render the person who participates in them vulgar. A task and also an art or a science must be deemed vulgar if it renders the body or soul or mind of free men useless for the employments and actions of virtue. Hence we entitle vulgar all such arts as deteriorate the condition of the body, and also the industries that earn wages; for they make the mind preoccupied and degraded. And even with the liberal sciences, although it is not illiberal to take part in some of them up to a point, to devote oneself to them too assiduously and carefully is liable to have the injurious results specified. Also it makes much difference what object one has in view in a pursuit or study; if none follows it for the sake of oneself or one's friends, or on moral grounds, it is not illiberal, but the man who follows the same pursuit because of other people would often appear to be acting in a menial and servile manner.

The branches of study at present established fall into both classes, as was said before. There are perhaps four customary subjects of education, reading and writing, gymnastics, music, and fourth, with some people, drawing; reading and writing and drawing being taught as being useful for the purposes of life and very serviceable, and gymnastics as contributing to manly courage; but as to music, here one might raise a question. For at present most people take part in it for the sake of pleasure; but those who originally included it in education did so because, as has often been said, nature itself seeks to be able not only to engage rightly in business but also to occupy leisure nobly; for—to speak about it yet again—this is the first principle of all things. For if although both business and leisure are necessary, yet leisure is more desirable and more fully an end than business, we must inquire what is the proper occupation of leisure. For assuredly it should not be employed in play, since it would follow that play is our end in life. But if this is impossible, and sports should rather be employed in our times of business (for a man who is at work needs rest, and rest is the object of play, while business is accompanied by toil and exertion), it follows that in introducing sports we must watch the right opportunity for their employment, since we are applying them to serve as medicine; for the activity of play is a relaxation of the soul, and serves as recreation because of its pleasantness. But leisure seems itself to contain pleasure and happiness and felicity of life. And this is not possessed by the busy but by the leisured; for the busy man busies himself for the sake of some end as not being in his possession, but happiness is an end achieved, which all men think is accompanied by pleasure and not by pain. But all men do not go on to define this pleasure in the same way, but according to their various natures and to their own characters, and the pleasure with which the best man thinks that happiness is conjoined is the best pleasure and the one arising from the noblest sources. So that it is clear that some subjects must be learnt and acquired merely with a view to the pleasure in their pursuit, and that these studies and these branches of learning are ends in themselves, while the forms of learning related to business are studied as necessary and as means to other things. Hence our predecessors included music in education not as a necessity (for there is nothing necessary about it), nor as useful (in the way in which reading and writing are useful

for business and for household management and for acquiring learning and for many pursuits of civil life, while drawing also seems to
be useful in making us better judges of the works of artists), nor yet
again as we pursue gymnastics, for the sake of health and strength
(for we do not see either of these things produced as a result of
music); it remains therefore that it is useful as a pastime in leisure,
which is evidently the purpose for which people actually introduce
it, for they rank it as a form of pastime that they think proper for
free men. For this reason Homer wrote thus:

> But him alone
> 'Tis meet to summon to the festal banquet

and after these words he speaks of certain others

> Who call the bard that he may gladden all.

And also in other verses Odysseus says that this is the best pastime,
when, as men are enjoying good cheer,

> The banqueters, seated in order due
> Throughout the hall, may hear a minstrel sing.

III. It is clear therefore that there is a form of education in
which boys should be trained not because it is useful or necessary
but as being liberal and noble; though whether there is one such
subject of education or several, and what these are and how they
are to be pursued, must be discussed later, but as it is we have made
this much progress on the way, that we have some testimony even
from the ancients, derived from the courses of education which
they founded—for the point is proved by music. And it is also clear
that some of the useful subjects as well ought to be studied by the
young not only because of their utility, like the study of reading and
writing, but also because they may lead on to many other branches
of knowledge; and similarly they should study drawing not in order
that they may not go wrong in their private purchases and may
avoid being cheated in buying and selling furniture, but rather because this study makes a man observant of bodily beauty; and to
seek for utility everywhere is entirely unsuited to men that are
great-souled and free.

THE LATER ETHICAL PERIOD

Socrates, Plato, and Aristotle were informed by an undoubted note of metaphysical optimism, not to say of romanticism. Socrates had confidently proclaimed in life that the real reason why anything happens is that it is better to be than not to be and at death that no harm can befall a good man, living or dead. Plato had insisted upon the power of intelligence to build a better world, and had held to his dream, even when circumstances ruled against the practicability, of an improved society guided by philosopher-kings. Aristotle had made great dents in ignorance through systematic research, and had generalized the deep optimism into a picture of nature that was all potentiality at the bottom and realized form at the top—a nature in which everything yearns for, and moves toward, perfection. This profound optimism was the glow and the afterglow of the Periclean age in Athens. But even while Aristotle taught, his former charge, Alexander the Great, was conquering the world and in the course of doing it was writing finis to the Greek city-state which had been the mother of great virtues, including this high hope that intelligence could be made to prevail in human affairs. The independence and pride of the city-state gone, the philosophers had left only the hope of making the best out of the worst. All the succeeding schools went back of Aristotle and Plato to find a basis for their teaching. If men cannot get what they want, there remains the humbler virtue of learning to want what they get. A way of life, a philosophy of salvation, seemed the course of wisdom. The authority of a personality, such as Socrates (later of Jesus), became more important than the authority of thought itself. The three great schools—Epicureanism, Stoicism, Skepticism—drew comfort either from Socrates or from those who had drawn comfort from Socrates, while they built each a philosophy of life upon a universe less friendly to human aspiration than that which Plato and Aristotle had assumed. It is well to remember, however, that in destroying provincialism, Alexander the Great furthered cosmopolitanism. So also those who in the name of philosophy drew man's attention from the course of the stars to a way of life deserve their meed of praise as servants of mankind. They may not all have become sages, but they elaborated an ideal of the Sage, the Wise Man, as the finest flowering of the human spirit.

CHAPTER II

THE CYRENAIC-EPICUREAN TRADITION

The Epicurean school, which we are now to examine, had its connection with a philosophical movement that dated back to Socrates and professed to draw its inspiration from him—the Cyrenaic school. Aristippus (ca. 435–355) was a disciple of Socrates, who after the master's death set up a school devoted to one aspect of that many-sided father of philosophy. Pleasure was to be counted the good, or, pleasure unattainable, a neutral state of feeling in which pain was absent; and intelligence was to serve as the art of mensuration of pleasure, which Plato's Socrates has so convincingly told us of in the "Protagoras." This hedonistic ethics rested by preference upon atomism much more materialistic than the metaphysics attributed by Plato to Socrates. Upon this general foundation Epicurus (341–270) builded his school in Athens after the city's loss of political independence. Drawing his metaphysics from Democritus, who had brought atomism to its most systematic form, he pictured a world in which pure chance reduced the hope of intelligence to humble proportions. If man could not improve a world, he might by retiring to the Gardens save himself from grievous hurt, and might even with kindred spirits preserve a little oasis in a vast desert of misery. Pleasure is still the good, though the surest hope is merely to escape pain. Fear is the greatest enemy of this minimum salvage, and since fear is often associated with the avenging gods, men may count their own mortality a boon. When men are, death is not; and when death comes, men are not. Moreover, the gods, though real, are wholly disinterested in human affairs. Social life is still possible, where men as individuals think it worth their while voluntarily to combine; but the less the combination the greater the security, and the greater the independence from want the less the risk of pain.

. . .

DIOGENES LAERTIUS ON EPICURUS
AND THE EPICUREANS

Epicurus. Hicks's translation ("Loeb Classical Library" series). No important part is omitted from this discussion.—T. V. S.

Epicurus was a most prolific author and eclipsed all before him in the number of his writings: for they amount to about three hundred rolls, and contain not a single citation from other authors; it is Epicurus himself who speaks throughout. Chrysippus tried to outdo him in authorship according to Carneades, who therefore calls him the literary parasite of Epicurus. "For every subject treated by Epicurus, Chrysippus in his contentiousness must treat at equal length; hence he has frequently repeated himself and set down the first thought that occurred to him, and in his haste has left things unrevised, and he has so many citations that they alone fill his books: nor is this unexampled in Zeno and Aristotle." Such, then, in number and character are the writings of Epicurus. . . . .

The views expressed in these works I will try to set forth by quoting three of his epistles, in which he has given an epitome of his whole system. I will also set down his *Sovran Maxims* and any other utterance of his that seems worth citing, that you may be in a position to study the philosopher on all sides and know how to judge him.

The first epistle is addressed to Herodotus and deals with physics; the second to Pythocles and deals with astronomy or meteorology; the third is addressed to Menoeceus and its subject is human life. We must begin with the first after some few preliminary reremarks upon his division of philosophy.

It is divided into three parts—Canonic, Physics, Ethics. Canonic forms the introduction to the system and is contained in a single work entitled *The Canon.* The physical part includes the entire theory of Nature: it is contained in the thirty-seven books *Of Nature* and, in a summary form, in the letters. The ethical part deals with the facts of choice and aversion: this may be found in the books *On Human Life*, in the letters, and in his treatise *Of the End.* The usual arrangement, however, is to conjoin canonic with physics, and the former they call the science which deals with the standard and the first principle, or the elementary part of philosophy, while physics proper, they say, deals with becoming and perishing and with nature; ethics, on the other hand, deals with things to be sought and avoided, with human life and with the end-in-chief.

They reject dialectic as superfluous; holding that in their inquiries the physicists should be content to employ the ordinary terms for things. Now in *The Canon* Epicurus affirms that our sensations and preconceptions and our feelings are the standards of truth; the Epicureans generally make perceptions of mental presentations to be also standards. His own statements are also to be found in the *Summary* addressed to Herodotus and in the *Sovran Maxims*. Every sensation, he says, is devoid of reason and incapable of memory; for neither is it self-caused nor, regarded as having an external cause, can it add anything thereto or take anything therefrom. Nor is there anything which can refute sensations or convict them of error: one sensation cannot convict another and kindred sensation, for they are equally valid; nor can one sensation refute another which is not kindred but heterogeneous, for the objects which the two senses judge are not the same; nor again can reason refute them, for reason is wholly dependent on sensation; nor can one sense refute another, since we pay equal heed to all. And the reality of separate perceptions guarantees the truth of our senses. But seeing and hearing are just as real as feeling pain. Hence it is from plain facts that we must start when we draw inferences about the unknown. For all our notions are derived from perceptions, either by actual contact or by analogy, or resemblance, or composition, with some slight aid from reasoning. And the objects presented to madmen and to people in dreams are true, for they produce effects—*i.e.* movements in the mind—which that which is unreal never does.

By preconception they mean a sort of apprehension or a right opinion or notion, or universal idea stored in the mind; that is, a recollection of an external object often presented, *e.g.* Such and such a thing is a man: for no sooner is the word "man" uttered than we think of his shape by an act of preconception, in which the senses take the lead. Thus the object primarily denoted by every term is then plain and clear. And we should never have started an investigation, unless we had known what it was that we were in search of. For example: The object standing yonder is a horse or a cow. Before making this judgement, we must at some time or other have known by preconception the shape of a horse or a cow. We should not have given anything a name, if we had not first learnt its form by way of preconception. It follows, then, that preconceptions are clear. The object of a judgement is derived from something previously clear, by reference to which we frame the proposition, *e.g.* "How do we know that this is a man?" Opinion they also call conception or assumption, and declare it to be true and false; for it is true if it is subsequently confirmed or if it is not contradicted by evidence, and false if it is not subsequently confirmed or is contradicted by evidence. Hence the introduction of the phrase, "that which awaits" confirmation, *e.g.* to wait and get close to the tower and then learn what it looks like at close quarters.

They affirm that there are two states of feeling, pleasure and pain, which arise in every animate being, and that the one is favourable and the other hostile to that being, and by their means choice and avoidance are determined; and that there are two kinds of inquiry, the one concerned with things, the other with nothing but words. So much, then, for his division and criterion in their main outline.

But we must return to the letter.[1]

"Epicurus to Herodotus, greeting.

"For those who are unable to study carefully all my physical writings or to go into the longer treatises at all, I have myself prepared an epitome[2] of the whole system, Herodotus, to preserve in the memory enough of the principal doctrines,[3] to the end that on every occasion they may be able to aid themselves on the most important points, so far as they take up the study of Physics. Those who have made some advance in the survey of the entire system ought to fix in their minds under the principal headings an elementary outline of the whole treatment of the subject. For a comprehensive view is often required, the details but seldom.

---

[1] This letter to Herodotus is the second and most valuable instalment of Epicurean doctrine. The manuscript seems to have been entrusted to a scribe to copy, just as it was: scholia and marginal notes, even where they interrupt the thread of the argument, have been faithfully reproduced. See §§ 39, 40, 43, 44, 50, 66, 71, 73, 74, 75.

[2] This, as the most authentic summary of Epicurean physics which we possess, serves as a groundwork in modern histories.

[3] Only the principal doctrines are contained in this epistle; more, both general and particular, was given in the *Larger Compendium*.

"To the former, then—the main heads—we must continually return, and must memorize them so far as to get a valid conception of the facts, as well as the means of discovering all the details exactly when once the general outlines are rightly understood and remembered; since it is the privilege of the mature student to make a ready use of his conceptions by referring every one of them to elementary facts and simple terms. For it is impossible to gather up the results of continuous diligent study of the entirety of things, unless we can embrace in short formulas and hold in mind all that might have been accurately expressed even to the minutest detail.

"Hence, since such a course is of service to all who take up natural science, I, who devote to the subject my continuous energy and reap the calm enjoyment of a life like this, have prepared for you just such an epitome and manual of the doctrines as a whole.

"In the first place, Herodotus, you must understand what it is that words denote, in order that by reference to this we may be in a position to test opinions, inquiries, or problems, so that our proofs may not run on untested *ad infinitum*, nor the terms we use be empty of meaning. For the primary signification of every term employed must be clearly seen, and ought to need no proving; this being necessary, if we are to have something to which the point at issue or the problem or the opinion before us can be referred.

"Next, we must by all means stick to our sensations, that is, simply to the present impressions whether of the mind or of any criterion whatever, and similarly to our actual feelings, in order that we may have the means of determining that which needs confirmation and that which is obscure.

"When this is clearly understood, it is time to consider generally things which are obscure. To begin with, nothing comes into being out of what is non-existent. For in that case anything would have arisen out of anything, standing as it would in no need of its proper germs. And if that which disappears had been destroyed and become non-existent, everything would have perished, that into which the things were dissolved being non-existent. Moreover, the sum total of things was always such as it is now, and such it will ever remain. For there is nothing into which it can change. For outside the sum of things there is nothing which could enter into it and bring about the change.

"Further [*this he says also in the Larger Epitome near the beginning and in his First Book "On Nature"*], the whole of being consists of bodies and space. For the existence of bodies is everywhere attested by sense itself, and it is upon sensation that reason must rely when it attempts to infer the unknown from the known. And if there were no space (which we call also void and place and intangible nature), bodies would have nothing in which to be and through which to move, as they are plainly seen to move. Beyond bodies and space there is nothing which by mental apprehension or on its analogy we can conceive to exist. When we speak of bodies and space, both are regarded as wholes or separate things, not as the properties or accidents of separate things.

"Again [*he repeats this in the First Book and in Books XIV. and XV. of the work "On Nature" and in the Larger Epitome*], of bodies some are composite, others the elements of which these composite bodies are made. These elements are indivisible and unchangeable, and necessarily so, if things are not all to be destroyed and pass into non-existence, but are to be strong enough to endure when the composite bodies are broken up, because they possess a solid nature and are incapable of being anywhere or anyhow dissolved. It follows that the first beginnings must be indivisible, corporeal entities.

"Again, the sum of things is infinite. For what is finite has an extremity, and the extremity of anything is discerned only by comparison with something else. ⟨Now the sum of things is not discerned by comparison with anything else:⟩ hence, since it has no extremity, it has no limit; and, since it has no limit, it must be unlimited or infinite.

"Moreover, the sum of things is unlimited both by reason of the multitude of the atoms and the extent of the void. For if the void were infinite and bodies finite, the bodies would not have stayed anywhere but would have been dispersed in their course through the infinite void, not having any supports or counterchecks to send them back on their upward rebound. Again, if the void were finite, the infinity of bodies would not have anywhere to be.

"Furthermore, the atoms, which have no void in them—out of which composite bodies arise and into which they are dissolved—vary indefinitely in their shapes; for so many varieties of things as we see could never have arisen out of a recurrence of a definite number of the same shapes. The like atoms of each shape are absolutely infinite; but the variety of shapes, though indefinitely large, is not absolutely infinite. [*For neither does the divisibility go on "ad infinitum," he says below; but he adds, since the qualities change, unless one is prepared to keep enlarging their magnitudes also simply "ad infinitum."*]

"The atoms are in continual motion through all eternity. [*Further, he says below, that the atoms move with equal speed, since the void makes way for the lightest and heaviest alike.*] Some of them rebound to a considerable distance from each other, while others merely oscillate in one place when they chance to have got entangled or to be enclosed by a mass of other atoms shaped for entangling.[4]

"This is because each atom is separated from the rest by void, which is incapable of offering any resistance to the rebound; while it is the solidity of the atom which makes it rebound after a collision, however short the distance to which it rebounds, when it finds itself imprisoned in a mass of entangling atoms. Of all this there is no beginning, since both atoms and void exist from everlasting. [*He says below that atoms have no quality at all except shape, size, and weight. But that colour varies with the arrangement of the atoms he states in his "Twelve Rudiments"; further, that they are not of any and every size; at any rate no atom has ever been seen by our sense.*]

"The repetition at such length of all that we are now recalling to mind furnishes an adequate outline for our conception of the nature of things.

"Moreover, there is an infinite number of worlds, some like this world, others unlike it.[5] For the atoms being infinite in number, as has just been proved, are borne ever further in their course. For the atoms out of which a world might arise, or by which a world might be formed, have not all been expended on one world or a finite number of worlds, whether like or unlike this one. Hence there will be nothing to hinder an infinity of worlds.

"Again, there are outlines or films, which are of the same shape as solid bodies, but of a thinness far exceeding that of any object that we see. For it is not impossible that there should be found in the surrounding air combinations of this kind, materials adapted

[4] Note the distinction between (1) solids, composed of interlacing atoms (which have got entangled), and (2) fluids, composed of atoms not interlaced, needing a sheath or container of other atoms, if they are to remain united. To (2) belongs Soul (§ 66).

[5] This remark is not misplaced. For infinity of worlds follows from the infinity of (*a*) atoms, (*b*) space; see *inf.* §§ 73, 89.

for expressing the hollowness and thinness of surfaces, and effluxes preserving the same relative position and motion which they had in the solid objects from which they come. To these films we give the name of 'images' or 'idols.' Furthermore, so long as nothing comes in the way to offer resistance, motion through the void accomplishes any imaginable distance in an inconceivably short time. For resistance encountered is the equivalent of slowness, its absence the equivalent of speed.

"Not that, if we consider the minute times perceptible by reason alone, the moving body itself arrives at more than one place simultaneously (for this too is inconceivable), although in time perceptible to sense it does arrive simultaneously, however different the point of departure from that conceived by us. For if it changed its direction, that would be equivalent to its meeting with resistance, even if up to that point we allow nothing to impede the rate of its flight. This is an elementary fact which in itself is well worth bearing in mind. In the next place the exceeding thinness of the images is contradicted by none of the facts under our observation. Hence also their velocities are enormous, since they always find a void passage to fit them. Besides, their incessant effluence meets with no resistance, or very little, although many atoms, not to say an unlimited number, do at once encounter resistance.

"Besides this, remember that the production of the images is as quick as thought. For particles are continually streaming off from the surface of bodies, though no diminution of the bodies is observed, because other particles take their place.[6] And those given off for a long time retain the position and arrangement which their atoms had when they formed part of the solid bodies, although occasionally they are thrown into confusion. Sometimes such films are formed very rapidly in the air, because they need not have any solid content; and there are other modes in which they may be formed. For there is nothing in all this which is contradicted by sensation, if we in some sort look at the clear evidence of sense, to which we should also refer the continuity of particles in the objects external to ourselves.

"We must also consider that it is by the entrance of something

[6] If vision is to be not merely intermittent but continuous, images must be perpetually streaming from the objects seen to our eyes; there must be a continual succession of similar images.

coming from external objects that we see their shapes and think of them. For external things would not stamp on us their own nature of colour and form through the medium of the air which is between them and us, or by means of rays of light or currents of any sort going from us to them, so well as by the entrance into our eyes or minds, to whichever their size is suitable, of certain films coming from the things themselves, these films or outlines being of the same colour and shape as the external things themselves. They move with rapid motion; and this again explains why they present the appearance of the single continuous object, and retain the mutual interconnexion which they had in the object, when they impinge upon the sense, such impact being due to the oscillation of the atoms in the interior of the solid object from which they come. And whatever presentation we derive by direct contact, whether it be with the mind or with the sense-organs, be it shape that is presented or other properties, this shape as presented is the shape of the solid thing, and it is due either to a close coherence of the image as a whole or to a mere remnant of its parts. Falsehood and error always depend upon the intrusion of opinion <when a fact awaits> confirmation or the absence of contradiction, which fact is afterwards frequently not confirmed <or even contradicted> [*following a certain movement in ourselves connected with, but distinct from, the mental picture presented—which is the cause of error.*]

"For the presentations which, *e.g.*, are received in a picture or arise in dreams, or from any other form of apprehension by the mind or by the other criteria of truth, would never have resembled what we call the real and true things, had it not been for certain actual things of the kind with which we come in contact. Error would not have occurred, if we had not experienced some other movement in ourselves, conjoined with, but distinct from, the perception of what is presented. And from this movement, if it be not confirmed or be contradicted, falsehood results; while, if it be confirmed or not contradicted, truth results.

"And to this view we must closely adhere, if we are not to repudiate the criteria founded on the clear evidence of sense, nor again to throw all these things into confusion by maintaining falsehood as if it were truth.[7]

"Again, hearing takes place when a current passes from the ob-

[7] Epicurus was a severe critic of the Sceptics; *cf.* §§ 146, 147.

ject, whether person or thing, which emits voice or sound or noise, or produces the sensation of hearing in any way whatever. This current is broken up into homogeneous particles, which at the same time preserve a certain mutual connexion and a distinctive unity extending to the object which emitted them, and thus, for the most part, cause the perception in that case or, if not, merely indicate the presence of the external object. For without the transmission from the object of a certain interconnexion of the parts no such sensation could arise. Therefore we must not suppose that the air itself is moulded into shape by the voice emitted or something similar; for it is very far from being the case that the air is acted upon by it in this way. The blow which is struck in us when we utter a sound causes such a displacement of the particles as serves to produce a current resembling breath, and this displacement gives rise to the sensation of hearing.

"Again, we must believe that smelling, like hearing, would produce no sensation, were there not particles conveyed from the object which are of the proper sort for exciting the organ of smelling, some of one sort, some of another, some exciting it confusedly and strangely, others quietly and agreeably.

"Moreover, we must hold that the atoms in fact possess none of the qualities belonging to things which come under our observation, except shape, weight, and size, and the properties necessarily conjoined with shape. For every quality changes, but the atoms do not change, since, when the composite bodies are dissolved, there must needs be a permanent something, solid and indissoluble, left behind, which makes change possible: not changes into or from the non-existent, but often through differences of arrangement, and sometimes through additions and subtractions of the atoms. Hence these somethings capable of being diversely arranged must be indestructible, exempt from change, but possessed each of its own distinctive mass and configuration. This must remain.

"For in the case of changes of configuration within our experience the figure is supposed to be inherent when other qualities are stripped off, but the qualities are not supposed, like the shape which is left behind, to inhere in the subject of change, but to vanish altogether from the body. Thus, then, what is left behind is sufficient to account for the differences in composite bodies, since something at least must necessarily be left remaining and be immune from annihilation.

"Again, you should not suppose that the atoms have any and every size,[8] lest you be contradicted by facts; but differences of size must be admitted; for this addition renders the facts of feeling and sensation easier of explanation. But to attribute any and every magnitude to the atoms does not help to explain the differences of quality in things; moreover, in that case atoms large enough to be seen ought to have reached us, which is never observed to occur; nor can we conceive how its occurrence should be possible, *i.e.* that an atom should become visible.

"Besides, you must not suppose that there are parts unlimited in number, be they ever so small, in any finite body. Hence not only must we reject as impossible subdivision *ad infinitum* into smaller and smaller parts, lest we make all things too weak and, in our conceptions of the aggregates, be driven to pulverize the things that exist, *i.e.* the atoms, and annihilate them; but in dealing with finite things we must also reject as impossible the progression *ad infinitum* by less and less increments.

"For when once we have said that an infinite number of particles, however small, are contained in anything, it is not possible to conceive how it could any longer be limited or finite in size. For clearly our infinite number of particles must have some size; and then, of whatever size they were, the aggregate they made would be infinite. And, in the next place, since what is finite has an extremity which is distinguishable, even if it is not by itself observable, it is not possible to avoid thinking of another such extremity next to this. Nor can we help thinking that in this way, by proceeding forward from one to the next in order, it is possible by such a progression to arrive in thought at infinity.

"We must consider the minimum perceptible by sense as not corresponding to that which is capable of being traversed, *i.e.* is extended, nor again as utterly unlike it, but as having something in common with the things capable of being traversed, though it is without distinction of parts. But when from the illusion created by this common property we think we shall distinguish something in the minimum, one part on one side and another part on the other side, it must be another minimum equal to the first which catches

[8] The opinion of Democritus.

our eye. In fact, we see these minima one after another, beginning with the first, and not as occupying the same space; nor do we see them touch one another's parts with their parts, but we see that by virtue of their own peculiar character (*i.e.* as being unit indivisibles) they afford a means of measuring magnitudes: there are more of them, if the magnitude measured is greater; fewer of them, if the magnitude measured is less.

"We must recognize that this analogy also holds of the minimum in the atom; it is only in minuteness that it differs from that which is observed by sense, but it follows the same analogy. On the analogy of things within our experience we have declared that the atom has magnitude; and this, small as it is, we have merely reproduced on a larger scale. And further, the least and simplest things must be regarded as extremities of lengths, furnishing from themselves as units the means of measuring lengths, whether greater or less, the mental vision being employed, since direct observation is impossible. For the community which exists between them and the unchangeable parts (*i.e.* the minimal parts of area or surface) is sufficient to justify the conclusion so far as this goes. But it is not possible that these minima of the atom should group themselves together through the possession of motion.

"Further, we must not assert 'up' or 'down' of that which is unlimited, as if there were a zenith or nadir. As to the space overhead, however, if it be possible to draw a line to infinity from the point where we stand, we know that never will this space—or, for that matter, the space below the supposed standpoint if produced to infinity—appear to us to be at the same time 'up' and 'down' with reference to the same point; for this is inconceivable. Hence it is possible to assume one direction of motion, which we conceive as extending upwards *ad infinitum*, and another downwards, even if it should happen ten thousand times that what moves from us to the spaces above our heads reaches the feet of those above us, or that which moves downwards from us the heads of those below us. None the less is it true that the whole of the motion in the respective cases is conceived as extending in opposite directions *ad infinitum*.

"When they are travelling through the void and meet with no resistance, the atoms must move with equal speed. Neither will heavy atoms travel more quickly than small and light ones, so long as nothing meets them, nor will small atoms travel more quickly

than large ones, provided they always find a passage suitable to
their size, and provided also that they meet with no obstruction.
Nor will their upward or their lateral motion, which is due to col-
lisions, nor again their downward motion, due to weight, affect their
velocity. As long as either motion obtains, it must continue, quick
as the speed of thought, provided there is no obstruction, whether
due to external collision or to the atoms' own weight counteracting
the force of the blow.

"Moreover, when we come to deal with composite bodies, one of
them will travel faster than another, although their atoms have
equal speed. This is because the atoms in the aggregates are
travelling in one direction during the shortest continuous time,
albeit they move in different directions in times so short as to be
appreciable only by the reason, but frequently collide until the
continuity of their motion is appreciated by sense. For the assumption that beyond the range of direct observation even the minute
times conceivable by reason will present continuity of motion is not
true in the case before us. Our canon is that direct observation by
sense and direct apprehension by the mind are alone invariably
true.

"Next, keeping in view our perceptions and feelings (for so shall
we have the surest grounds for belief), we must recognize generally
that the soul is a corporeal thing, composed of fine particles, dispersed all over the frame, most nearly resembling wind with an admixture of heat, in some respects like wind, in others like heat. But,
again, there is the third part which exceeds the other two in the
fineness of its particles and thereby keeps in closer touch with the
rest of the frame. And this is shown by the mental faculties
and feelings, by the ease with which the mind moves, and by
thoughts, and by all those things the loss of which causes death.
Further, we must keep in mind that soul has the greatest share in
causing sensation. Still, it would not have had sensation, had it not
been somehow confined within the rest of the frame. But the rest
of the frame, though it provides this indispensable condition for
the soul, itself also has a share, derived from the soul, of the said
quality; and yet does not possess all the qualities of soul. Hence
on the departure of the soul it loses sentience. For it had not this
power in itself; but something else, congenital with the body, supplied it to body: which other thing, through the potentiality actual-

ized in it by means of motion, at once acquired for itself a quality of sentience, and, in virtue of the neighbourhood and interconnexion between them, imparted it (as I said) to the body also.

"Hence, so long as the soul is in the body, it never loses sentience through the removal of some other part. The containing sheath may be dislocated in whole or in part, and portions of the soul may thereby be lost; yet in spite of this the soul, if it manage to survive, will have sentience. But the rest of the frame, whether the whole of it survives or only a part, no longer has sensation, when once those atoms have departed, which, however few in number, are required to constitute the nature of soul. Moreover, when the whole frame is broken up, the soul is scattered and has no longer the same powers as before, nor the same motions; hence it does not possess sentience either.

"For we cannot think of it as sentient, except it be in this composite whole and moving with these movements; nor can we so think of it when the sheaths which enclose and surround it are not the same as those in which the soul is now located and in which it performs these movements. [*He says elsewhere that the soul is composed of the smoothest and roundest of atoms, far superior in both respects to those of fire; that part of it is irrational, this being scattered over the rest of the frame, while the rational part resides in the chest, as is manifest from our fears and our joy; the sleep occurs when the parts of the soul which have been scattered all over the composite organism are held fast in it or dispersed, and afterwards collide with one another by their impacts. The semen is derived from the whole of the body.*]

"There is the further point to be considered, what the incorporeal can be, if, I mean, according to current usage the term is applied to what can be conceived as self-existent. But it is impossible to conceive anything that is incorporeal as self-existent except empty space. And empty space cannot itself either act or be acted upon, but simply allows body to move through it. Hence those who call soul incorporeal speak foolishly. For if it were so, it could neither act nor be acted upon. But, as it is, both these properties, you see, plainly belong to soul.

"If, then, we bring all these arguments concerning soul to the criterion of our feelings and perceptions, as if we keep in mind the proposition stated at the outset, we shall see that the subject has been adequately comprehended in outline: which will enable us to determine the details with accuracy and confidence.

"Moreover, shapes and colours, magnitudes and weights, and in short all those qualities which are predicated of body, in so far as they are perpetual properties either of all bodies or of visible bodies, are knowable by sensation of these very properties: these, I say, must not be supposed to exist independently by themselves (for that is inconceivable), nor yet to be non-existent, nor to be some other and incorporeal entities cleaving to body, nor again to be parts of body. We must consider the whole body in a general way to derive its permanent nature from all of them, though it is not, as it were, formed by grouping them together in the same way as when from the particles themselves a larger aggregate is made up, whether these particles be primary or any magnitudes whatsoever less than the particular whole. All these qualities, I repeat, merely give the body its own permanent nature. They all have their own characteristic modes of being perceived and distinguished, but always along with the whole body in which they inhere and never in separation from it; and it is in virtue of this complete conception of the body as a whole that it is so designated.

"Again, qualities often attach to bodies without being permanent concomitants. They are not to be classed among invisible entities nor are they incorporeal. Hence, using the term 'accidents' in the commonest sense, we say plainly that 'accidents' have not the nature of the whole thing to which they belong, and to which, conceiving it as a whole, we give the name of body, nor that of the permanent properties without which body cannot be thought of. And in virtue of certain peculiar modes of apprehension into which the complete body always enters, each of them can be called an accident. But only as often as they are seen actually to belong to it, since such accidents are not perpetual concomitants. There is no need to banish from reality this clear evidence that the accident has not the nature of that whole—by us called body—to which it belongs, nor of the permanent properties which accompany the whole. Nor, on the other hand, must we suppose the accident to have independent existence (for this is just as inconceivable in the case of accidents as in that of the permanent properties); but, as is manifest, they should all be regarded as accidents, not as permanent concomitants, of bodies, nor yet as having the rank of independent existence. Rather they are seen to be exactly as and what sensation itself makes them individually claim to be.

"There is another thing which we must consider carefully. We must not investigate time as we do the other accidents which we investigate in a subject, namely, by referring them to the preconceptions envisaged in our minds; but we must take into account the plain fact itself, in virtue of which we speak of time as long or short, linking to it in intimate connexion this attribute of duration. We need not adopt any fresh terms as preferable, but should employ the usual expressions about it. Nor need we predicate anything else of time, as if this something else contained the same essence as is contained in the proper meaning of the word 'time' (for this also is done by some). We must chiefly reflect upon that to which we attach this peculiar character of time, and by which we measure it. No further proof is required: we have only to reflect that we attach the attribute of time to days and nights and their parts, and likewise to feelings of pleasure and pain and to neutral states, to states of movement and states of rest, conceiving a peculiar accident of these to be this very characteristic which we express by the word 'time'. [*He says this both in the second book "On Nature" and in the Larger Epitome.*]

"After the foregoing we have next to consider that the worlds and every finite aggregate which bears a strong resemblance to things we commonly see have arisen out of the infinite. For all these, whether small or great, have been separated off from special conglomerations of atoms; and all things are again dissolved, some faster, some slower, some through the action of one set of causes, others through the action of another. [*It is clear, then, that he also makes the worlds perishable, as their parts are subject to change. Elsewhere he says the earth is supported on the air.*]

"And further, we must not suppose that the worlds have necessarily one and the same shape. [*On the contrary, in the twelfth book "On Nature" he himself says that the shapes of the worlds differ, some being spherical, some oval, others again of shapes different from these. They do not, however, admit of every shape. Nor are they living beings which have been separated from the infinite.*] For nobody can prove that in one sort of world there might not be contained, whereas in another sort of world there could not possibly be, the seeds out of which animals and plants arise and all the rest of the things we see.

[*And the same holds good for their nurture in a world after they have arisen. And so too we must think it happens upon the earth also.*]

"Again, we must suppose that nature too has been taught and forced to learn many various lessons by the facts themselves, that reason subsequently develops what it has thus received and makes fresh discoveries, among some tribes more quickly, among others more slowly, the progress thus made being at certain times and seasons greater, at others less.

"Hence even the names of things were not originally due to convention, but in the several tribes under the impulse of special feelings and special presentations of sense primitive man uttered special cries. The air thus emitted was moulded by their individual feelings or sense-presentations, and differently according to the difference of the regions which the tribes inhabited. Subsequently whole tribes adopted their own special names, in order that their communications might be less ambiguous to each other and more briefly expressed. And as for things not visible, so far as those who were conscious of them tried to introduce any such notion, they put in circulation certain names for them, either sounds which they were instinctively compelled to utter or which they selected by reason on analogy according to the most general cause there can be for expressing oneself in such a way.

"Nay more: we are bound to believe that in the sky revolutions, solstices, eclipses, risings and settings, and the like, take place without the ministration or command, either now or in the future, of any being who at the same time enjoys **perfect** bliss along with immortality. For troubles and anxieties and feelings of anger and partiality do not accord with bliss, but always imply weakness and fear and dependence upon one's neighbours. Nor, again, must we hold that things which are no more than globular masses of fire, being at the same time endowed with bliss, assume these motions at will. Nay, in every term we use we must hold fast to all the majesty which attaches to such notions as bliss and immortality, lest the terms should generate opinions inconsistent with this majesty. Otherwise such inconsistency will of itself suffice to produce the worst disturbance in our minds. Hence, where we find phenomena invariably recurring, the invariableness of the recurrence must be ascribed to the original interception and conglomeration of atoms whereby the world was formed.

"Further, we must hold that to arrive at accurate knowledge of the cause of things of most moment is the business of natural science, and that happiness depends on this (viz. on the knowledge of celestial and atmospheric phenomena), and upon knowing what the heavenly bodies really are, and any kindred facts contributing to exact knowledge in this respect.

"Further, we must recognize on such points as this no plurality of causes or contingency, but must hold that nothing suggestive of conflict or disquiet is compatible with an immortal and blessed nature. And the mind can grasp the absolute truth of this.

"But when we come to subjects for special inquiry, there is nothing in the knowledge of risings and settings and solstices and eclipses and all kindred subjects that contributes to our happiness; but those who are well-informed about such matters and yet are ignorant what the heavenly bodies really are, and what are the most important causes of phenomena, feel quite as much fear as those who have no such special information—nay, perhaps even greater fear, when the curiosity excited by this additional knowledge cannot find a solution or understand the subordination of these phenomena to the highest causes.

"Hence, if we discover more than one cause that may account for solstices, settings and risings, eclipses and the like, as we did also in particular matters of detail, we must not suppose that our treatment of these matters fails of accuracy, so far as it is needful to ensure our tranquillity and happiness. When, therefore, we investigate the causes of celestial and atmospheric phenomena, as of all that is unknown, we must take into account the variety of ways in which analogous occurrences happen within our experience; while as for those who do not recognize the difference between what is or comes about from a single cause and that which may be the effect of any one of several causes, overlooking the fact that the objects are only seen at a distance, and are moreover ignorant of the conditions that render, or do not render, peace of mind impossible—all such persons we must treat with contempt. If then we think that an event could happen in one or other particular way out of several, we shall be as tranquil when we recognize that it actually comes about in more ways than one as if we knew that it happens in this particular way.

"There is yet one more point to seize, namely, that the greatest anxiety of the human mind arises through the belief that the heavenly bodies are blessed and indestructible, and that at the same time they have volitions and actions and causality inconsistent with this belief; and through expecting or apprehending some everlasting evil, either because of the myths, or because we are in dread of the mere insensibility of death, as if it had to do with us; and through being reduced to this state not by conviction but by a certain irrational perversity, so that, if men do not set bounds to their terror, they endure as much or even more intense anxiety than the man whose views on these matters are quite vague. But mental tranquillity means being released from all these troubles and cherishing a continual remembrance of the highest and most important truths.

"Hence we must attend to present feelings and sense perceptions, whether those of mankind in general or those peculiar to the individual, and also attend to all the clear evidence available, as given by each of the standards of truth. For by studying them we shall rightly trace to its cause and banish the source of disturbance and dread, accounting for celestial phenomena and for all other things which from time to time befall us and cause the utmost alarm to the rest of mankind.

"Here then, Herodotus, you have the chief doctrines of Physics in the form of a summary. So that, if this statement be accurately retained and take effect, a man will, I make no doubt, be incomparably better equipped than his fellows, even if he should never go into all the exact details. For he will clear up for himself many of the points which I have worked out in detail in my complete exposition; and the summary itself, if borne in mind, will be of constant service to him.

"It is of such a sort that those who are already tolerably, or even perfectly, well acquainted with the details can, by analysis of what they know into such elementary perceptions as these, best prosecute their researches in physical science as a whole; while those, on the other hand, who are not altogether entitled to rank as mature students can in silent fashion and as quick as thought run over the doctrines most important for their peace of mind."

Such is his epistle on Physics. Next comes the epistle on Celestial Phenomena.

"Epicurus to Pythocles, greeting.

"In your letter to me, of which Cleon was the bearer, you continue to show me affection which I have merited by my devotion to you, and you try, not without success, to recall the considerations which make for a happy life. To aid your memory you ask me for a clear and concise statement respecting celestial phenomena; for what we have written on this subject elsewhere is, you tell me, hard to remember, although you have my books constantly with you. I was glad to receive your request and am full of pleasant expectations. We will then complete our writing and grant all you ask. Many others besides you will find these reasonings useful, and especially those who have but recently made acquaintance with the true story of nature and those who are attached to pursuits which go deeper than any part of ordinary education. So you will do well to take and learn them and get them up quickly along with the short epitome in my letter to Herodotus.

"In the first place, remember that, like everything else, knowledge of celestial phenomena, whether taken along with other things or in isolation, has no other end in view than peace of mind and firm conviction.[9] We do not seek to wrest by force what is impossible, nor to understand all matters equally well, nor make our treatment always as clear as when we discuss human life or explain the principles of physics in general—for instance, that the whole of being consists of bodies and intangible nature, or that the ultimate elements of things are indivisible, or any other proposition which admits only one explanation of the phenomena to be possible. But this is not the case with celestial phenomena: these at any rate admit of manifold causes for their occurrence and manifold accounts, none of them contradictory of sensation, of their nature.

"For in the study of nature we must not conform to empty assumptions and arbitrary laws, but follow the promptings of the facts; for our life has no need now of unreason and false opinion; our one need is untroubled existence. All things go on uninterruptedly, if all be explained by the method of plurality of causes in conformity with the facts, so soon as we duly understand what may be plausibly alleged respecting them. But when we pick and choose among them, rejecting one equally consistent with the phe-

[9] Philosophy is defined as "an activity which by words and arguments secures the happy life."

nomena, we clearly fall away from the study of nature altogether and tumble into myth. Some phenomena within our experience afford evidence by which we may interpret what goes on in the heavens. We see how the former really take place, but not how the celestial phenomena take place, for their occurrence may possibly be due to a variety of causes. However, we must observe each fact as presented, and further separate from it all the facts presented along with it, the occurrence of which from various causes is not contradicted by facts within our experience.

"A world is a circumscribed portion of the universe, which contains stars and earth and all other visible things, cut off from the infinite, and terminating [*and terminating in a boundary which may be either thick or thin, a boundary whose dissolution will bring about the wreck of all within it*] in an exterior which may either revolve or be at rest, and be round or triangular or of any other shape whatever. All these alternatives are possible: they are contradicted by none of the facts in this world, in which an extremity can nowhere be discerned.

"That there is an infinite number of such worlds can be perceived, and that such a world may arise in a world or in one of the *intermundia* (by which term we mean the spaces between worlds) in a tolerably empty space and not, as some maintain, in a vast space perfectly clear and void. It arises when certain suitable seeds rush in from a single world or *intermundium*, or from several, and undergo gradual additions or articulations or changes of place, it may be, and waterings from appropriate sources, until they are matured and firmly settled in so far as the foundations laid can receive them. For it is not enough that there should be an aggregation or a vortex in the empty space in which a world may arise, as the necessitarians hold, and may grow until it collide with another, as one of the so-called physicists says. For this is in conflict with facts.

"The sun and moon and the stars generally were not of independent origin and later absorbed within our world, [such parts of it at least as serve at all for its defence]; but they at once began to take form and grow [and so too did earth and sea] by the accretions and whirling motions of certain substances of finest texture, of the nature either of wind or fire, or of both; for thus sense itself suggests.

"The size of the sun and the remaining stars relatively to us is just as great as it appears. [*This he states in the eleventh book "On*

Nature." For, says he, if it had diminished in size on account of the distance, it would much more have diminished its brightness; for indeed there is no distance more proportionate to this diminution of size than is the distance at which the brightness begins to diminish.] But in itself and actually it may be a little larger or a little smaller, or precisely as great as it is seen to be. For so too fires of which we have experience are seen by sense when we see them at a distance. And every objection brought against this part of the theory will easily be met by anyone who attends to plain facts, as I show in my work *On Nature*. And the rising and setting of the sun, moon, and stars may be due to kindling and quenching, provided that the circumstances are such as to produce this result in each of the two regions, east and west: for no fact testifies against this. Or the result might be produced by their coming forward above the earth and again by its intervention to hide them: for no fact testifies against this either. And their motions may be due to the rotation of the whole heaven, or the heaven may be at rest and they alone rotate according to some necessary impulse to rise, implanted at first when the world was made . . . . and this through excessive heat, due to a certain extension of the fire which always encroaches upon that which is near it.

"The turnings of the sun and moon in their course may be due to the obliquity of the heaven, whereby it is forced back at these times. Again, they may equally be due to the contrary pressure of the air or, it may be, to the fact that either the fuel from time to time necessary has been consumed in the vicinity or there in a dearth of it. Or even because such a whirling motion was from the first inherent in these stars so that they move in a sort of spiral. For all such explanations and the like do not conflict with any clear evidence, if only in such details we hold fast to what is possible, and can bring each of these explanations into accord with the facts, unmoved by the servile artifices of the astronomers.

"The waning of the moon and again her waxing might be due to the rotation of the moon's body, and equally well to configurations which the air assumes; further, it may be due to the interposition of certain bodies. In short, it may happen in any of the ways in which the facts within our experience suggest such an appearance to be explicable. But one must not be so much in love with the explanation by a single way as wrongly to reject all the others from ignorance of what can, and what cannot, be within human knowledge, and consequent longing to discover the indiscoverable. Further, the moon may possibly shine by her own light, just as possibly she may derive her light from the sun; for in our own experience we see many things which shine by their own light and many also which shine by borrowed light. And none of the celestial phenomena stand in the way, if only we always keep in mind the method of plural explanation and the several consistent assumptions and causes, instead of dwelling on what is inconsistent and giving it a false importance so as always to fall back in one way or another upon the single explanation. The appearance of the face in the moon may equally well arise from interchange of parts, or from interposition of something, or in any other of the ways which might be seen to accord with the facts. For in all the celestial phenomena such a line of research is not to be abandoned; for, if you fight against clear evidence, you never can enjoy genuine peace of mind.

"An eclipse of the sun or moon may be due to the extinction of their light, just as within our own experience this is observed to happen; and again by interposition of something else—whether it be the earth or some other invisible body like it. And thus we must take in conjunction the explanations which agree with one another, and remember that the concurrence of more than one at the same time may not impossibly happen. [*He says the same in Book XII. of his "De Natura," and further that the sun is eclipsed when the moon throws her shadow over him, and the moon is eclipsed by the shadow of the earth; or again, eclipse may be due to the moon's withdrawal, and this is cited by Diogenes the Epicurean in the first book of his "Epilecta."*]

"And further, let the regularity of their orbits be explained in the same way as certain ordinary incidents within our own experience; the divine nature must not on any account be adduced to explain this, but must be kept free from the task and in perfect bliss. Unless this be done, the whole study of celestial phenomena will be in vain, as indeed it has proved to be with some who did not lay hold of a possible method, but fell into the folly of supposing that these events happen in one single way only and of rejecting all the others which are possible, suffering themselves to be carried into the realm of the unintelligible, and being unable to take a comprehensive view of the facts which must be taken as clues to the rest.

"The variations in the length of nights and days may be due to the swiftness and again to the slowness of the sun's motion in the sky, owing to the variations in the length of spaces traversed and to his accomplishing some distances more swiftly or more slowly, as happens sometimes within our own experience; and with these facts our explanation of celestial phenomena must agree; whereas those who adopt only one explanation are in conflict with the facts and are utterly mistaken as to the way in which man can attain knowledge.

"The signs in the sky which betoken the weather may be due to mere coincidence of the seasons, as is the case with signs from animals seen on earth, or they may be caused by changes and alterations in the air. For neither the one explanation nor the other is in conflict with facts, and it is not easy to see in which cases the effect is due to one cause or to the other.

"Clouds may form and gather either because the air is condensed under the pressure of winds, or because atoms which hold together and are suitable to produce this result become mutually entangled, or because currents collect from the earth and the waters; and there are several other ways in which it is not impossible for the aggregations of such bodies into clouds to be brought about. And that being so, rain may be produced from them sometimes by their compression, sometimes by their transformation; or again may be caused by exhalations of moisture rising from suitable places through the air, while a more violent inundation is due to certain accumulations suitable for such discharge. Thunder may be due to the rolling of wind in the hollow parts of the clouds, as it is sometimes imprisoned in vessels which we use; or to the roaring of fire in them when blown by a wind, or to the rending and disruption of clouds, or to the friction and splitting up of clouds when they have become as firm as ice. As in the whole survey, so in this particular point, the facts invite us to give a plurality of explanations. Lightnings too happen in a variety of ways. For when the clouds rub against each other and collide, that collocation of atoms which is the cause of fire generates lightning; or it may be due to the flashing forth from the clouds, by reason of winds, of particles capable of producing this brightness; or else it is squeezed out of the clouds when they have been condensed either by their own action or by that of the winds; or again, the light diffused from the stars may be enclosed in the clouds, then driven about by their motion and by that of the winds, and finally make its escape from the clouds; or light of the finest texture may be filtered through the clouds (whereby the clouds may be set on fire and thunder produced), and the motion of this light may make lightning; or it may arise from the combustion of wind brought about by the violence of its motion and the intensity of its compression; or, when the clouds are rent asunder by winds, and the atoms which generate fire are expelled, these likewise cause lightning to appear. And it may easily be seen that its occurrence is possible in many other ways, so long as we hold fast to facts and take a general view of what is analogous to them. Lightning precedes thunder, when the clouds are constituted as mentioned above and the configuration which produces lightning is expelled at the moment when the wind falls upon the cloud, and the wind being rolled up afterwards produces the roar of thunder; or, if both are simultaneous, the lightning moves with a greater velocity towards us and the thunder lags behind, exactly as when persons who are striking blows are observed from a distance. A thunderbolt is caused when winds are repeatedly collected, imprisoned, and violently ignited; or when a part is torn asunder and is more violently expelled downwards, the rending being due to the fact that the compression of the clouds has made the neighbouring parts more dense; or again it may be due like thunder merely to the expulsion of the imprisoned fire, when this has accumulated and been more violently inflated with wind and has torn the cloud, being unable to withdraw to the adjacent parts because it is continually more and more closely compressed—[generally by some high mountain where thunderbolts mostly fall]. And there are several other ways in which thunderbolts may possibly be produced. Exclusion of myth is the sole condition necessary; and it will be excluded, if one properly attends to the facts and hence draws inferences to interpret what is obscure.

"Fiery whirlwinds are due to the descent of a cloud forced downwards like a pillar by the wind in full force and carried by a gale round and round, while at the same time the outside wind gives the cloud a lateral thrust; or it may be due to a change of the wind which veers to all points of the compass as a current of air from above helps to force it to move; or it may be that a strong eddy of winds has been started and is unable to burst through laterally because the air around is closely condensed. And when they descend upon land, they cause what are called tornadoes, in accordance with the various ways in which they are produced through the force of the wind; and when let down upon the sea, they cause waterspouts.

"Earthquakes may be due to the imprisonment of wind underground, and to its being interspersed with small masses of earth and then set in continuous motion, thus causing the earth to tremble. And the earth either takes in this wind from without or from the falling in of foundations, when undermined, into subterranean caverns, thus raising a wind in the imprisoned air. Or they may be due to the propagation of movement arising from the fall of many foundations and to its being again checked when it encounters the more solid resistance of earth. And there are many other causes to which these oscillations of the earth may be due.

"Winds arise from time to time when foreign matter continually and gradually finds its way into the air; also through the gathering of great store of water. The rest of the winds arise when a few of them fall into the many hollows and they are thus divided and multiplied.

"Hail is caused by the firmer congelation and complete transformation, and subsequent distribution into drops, of certain particles resembling wind: also by the slighter congelation of certain particles of moisture and the vicinity of certain particles of wind which at one and the same time forces them together and makes them burst, so that they become frozen in parts and in the whole mass. The round shape of hailstones is not impossibly due to the extremities on all sides being melted and to the fact that, as explained, particles either of moisture or of wind surround them evenly on all sides and in every quarter, when they freeze.

"Snow may be formed when a fine rain issues from the clouds because the pores are symmetrical and because of the continuous and violent pressure of the winds upon clouds which are suitable; and then this rain has been frozen on its way because of some violent change to coldness in the regions below the clouds. Or again, by congelation in clouds which have uniform density a fall of snow might occur through the clouds which contain moisture being densely packed in close proximity to each other; and these clouds produce a sort of compression and cause hail, and this happens mostly in

spring. And when frozen clouds rub against each other, this accumulation of snow might be thrown off. And there are other ways
in which snow might be formed.

"Dew is formed when such particles as are capable of producing
this sort of moisture meet each other from the air: again by their
rising from moist and damp places, the sort of place where dew is
chiefly formed, and their subsequent coalescence, so as to create
moisture and fall downwards, just as in several cases something
similar is observed to take place under our eyes. And the formation of hoar-frost is not different from that of dew, certain particles
of such a nature becoming in some such way congealed owing to a
certain condition of cold air.

"Ice is formed by the expulsion from the water of the circular,
and the compression of the scalene and acute-angled atoms contained in it; further by the accretion of such atoms from without,
which being driven together cause the water to solidify after the
expulsion of a certain number of round atoms.

"The rainbow arises when the sun shines upon humid air; or
again by a certain peculiar blending of light with air, which will
cause either all the distinctive qualities of these colours or else some
of them belonging to a single kind, and from the reflection of this light
the air all around will be coloured as we see it to be, as the sun shines
upon its parts. The circular shape which it assumes is due to the
fact that the distance of every point is perceived by our sight to be
equal; or it may be because, the atoms in the air or in the clouds and
deriving from the sun having been thus united, the aggregate of
them presents a sort of roundness.

"A halo round the moon arises because the air on all sides extends
to the moon; or because it equably raises upwards the currents
from the moon so high as to impress a circle upon the cloudy mass
and not to separate it altogether; or because it raises the air which
immediately surrounds the moon symmetrically from all sides up to
a circumference round her and there forms a thick ring. And this
happens at certain parts either because a current has forced its
way in from without or because the heat has gained possession of
certain passages in order to effect this.

"Comets arise either because fire is nourished in certain places
at certain intervals in the heavens, if circumstances are favourable;
or because at times the heaven has a particular motion above us so

that such stars appear; or because the stars themselves are set in motion under certain conditions and come to our neighbourhood and show themselves. And their disappearance is due to the causes which are the opposite of these. Certain stars may revolve without setting not only for the reason alleged by some, because this is the part of the world round which, itself unmoved, the rest revolves, but it may also be because a circular eddy of air surrounds this part, which prevents them from travelling out of sight like other stars; or because there is a dearth of necessary fuel farther on, while there is abundance in that part where they are seen to be. Moreover there are several other ways in which this might be brought about, as may be seen by anyone capable of reasoning in accordance with the facts. The wanderings of certain stars, if such wandering is their actual motion, and the regular movement of certain other stars, may be accounted for by saying that they originally moved in a circle and were constrained, some of them to be whirled round with the same uniform rotation and others with a whirling motion which varied; but it may also be that according to the diversity of the regions traversed in some places there are uniform tracts of air, forcing them forward in one direction and burning uniformly, in others these tracts present such irregularities as cause the motions observed. To assign a single cause for these effects when the facts suggest several causes is madness and a strange inconsistency; yet it is done by adherents of rash astronomy, who assign meaningless causes for the stars whenever they persist in saddling the divinity with burdensome tasks. That certain stars are seen to be left behind by others may be because they travel more slowly, though they go the same round as the others; or it may be that they are drawn back by the same whirling motion and move in the opposite direction; or again it may be that some travel over a larger and others over a smaller space in making the same revolution. But to lay down as assured a single explanation of these phenomena is worthy of those who seek to dazzle the multitude with marvels.

"Falling stars, as they are called, may in some cases be due to the mutual friction of the stars themselves, in other cases to the expulsion of certain parts when that mixture of fire and air takes place which was mentioned when we were discussing lightning; or it may be due to the meeting of atoms capable of generating fire, which accord so well as to produce this result, and their subsequent motion wherever the impulse which brought them together at first leads them; or it may be that wind collects in certain dense mist-like masses and, since it is imprisoned, ignites and then bursts forth upon whatever is round about it, and is carried to that place to which its motion impels it. And there are other ways in which this can be brought about without recourse to myths.

"The fact that the weather is sometimes foretold from the behaviour of certain animals is a mere coincidence in time. For the animals offer no necessary reason why a storm should be produced; and no divine being sits observing when these animals go out and afterwards fulfilling the signs which they have given. For such folly as this would not possess the most ordinary being if ever so little enlightened, much less one who enjoys perfect felicity.

"All this, Pythocles, you should keep in mind; for then you will escape a long way from myth, and you will be able to view in their connexion the instances which are similar to these. But above all give yourself up to the study of first principles and of infinity and of kindred subjects, and further of the standards and of the feelings and of the end for which we choose between them. For to study these subjects together will easily enable you to understand the causes of the particular phenomena. And those who have not fully accepted this, in proportion as they have not done so, will be ill acquainted with these very subjects, nor have they secured the end for which they ought to be studied." Such are his views on celestial phenomena.

But as to the conduct of life, what we ought to avoid and what to choose, he writes as follows. Before quoting his words, however, let me go into the views of Epicurus himself and his school concerning the wise man.

There are three motives to injurious acts among men—hatred, envy, and contempt; and these the wise man overcomes by reason. Moreover, he who has once become wise never more assumes the opposite habit, not even in semblance, if he can help it. He will be more susceptible of emotion than other men: that will be no hindrance to his wisdom. However, not every bodily constitution nor every nationality would permit a man to become wise. Even on the rack the wise man is happy. He alone will feel gratitude towards friends, present and absent alike, and show it by word and deed. When on the rack, however, he will give vent to cries and groans.

As regards women he will submit to the restrictions imposed by the law, as Diogenes says in his epitome of Epicurus' ethical doctrines. Nor will he punish his servants; rather he will pity them and make allowance on occasion for those who are of good character. The Epicureans do not suffer the wise man to fall in love; nor will he trouble himself about funeral rites; according to them love does not come by divine inspiration: so Diogenes in his twelfth book. The wise man will not make fine speeches. No one was ever the better for sexual indulgence, and it is well if he be not the worse.

Nor, again, will the wise man marry and rear a family: so Epicurus says in the *Problems* and in the *De Natura*. Occasionally he may marry owing to special circumstances in his life. Some too will turn aside from their purpose. Nor will he drivel, when drunken: so Epicurus says in the *Symposium*. Nor will he take part in politics, as is stated in the first book *On Life;* nor will he make himself a tyrant; nor will he turn Cynic (so the second book *On Life* tells us); nor will he be a mendicant. But even when he has lost his sight, he will not withdraw himself from life: this is stated in the same book. The wise man will also feel grief, according to Diogenes in the fifth book of his *Epilecta*. And he will take a suit into court. He will leave written words behind him, but will not compose panegyric. He will have regard to his property and to the future. He will be fond of the country. He will be armed against fortune and will never give up a friend. He will pay just so much regard to his reputation as not to be looked down upon. He will take more delight than other men in state festivals.

The wise man will set up votive images. Whether he is well off or not will be matter of indifference to him. Only the wise man will be able to converse correctly about music and poetry, without however actually writing poems himself. One wise man does not move more wisely than another. And he will make money, but only by his wisdom, if he should be in poverty, and he will pay court to a king, if need be. He will be grateful to anyone when he is corrected. He will found a school, but not in such a manner as to draw the crowd after him; and will give readings in public, but only by request. He will be a dogmatist but not a mere sceptic; and he will be like himself even when asleep. And he will on occasion die for a friend.

The school holds that sins are not all equal; that health is in some cases a good, in others a thing indifferent; that courage is not a natural gift but comes from calculation of expediency; and that friendship is prompted by our needs. One of the friends, however, must make the first advances (just as we have to cast seed into the earth), but it is maintained by a partnership in the enjoyment of life's pleasures.

Two sorts of happiness can be conceived, the one the highest possible, such as the gods enjoy, which cannot be augmented, the other admitting addition and subtraction of pleasures.

We must now proceed to his letter.

"Epicurus to Menoeceus, greeting.

"Let no one be slow to seek wisdom when he is young nor weary in the search thereof when he is grown old. For no age is too early or too late for the health of the soul. And to say that the season for studying philosophy has not yet come, or that it is past and gone, is like saying that the season for happiness is not yet or that it is now no more. Therefore, both old and young ought to seek wisdom, the former in order that, as age comes over him, he may be young in good things because of the grace of what has been, and the latter in order that, while he is young, he may at the same time be old, because he has no fear of the things which are to come. So we must exercise ourselves in the things which bring happiness, since, if that be present, we have everything, and, if that be absent, all our actions are directed toward attaining it.

"Those things which without ceasing I have declared unto thee, those do, and exercise thyself therein, holding them to be the elements of right life. First believe that God is a living being immortal and blessed, according to the notion of a god indicated by the common sense of mankind; and so believing, thou shalt not affirm of him aught that is foreign to his immortality or that agrees not with blessedness, but shalt believe about him whatever may uphold both his blessedness and his immortality. For verily there are gods, and the knowledge of them is manifest; but they are not such as the multitude believe, seeing that men do not steadfastly maintain the notions they form respecting them. Not the man who denies the gods worshipped by the multitude, but he who affirms of the gods what the multitude believes about them is truly impious. For the utterances of the multitude about the gods are not true preconceptions but false assumptions; hence it is that the greatest evils happen to the wicked and the greatest blessings happen to the good from the hand of the gods, seeing that they are always favourable to their own good qualities and take pleasure in men like unto themselves, but reject as alien whatever is not of their kind.

"Accustom thyself to believe that death is nothing to us, for good and evil imply sentience, and death is the privation of all sentience; therefore a right understanding that death is nothing to us makes the mortality of life enjoyable, not by adding to life an illimitable time, but by taking away the yearning after immortality. For life has no terrors for him who has thoroughly apprehended that there are no terrors for him in ceasing to live. Foolish, therefore, is the man who says that he fears death, not because it will pain when it comes, but because it pains in the prospect. Whatsoever causes no annoyance when it is present, causes only a groundless pain in the expectation. Death, therefore, the most awful of evils, is nothing to us, seeing that, when we are, death is not come, and, when death is come, we are not. It is nothing, then, either to the living or to the dead, for with the living it is not and the dead exist no longer. But in the world, at one time men shun death as the greatest of all evils, and at another time choose it as a respite from the evils in life. The wise man does not deprecate life nor does he fear the cessation of life. The thought of life is no offence to him, nor is the cessation of life regarded as an evil. And even as men choose of food not merely and simply the larger portion, but the more pleasant, so the wise seek to enjoy the time which is most pleasant and not merely that which is longest. And he who admonishes the young to live well and the old to make a good end speaks foolishly, not merely because of the desirableness of life, but because the same exercise at once teaches to live well and to die well. Much worse is he who says that it were good not to be born, but when once one is born to pass with all speed through the gates of Hades. For if he truly believes this, why does he not depart from life? It were easy for him to do so, if once he were firmly convinced. If he speaks only in mockery, his words are foolishness, for those who hear believe him not.

"We must remember that the future is neither wholly ours nor wholly not ours, so that neither must we count upon it as quite certain to come nor despair of it as quite certain not to come.

"We must also reflect that of desires some are natural, others are groundless; and that of the natural some are necessary as well as natural, and some natural only. And of the necessary desires some are necessary if we are to be happy, some if the body is to be rid of uneasiness, some if we are even to live. He who has a clear and certain understanding of these things will direct every preference and aversion toward securing health of body and tranquillity of mind, seeing that this is the sum and end of a blessed life. For the end of all our actions is to be free from pain and fear, and, when once we have attained all this, the tempest of the soul is laid; seeing that the living creature has no need to go in search of something that is lacking, nor to look for anything else by which the good of the soul and of the body will be fulfilled. When we are pained because of the absence of pleasure, then, and then only, do we feel the need of pleasure. Wherefore we call pleasure the alpha and omega of a blessed life. Pleasure is our first and kindred good. It is the starting-point of every choice and of every aversion, and to it we come back, inasmuch as we make feeling the rule by which to judge of every good thing. And since pleasure is our first and native good, for that reason we do not choose every pleasure whatsoever, but ofttimes pass over many pleasures when a greater annoyance ensues from them. And ofttimes we consider pains superior to pleasures when submission to the pains for a long time brings us as a consequence a greater pleasure. While therefore all pleasure because it is naturally akin to us is good, not all pleasure is choiceworthy, just as all pain is an evil and yet not all pain is to be shunned. It is, however, by measuring one against another, and by looking at the conveniences and inconveniences, that all these matters must be judged. Sometimes we treat the good as an evil, and the evil, on the contrary, as a good. Again, we regard independence of outward things as a great good, not so as in all cases to use little, but so as to be contented with little if we have not much, being honestly persuaded that they have the sweetest enjoyment of luxury who stand least in need of it, and that whatever is natural is easily procured and only the vain and worthless hard to win. Plain fare gives as much pleasure as a costly diet, when once the pain of want has been removed, while bread and water confer the highest possible pleasure when they are brought to hungry lips. To habituate one's self, therefore, to simple and inexpensive diet supplies all that is needful for health, and enables a man to meet the necessary requirements of life without shrinking, and it places us in a better condition when we approach at intervals a costly fare and renders us fearless of fortune.

"When we say, then, that pleasure is the end and aim, we do not mean the pleasures of the prodigal or the pleasures of sensuality, as we are understood to do by some through ignorance, prejudice, or wilful misrepresentation. By pleasure we mean the absence of pain in the body and of trouble in the soul. It is not an unbroken succession of drinking-bouts and of revelry, not sexual love, not the enjoyment of the fish and other delicacies of a luxurious table, which produce a pleasant life; it is sober reasoning, searching out the grounds of every choice and avoidance, and banishing those beliefs through which the greatest tumults take possession of the soul. Of all this the beginning and the greatest good is prudence. Wherefore prudence is a more precious thing even than philosophy; from it spring all the other virtues, for it teaches that we cannot lead a life of pleasure which is not also a life of prudence, honour, and justice; nor lead a life of prudence, honour, and justice, which is not also a life of pleasure. For the virtues have grown into one with a pleasant life, and a pleasant life is inseparable from them.

"Who, then, is superior in thy judgement to such a man? He holds a holy belief concerning the gods, and is altogether free from the fear of death. He has diligently considered the end fixed by nature, and understands how easily the limit of good things can be reached and attained, and how either the duration or the intensity of evils is but slight. Destiny, which some introduce as sovereign over all things, he laughs to scorn, affirming rather that some things happen of necessity, others by chance, others through our own agency. For he sees that necessity destroys responsibility and that chance or fortune is inconstant; whereas our own actions are free, and it is to them that praise and blame naturally attach. It were better, indeed, to accept the legends of the gods than to bow beneath that yoke of destiny which the natural philosophers have imposed. The one holds out some faint hope that we may escape if we honour the gods, while the necessity of the naturalists is deaf to all entreaties. Nor does he hold chance to be a god, as the world in general does, for in the acts of a god there is no disorder; nor to be a cause, though an uncertain one, for he believes that no good or evil is dispensed by chance to men so as to make life blessed, though it supplies the starting-point of great good and great evil. He believes that the misfortune of the wise is better than the prosperity of the fool. It is better, in short, that what is well judged in action should not owe its successful issue to the aid of chance.

"Exercise thyself in these and kindred precepts day and night, both by thyself and with him who is like unto thee; then never, either in waking or in dream, wilt thou be disturbed, but wilt live as a god among men. For man loses all semblance of mortality by living in the midst of immortal blessings."

Elsewhere he rejects the whole of divination, as in the short epitome, and says, "No means of predicting the future really exists, and if it did, we must regard what happens according to it as nothing to us."

Such are his views on life and conduct; and he has discoursed upon them at greater length elsewhere.

He differs from the Cyrenaics[10] with regard to pleasure. They do not include under the term the pleasure which is a state of rest, but only that which consists in motion. Epicurus admits both; also pleasure of mind as well as of body, as he states in his work *On Choice and Avoidance* and in that *On the Ethical End*, and in the first book of his work *On Human Life* and in the epistle to his philosopher friends in Mytilene. So also Diogenes in the seventeenth book of his *Epilecta*, and Metrodorus in his *Timocrates*, whose actual words are: "Thus pleasure being conceived both as that species which consists in motion and that which is a state of rest." The words of Epicurus in his work *On Choice* are: "Peace of mind and freedom from pain are pleasures which imply a state of rest; joy and delight are seen to consist in motion and activity."

He further disagrees with the Cyrenaics in that they hold that pains of body are worse than mental pains; at all events evil-doers are made to suffer bodily punishment; whereas Epicurus holds the pains of the mind to be the worse; at any rate the flesh endures the storms of the present alone, the mind those of the past and future as well as the present. In this way also he holds mental pleasures to be greater than those of the body. And as proof that pleasure is the end he adduces the fact that living things, so soon as they are born, are well content with pleasure and are at enmity with pain, by the prompting of nature and apart from reason. Left to our own feel-

[10] Next come excerpts dealing with the difference between Epicurean and Cyrenaic ethics.

ings, then, we shun pain; as when even Heracles, devoured by the poisoned robe, cries aloud,

> And bites and yells, and rock to rock resounds,
> Headlands of Locris and Euboean cliffs.

And we choose the virtues too on account of pleasure and not for their own sake, as we take medicine for the sake of health. So too in the twentieth book of his *Epilecta* says Diogenes, who also calls education recreation. Epicurus describes virtue as the *sine qua non* of pleasure, *i.e.* the one thing without which pleasure cannot be, everything else, food, for instance, being separable, *i.e.* not indispensable to pleasure.

Come, then, let me set the seal, so to say, on my entire work as well as on this philosopher's life by citing his Sovran Maxims, therewith bringing the whole work to a close and making the end of it to coincide with the beginning of happiness.

1. A blessed and eternal being has no trouble himself and brings no trouble upon any other being; hence he is exempt from movements of anger and partiality, for every such movement implies weakness. [*Elsewhere he says that the gods are discernible by reason alone, some being numerically distinct, while others result uniformly from the continuous influx of similar images directed to the same spot and in human form.*]

2. Death is nothing to us; for the body, when it has been resolved into its elements, has no feeling, and that which has no feeling is nothing to us.

3. The magnitude of pleasure reaches its limit in the removal of all pain. When pleasure is present, so long as it is uninterrupted, there is no pain either of body or of mind or of both together.

4. Continuous pain does not last long in the flesh; on the contrary, pain, if extreme, is present a very short time, and even that degree of pain which barely outweighs pleasure in the flesh does not last for many days together. Illnesses of long duration even permit of an excess of pleasure over pain in the flesh.

5. It is impossible to live a pleasant life without living wisely and well and justly, and it is impossible to live wisely and well and justly without living pleasantly. Whenever any one of these is lacking, when, for instance, the man is not able to live wisely,

though he lives well and justly, it is impossible for him to live a pleasant life.

6. In order to obtain security from any other men any means whatsoever of procuring this was a natural good.

7. Some men have sought to become famous and renowned, thinking that thus they would make themselves secure against their fellow-men. If, then, the life of such persons really was secure, they attained natural good; if, however, it was insecure, they have not attained the end which by nature's own prompting they originally sought.

8. No pleasure is in itself evil, but the things which produce certain pleasures entail annoyances many times greater than the pleasures themselves.

9. If all pleasure had been capable of accumulation,—if this had gone on not only by recurrence in time, but all over the frame or, at any rate, over the principal parts of man's nature, there would never have been any difference between one pleasure and another, as in fact there is.

10. If the objects which are productive of pleasures to profligate persons really freed them from fears of the mind,—the fears, I mean, inspired by celestial and atmospheric phenomena, the fear of death, the fear of pain; if, further, they taught them to limit their desires, we should never have any fault to find with such persons, for they would then be filled with pleasures to overflowing on all sides and would be exempt from all pain, whether of body or mind, that is, from all evil.

11. If we had never been molested by alarms at celestial and atmospheric phenomena, nor by the misgiving that death somehow affects us, nor by neglect of the proper limits of pains and desires, we should have had no need to study natural science.

12. It would be impossible to banish fear on matters of the highest importance, if a man did not know the nature of the whole universe, but lived in dread of what the legends tell us. Hence without the study of nature there was no enjoyment of unmixed pleasures.

13. There would be no advantage in providing security against our fellow-men, so long as we were alarmed by occurrences over our

heads or beneath the earth or in general by whatever happens in the boundless universe.

14. When tolerable security against our fellow-men is attained, then on a basis of power sufficient to afford support and of material prosperity arises in most genuine form the security of a quiet private life withdrawn from the multitude.

15. Nature's wealth at once has its bounds and is easy to procure; but the wealth of vain fancies recedes to an infinite distance.

16. Fortune but seldom interferes with the wise man; his greatest and highest interests have been, are, and will be, directed by reason throughout the course of his life.

17. The just man enjoys the greatest peace of mind, while the unjust is full of the utmost disquietude.

18. Pleasure in the flesh admits no increase when once the pain of want has been removed; after that it only admits of variation. The limit of pleasure in the mind, however, is reached when we reflect on the things themselves and their congeners which cause the mind the greatest alarms.

19. Unlimited time and limited time afford an equal amount of pleasure, if we measure the limits of that pleasure by reason.

20. The flesh receives as unlimited the limits of pleasure; and to provide it requires unlimited time. But the mind, grasping in thought what the end and limit of the flesh is, and banishing the terrors of futurity, procures a complete and perfect life, and has no longer any need of unlimited time. Nevertheless it does not shun pleasure, and even in the hour of death, when ushered out of existence by circumstances, the mind does not lack enjoyment of the best life.

21. He who understands the limits of life knows how easy it is to procure enough to remove the pain of want and make the whole of life complete and perfect. Hence he has no longer any need of things which are not to be won save by labour and conflict.

22. We must take into account as the end all that really exists and all clear evidence of sense to which we refer our opinions; for otherwise everything will be full of uncertainty and confusion.

23. If you fight against all your sensations, you will have no standard to which to refer, and thus no means of judging even those judgements which you pronounce false.

24. If you reject absolutely any single sensation without stop-

ping to discriminate with respect to that which awaits confirmation between matter of opinion and that which is already present, whether in sensation or in feelings or in any presentative perception of the mind, you will throw into confusion even the rest of your sensations by your groundless belief and so you will be rejecting the standard of truth altogether. If in your ideas based upon opinion you hastily affirm as true all that awaits confirmation as well as that which does not, you will not escape error, as you will be maintaining complete ambiguity whenever it is a case of judging between right and wrong opinion.

25. If you do not on every separate occasion refer each of your actions to the end prescribed by nature, but instead of this in the act of choice or avoidance swerve aside to some other end, your acts will not be consistent with your theories.

26. All such desires as lead to no pain when they remain ungratified are unnecessary, and the longing is easily got rid of, when the thing desired is difficult to procure or when the desires seem likely to produce harm.

27. Of all the means which are procured by wisdom to ensure happiness throughout the whole of life, by far the most important is the acquisition of friends.

28. The same conviction which inspires confidence that nothing we have to fear is eternal or even of long duration, also enables us to see that even in our limited conditions of life nothing enhances our security so much as friendship.

29. Of our desires some are natural and necessary; others are natural, but not necessary; others, again, are neither natural nor necessary, but are due to illusory opinion. [Epicurus regards as natural and necessary desires which bring relief from pain, as *e.g.* drink when we are thirsty; while by natural and not necessary he means those which merely diversify the pleasure without removing the pain, as *e.g.* costly viands; by the neither natural nor necessary he means desires for crowns and the erection of statues in one's honour.—Schol.]

30. Those natural desires which entail no pain when not gratified, though their objects are vehemently pursued, are also due to illusory opinion; and when they are not got rid of, it is not because of their own nature, but because of the man's illusory opinion.

31. Natural justice is a symbol or expression of expediency, to prevent one man from harming or being harmed by another.

32. Those animals which are incapable of making covenants with one another, to the end that they may neither inflict nor suffer harm, are without either justice or injustice. And those tribes which either could not or would not form mutual covenants to the same end are in like case.

33. There never was an absolute justice, but only an agreement made in reciprocal intercourse in whatever localities now and again from time to time, providing against the infliction or suffering of harm.

34. Injustice is not in itself an evil, but only in its consequence, viz. the terror which is excited by apprehension that those appointed to punish such offences will discover the injustice.

35. It is impossible for the man who secretly violates any article of the social compact to feel confident that he will remain undiscovered, even if he has already escaped ten thousand times; for right on to the end of his life he is never sure he will not be detected.

36. Taken generally, justice is the same for all, to wit, something found expedient in mutual intercourse; but in its application to particular cases of locality or conditions of whatever kind, it varies under different circumstances.

37. Among the things accounted just by conventional law, whatever in the needs of mutual intercourse is attested to be expedient, is thereby stamped as just, whether or not it be the same for all; and in case any law is made and does not prove suitable to the expediencies of mutual intercourse, then this is no longer just. And should the expediency which is expressed by the law vary and only for a time correspond with the prior conception, nevertheless for the time being it was just, so long as we do not trouble ourselves about empty words, but look simply at the facts.

38. Where without any change in circumstances the conventional laws, when judged by their consequences, were seen not to correspond with the notion of justice, such laws were not really just; but wherever the laws have ceased to be expedient in consequence of a change in circumstances, in that case the laws were for the time being just when they were expedient for the mutual intercourse of the citizens, and subsequently ceased to be just when they ceased to be expedient.

39. He who best knew how to meet fear of external foes made into one family all the creatures he could; and those he could not, he at any rate did not treat as aliens; and where he found even this impossible, he avoided all intercourse, and, so far as was expedient, kept them at a distance.

40. Those who were best able to provide themselves with the means of security against their neighbours, being thus in possession of the surest guarantee, passed the most agreeable life in each other's society; and their enjoyment of the fullest intimacy was such that, if one of them died before his time, the survivors did not lament his death as if it called for commiseration.

CHAPTER III
THE CYNIC-STOIC TRADITION

*Stoicism had also its connection with a philosophical move-
ment that dated back to Socrates and professed to exemplify his
spirit—the Cynic tradition. Though not professing disdain
for the pleasures of the body or the goods of life, Socrates needed
little of either to make him content; he could with equanimity
withstand great odds against his contentment. Antisthenes
(445-365) undertook to propagate as a way of life this side of
his master, Socrates, though it was Diogenes, of tub fame, whom
popular reputation made the exponent of the view that the best life
is the one that can get along with the least. Stoicism, which ties to
this earlier movement much as Epicureanism ties to the earlier
Cyrenaic, was founded in Aristotle's time by Zeno of Citium
(ca. 340-265), and perpetuated in succession by two able men,
Cleanthes (ca. 250-?) and Chrysippus (280-207). Perhaps
indebted to Semitic sources, Stoicism is not merely a philosophy,
but a religion raised upon the ruins of popular polytheism.
Speculation here, as in Epicureanism, is turned to practical
ends, the making of the best life and in the end production of the
Wise Man. Drawing upon a Heraclitean physics, Stoicism
orients the soul as fiery atoms in a universe likewise materialistic, though always conceived as reason and sometimes described
as God. Knowledge of the world flows from the likeness of the
soul to the world, and moral idealism arises from a faith in the
reach of Providence (an order more austere, however, than this
term is likely to suggest to a modern reader) throughout the
whole of nature. The Wise Man will achieve the best life, which
is a life in harmony with nature and a devotion to virtue for
virtue's sake. Man can graciously accept his world since he is
of it, and he can be resigned—not to say happy—however little
it gives him. Whether little or much, he knows that all is for the
best. This continuity between man and nature laid the basis*

*for a theoretical cosmopolitanism which was destined to flower
practically in later Roman times and to be permanently of influence in the West.*

. . .

DIOGENES LAERTIUS ON ZENO AND THE STOICS

Zeno. Hicks's translation ("Loeb Classical Library" series).

I have decided to give a general account of all the Stoic doctrines
in the life of Zeno because he was the founder of the School. I have
already given a list of his numerous writings, in which he has
spoken as has no other of the Stoics. And his tenets in general are
as follows. In accordance with my usual practice a summary statement must suffice.

Philosophic doctrine, say the Stoics, falls into three parts:[1] one
physical, another ethical, and the third logical. Zeno of Citium was
the first to make this division in his *Exposition of Doctrine*, and
Chrysippus too did so in the first book of his *Exposition of Doctrine*
and the first book of his *Physics;* and so too Apollodorus and Syllus
in the first part of their *Introductions to Stoic Doctrine*, as also
Eudromus in his *Elementary Treatise on Ethics*, Diogenes the Baby-
lonian, and Posidonius.

. . . .

The ethical branch of philosophy they divide as follows: (1)
the topic of impulse; (2) the topic of things good and evil; (3) that
of the passions; (4) that of virtue; (5) that of the end; (6) that of
primary value and of actions; (7) that of duties or the befitting; and
(8) of inducements to act or refrain from acting. The foregoing is
the subdivision adopted by Chrysippus, Archedemus, Zeno of
Tarsus, Apollodorus, Diogenes, Antipater, and Posidonius, and
their disciples. Zeno of Citium and Cleanthes treated the subject
somewhat less elaborately, as might be expected in an older generation. They, however, did subdivide Logic and Physics as well as
Ethics.

An animal's first impulse, say the Stoics, is to self-preservation,

[1] The two discussions of the physical and the logical aspects of the Stoic doctrine
I am obliged to omit here. They are of the detailed order of the discussion on ethics
here given in full.—T. V. S.

because nature from the outset endears it to itself, as Chrysippus affirms in the first book of his work *On Ends:* his words are, "The dearest thing to every animal is its own constitution and its consciousness thereof"; for it was not likely that nature should estrange the living thing from itself or that she should leave the creature she has made without either estrangement from or affection for its own constitution. We are forced then to conclude that nature in constituting the animal made it near and dear to itself; for so it comes to repel all that is injurious and give free access to all that is serviceable or akin to it.

As for the assertion made by some people that pleasure is the object to which the first impulse of animals is directed, it is shown by the Stoics to be false. For pleasure, if it is really felt, they declare to be a by-product, which never comes until nature by itself has sought and found the means suitable to the animal's existence or constitution; it is an aftermath comparable to the condition of animals thriving and plants in full bloom. And nature, they say, made no difference originally between plants and animals, for she regulates the life of plants too, in their case without impulse and sensation, just as also certain processes go on of a vegetative kind in us. But when in the case of animals impulse has been superadded, whereby they are enabled to go in quest of their proper aliment, for them, say the Stoics, Nature's rule is to follow the direction of impulse. But when reason by way of a more perfect leadership has been bestowed on the beings we call rational, for them life according to reason rightly becomes the natural life. For reason supervenes to shape impulse scientifically.

This is why Zeno was the first (in his treatise *On the Nature of Man*) to designate as the end "life in agreement with nature" (or living agreeably to nature), which is the same as a virtuous life, virtue being the goal towards which nature guides us. So too Cleanthes in his treatise *On Pleasure*, as also Posidonius, and Hecato in his work *On Ends*. Again, living virtuously is equivalent to living in accordance with experience of the actual course of nature, as Chrysippus says in the first book of his *De finibus;* for our individual natures are parts of the nature of the whole universe. And this is why the end may be defined as life in accordance with nature, or, in other words, in accordance with our own human nature as well as that of the universe, a life in which we refrain from every action forbidden by the law common to all things, that is to say, the right reason which pervades all things, and is identical with this Zeus, lord and ruler of all that is. And this very thing constitutes the virtue of the happy man and the smooth current of life, when all actions promote the harmony of the spirit dwelling in the individual man with the will of him who orders the universe. Diogenes then expressly declares the end to be to act with good reason in the selection of what is natural. Archedemus says the end is to live in the performance of all befitting actions.

By the nature with which our life ought to be in accord, Chrysippus understands both universal nature and more particularly the nature of man, whereas Cleanthes takes the nature of the universe alone as that which should be followed, without adding the nature of the individual.

And virtue, he holds, is a harmonious disposition, choice-worthy for its own sake and not from hope or fear or any external motive. Moreover, it is in virtue that happiness consists; for virtue is the state of mind which tends to make the whole of life harmonious. When a rational being is perverted, this is due to the deceptiveness of external pursuits or sometimes to the influence of associates. For the starting-points of nature are never perverse.

Virtue, in the first place, is in one sense the perfection of anything in general, say of a statue; again, it may be non-intellectual, like health, or intellectual, like prudence. For Hecato says in his first book *On the Virtues* that some are scientific and based upon theory, namely, those which have a structure of theoretical principles, such as prudence and justice; others are non-intellectual, those that are regarded as co-extensive and parallel with the former, like health and strength. For health is found to attend upon and be co-extensive with the intellectual virtue of temperance, just as strength is a result of the building of an arch. These are called non-intellectual, because they do not require the mind's assent; they supervene and they occur even in bad men: for instance, health, courage. The proof, says Posidonius in the first book of his treatise on *Ethics*, that virtue really exists is the fact that Socrates, Diogenes, and Antisthenes and their followers made moral progress. And for the existence of vice as a fundamental fact the proof is that it is the opposite of virtue. That it, virtue, can be taught is laid down by Chrysippus in the first book of his work *On the End*, by

Cleanthes, by Posidonius in his *Protreptica*, and by Hecato; that it can be taught is clear from the case of bad men becoming good.

Panaetius, however, divides virtue into two kinds, theoretical and practical; others make a threefold division of it into logical, physical, and ethical; while by the school of Posidonius four types are recognized and more than four by Cleanthes, Chrysippus, Antipater, and their followers. Apollophanes for his part counts but one, namely, practical wisdom.

Amongst the virtues some are primary, some are subordinate to these. The following are the primary: wisdom, courage, justice, temperance. Particular virtues are magnanimity, continence, endurance, presence of mind, good counsel. And wisdom they define as the knowledge of things good and evil and of what is neither good nor evil; courage as knowledge of what we ought to choose, what we ought to beware of, and what is indifferent; justice . . . . ; magnanimity as the knowledge or habit of mind which makes one superior to anything that happens, whether good or evil equally; continence as a disposition never overcome in that which concerns right reason, or a habit which no pleasures can get the better of; endurance as a knowledge or habit which suggests what we are to hold fast to, what not, and what is indifferent; presence of mind as a habit prompt to find out what is meet to be done at any moment; good counsel as knowledge by which we see what to do and how to do it if we would consult our own interests.

Similarly, of vices some are primary, others subordinate: *e.g.* folly, cowardice, injustice, profligacy are accounted primary; but incontinence, stupidity, ill-advisedness subordinate. Further, they hold that the vices are forms of ignorance of those things whereof the corresponding virtues are the knowledge.

Good in general is that from which some advantage comes, and more particularly what is either identical with or not distinct from benefit. Whence it follows that virtue itself and whatever partakes of virtue is called good in these three senses—viz. as being (1) the source from which benefit results; or (2) that in respect of which benefit results, *e.g.* the virtuous act; or (3) that by the agency of which benefit results, *e.g.* the good man who partakes in virtue.

Another particular definition of good which they give is "the natural perfection of a rational being *qua* rational." To this answers virtue and, as being partakers in virtue, virtuous acts and good men; as also its supervening accessories, joy and gladness and the like. So with evils: either they are vices, folly, cowardice, injustice, and the like; or things which partake of vice, including vicious acts and wicked persons as well as their accompaniments, despair, moroseness, and the like.

Again, some goods are goods of the mind and others external, while some are neither mental nor external. The former include the virtues and virtuous acts; external goods are such as having a good country or a good friend, and the prosperity of such. Whereas to be good and happy oneself is of the class of goods neither mental nor external. Similarly of things evil some are mental evils, namely, vices and vicious actions; others are outward evils, as to have a foolish country or a foolish friend and the unhappiness of such; other evils again are neither mental nor outward, *e.g.* to be yourself bad and unhappy.

Again, goods are either of the nature of ends or they are the means to these ends, or they are at the same time end and means. A friend and the advantages derived from him are means to good, whereas confidence, high-spirit, liberty, delight, gladness, freedom from pain, and every virtuous act are of the nature of ends.

The virtues (they say) are goods of the nature at once of ends and of means. On the one hand, in so far as they cause happiness they are means, and on the other hand, in so far as they make it complete, and so are themselves part of it, they are ends. Similarly of evils some are of the nature of ends and some of means, while others are at once both means and ends. Your enemy and the harm he does you are means; consternation, abasement, slavery, gloom, despair, excess of grief, and every vicious action are of the nature of ends. Vices are evils both as ends and as means, since in so far as they cause misery they are means, but in so far as they make it complete, so that they become part of it, they are ends.

Of mental goods some are habits, others are dispositions, while others again are neither the one nor the other. The virtues are dispositions, while accomplishments or avocations are matters of habit, and activities as such or exercise of faculty neither the one nor the other. And in general there are some mixed goods: *e.g.* to be happy in one's children or in one's old age. But knowledge is a pure good. Again, some goods are permanent like the virtues, others transitory like joy and walking-exercise.

All good (they say) is expedient, binding, profitable, useful, serviceable, beautiful, beneficial, desirable, and just or right. It is expedient, because it brings about things of such a kind that by their occurrence we are benefited. It is binding, because it causes unity where unity is needed; profitable, because it defrays what is expended on it, so that the return yields a balance of benefit on the transaction. It is useful, because it secures the use of benefit; it is serviceable, because the utility it affords is worthy of all praise. It is beautiful, because the good is proportionate to the use made of it; beneficial, because by its inherent nature it benefits; choiceworthy, because it is such that to choose it is reasonable. It is also just or right, inasmuch as it is in harmony with law and tends to draw men together.

The reason why they characterize the perfect good as beautiful is that it has in full all the "factors" required by nature or has perfect proportion. Of the beautiful there are (say they) four species, namely, what is just, courageous, orderly and wise; for it is under these forms that fair deeds are accomplished. Similarly there are four species of the base or ugly, namely, what is unjust, cowardly, disorderly, and unwise. By the beautiful is meant properly and in an unique sense that good which renders its possessors praiseworthy, or briefly, good which is worthy of praise; though in another sense it signifies a good aptitude for one's proper function; while in yet another sense the beautiful is that which lends new grace to anything, as when we say of the wise man that he alone is good and beautiful.

And they say that only the morally beautiful is good. So Hecato in his treatise *On Goods*, book iii., and Chrysippus in his work *On the Morally Beautiful*. They hold, that is, that virtue and whatever partakes of virtue consists in this: which is equivalent to saying that all that is good is beautiful, or that the term "good" has equal force with the term "beautiful," which comes to the same thing. "Since a thing is good, it is beautiful; now it is beautiful, therefore it is good." They hold that all goods are equal and that all good is desirable in the highest degree and admits of no lowering or heightening of intensity. Of things that are, some, they say, are good, some are evil, and some neither good nor evil (that is, morally indifferent).

Goods comprise the virtues of prudence, justice, courage, temperance, and the rest; while the opposites of these are evils, namely, folly, injustice, and the rest. Neutral (neither good nor evil, that is) are all those things which neither benefit nor harm a man: such as life, health, pleasure, beauty, strength, wealth, fair fame and noble birth, and their opposites, death, disease, pain, ugliness, weakness, poverty, ignominy, low birth, and the like. This Hecato affirms in his *De fine*, book vii., and also Apollodorus in his *Ethics*, and Chrysippus. For, say they, such things (as life, health, and pleasure) are not in themselves goods, but are morally indifferent, though falling under the species or subdivision "things preferred." For as the property of hot is to warm, not to cool, so the property of good is to benefit, not to injure; but wealth and health do no more benefit than injury, therefore neither wealth nor health is good. Further, they say that that is not good of which both good and bad use can be made; but of wealth and health both good and bad use can be made; therefore wealth and health are not goods. On the other hand, Posidonius maintains that these things too are among goods. Hecato in the ninth book of his treatise *On Goods*, and Chrysippus in his work *On Pleasure*, deny that pleasure is a good either; for some pleasures are disgraceful, and nothing disgraceful is good. To benefit is to set in motion or sustain in accordance with virtue; whereas to harm is to set in motion or sustain in accordance with vice.

The term "indifferent" has two meanings: in the first it denotes the things which do not contribute either to happiness or to misery, as wealth, fame, health, strength, and the like; for it is possible to be happy without having these, although, if they are used in a certain way, such use of them tends to happiness or misery. In quite another sense those things are said to be indifferent which are without the power of stirring inclination or aversion; *e.g.* the fact that the number of hairs on one's head is odd or even or whether you hold out your finger straight or bent. But it was not in this sense that the things mentioned above were termed indifferent, they being quite capable of exciting inclination or aversion. Hence of these latter some are taken by preference, others are rejected, whereas indifference in the other sense affords no ground for either choosing or avoiding.

Of things indifferent, as they express it, some are "preferred," others "rejected." Such as have value, they say, are "preferred," while such as have negative, instead of positive, value are "rejected." Value they define as, first, any contribution to harmonious living, such as attaches to every good; secondly, some faculty or use which indirectly contributes to the life according to nature: which is as much as to say "any assistance brought by wealth or health towards living a natural life"; thirdly, value is the full equivalent of an appraiser, as fixed by an expert acquainted with the facts—as when it is said that wheat exchanges for so much barley with a mule thrown in.

Thus things of the preferred class are those which have positive value, *e.g.* amongst mental qualities, natural ability, skill, moral improvement, and the like; among bodily qualities, life, health, strength, good condition, soundness of organs, beauty, and so forth; and in the sphere of external things, wealth, fame, noble birth, and the like. To the class of things "rejected" belong, of mental qualities, lack of ability, want of skill and the like; among bodily qualities, death, disease, weakness, being out of condition, mutilation, ugliness, and the like; in the sphere of external things, poverty, ignominy, low birth, and so forth. But again there are things belonging to neither class; such are not preferred, neither are they rejected.

Again, of things preferred some are preferred for their own sake, some for the sake of something else, and others again both for their own sake and for the sake of something else. To the first of these classes belong natural ability, moral improvement, and the like; to the second wealth, noble birth, and the like; to the last strength, perfect faculties, soundness of bodily organs. Things are preferred for their own sake because they accord with nature; not for their own sake, but for the sake of something else, because they secure not a few utilities. And similarly with the class of things rejected under the contrary heads.

Furthermore, the term Duty is applied to that for which, when done, a reasonable defence can be adduced, *e.g.* harmony in the tenor of life's process, which indeed pervades the growth of plants and animals. For even in plants and animals, they hold, you may discern fitness of behaviour.

Zeno was the first to use this term καθῆκον of conduct. Etymologically it is derived from κατά τινας ἥκειν, *i.e.* reaching as far as, being up to, or incumbent on so and so. And it is an action in itself adapted to nature's arrangements. For of the acts done at the prompting of impulse some, they observe, are fit and meet, others the reverse, while there is a third class which is neither the one nor the other.

Befitting acts are all those which reason prevails with us to do; and this is the case with honouring one's parents, brothers and country, and intercourse with friends. Unbefitting, or contrary to duty, are all acts that reason deprecates, *e.g.* to neglect one's parents, to be indifferent to one's brothers, not to agree with friends, to disregard the interests of one's country, and so forth. Acts which fall under neither of the foregoing classes are those which reason neither urges us to do nor forbids, such as picking up a twig, holding a style or a scraper, and the like.

Again, some duties are incumbent unconditionally, others in certain circumstances. Unconditional duties are the following: to take proper care of health and one's organs of sense, and things of that sort. Duties imposed by circumstances are such as maiming oneself and sacrifice of property. And so likewise with acts which are violations of duty. Another division is into duties which are always incumbent and those which are not. To live in accordance with virtue is always a duty, whereas dialectic by question and answer or walking-exercise and the like are not at all times incumbent. The same may be said of the violations of duty. And in things intermediate also there are duties; as that boys should obey the attendants who have charge of them.

According to the Stoics there is an eight-fold division of the soul: the five senses, the faculty of speech, the intellectual faculty, which is the mind itself, and the generative faculty, being all parts of the soul. Now from falsehood there results perversion, which extends to the mind; and from this perversion arise many passions or emotions, which are causes of instability. Passion, or emotion, is defined by Zeno as an irrational and unnatural movement in the soul, or again as impulse in excess.

The main, or most universal, emotions, according to Hecato in his treatise *On the Passions*, book ii., and Zeno in his treatise with the same title, constitute four great classes, grief, fear, desire or craving, pleasure. They hold the emotions to be judgements, as is stated by Chrysippus in his treatise *On the Passions:* avarice being a supposition that money is a good, while the case is similar with drunkenness and profligacy and all the other emotions.

And grief or pain they hold to be an irrational mental contraction. Its species are pity, envy, jealousy, rivalry, heaviness, annoyance, distress, anguish, distraction. Pity is grief felt at undeserved suffering; envy, grief at others' prosperity; jealousy, grief at the possession by another of that which one desires for oneself; rivalry, pain at the possession by another of what one has oneself. Heaviness or vexation is grief which weighs us down, annoyance that which coops us up and straitens us for want of room, distress a pain brought on by anxious thought that lasts and increases, anguish painful grief, distraction irrational grief, rasping and hindering us from viewing the situation as a whole.

Fear is an expectation of evil. Under fear are ranged the following emotions: terror, nervous shrinking, shame, consternation, panic, mental agony. Terror is a fear which produces fright; shame is fear of disgrace; nervous shrinking is a fear that one will have to act; consternation is fear due to a presentation of some unusual occurrence; panic is fear with pressure exercised by sound; mental agony is fear felt when some issue is still in suspense.

Desire or craving is irrational appetency, and under it are ranged the following states: want, hatred, contentiousness, anger, love, wrath, resentment. Want, then, is a craving when it is baulked and, as it were, cut off from its object, but kept at full stretch and attracted towards it in vain. Hatred is a growing and lasting desire or craving that it should go ill with somebody. Contentiousness is a craving or desire connected with partisanship; anger a craving or desire to punish one who is thought to have done you an undeserved injury. The passion of love is a craving from which good men are free; for it is an effort to win affection due to the visible presence of beauty. Wrath is anger which has long rankled and has become malicious, waiting for its opportunity, as is illustrated by the lines:

Even though for the one day he swallow his anger, yet doth he still keep his displeasure thereafter in his heart, till he accomplish it.

Resentment is anger in an early stage.

Pleasure is an irrational elation at the accruing of what seems to be choiceworthy; and under it are ranged ravishment, malevolent joy, delight, transport. Ravishment is pleasure which charms the ear. Malevolent joy is pleasure at another's ills. Delight is the mind's propulsion to weakness, its name in Greek (τέρψις) being akin to τρέψις or turning. To be in transports of delight is the melting away of virtue.

And as there are said to be certain infirmities in the body, as for instance gout and arthritic disorders, so too there is in the soul love of fame, love of pleasure, and the like. By infirmity is meant disease accompanied by weakness; and by disease is meant a fond imagining of something that seems desirable. And as in the body there are tendencies to certain maladies such as colds and diarrhoea, so it is with the soul, there are tendencies like enviousness, pitifulness, quarrelsomeness, and the like.

Also they say that there are three emotional states which are good, namely, joy, caution, and wishing. Joy, the counterpart of pleasure, is rational elation; caution, the counterpart of fear, rational avoidance; for though the wise man will never feel fear, he will yet use caution. And they make wishing the counterpart of desire (or craving), inasmuch as it is rational appetency. And accordingly, as under the primary passions are classed certain others subordinate to them, so too is it with the primary eupathies or good emotional states. Thus under wishing they bring well-wishing .or benevolence, friendliness, respect, affection; under caution, reverence and modesty; under joy, delight, mirth, cheerfulness.

Now they say that the wise man is passionless, because he is not prone to fall into such infirmity. But they add that in another sense the term apathy is applied to the bad man, when, that is, it means that he is callous and relentless. Further, the wise man is said to be free from vanity; for he is indifferent to good or evil report. However, he is not alone in this, there being another who is also free from vanity, he who is ranged among the rash, and that is the bad man. Again, they tell us that all good men are austere or harsh, because they neither have dealings with pleasure themselves nor tolerate those who have. The term harsh is applied, however, to others as well, and in much the same sense as a wine is said to be harsh when it is employed medicinally and not for drinking at all.

Again, the good are genuinely in earnest and vigilant for their own improvement, using a manner of life which banishes evil out of sight and makes what good there is in things appear. At the same time they are free from pretence; for they have stripped off all pretence or "make-up" whether in voice or in look. Free too are they from all business cares, declining to do anything which conflicts with duty. They will take wine, but not get drunk. Nay more, they will not be liable to madness either; not but what there will at times occur to the good man strange impressions due to melancholy or delirium, ideas not determined by the principle of what is choiceworthy but contrary to nature. Nor indeed will the wise man ever feel grief; seeing that grief is irrational contraction of the soul, as Apollodorus says in his *Ethics*.

They are also, it is declared, godlike; for they have a something divine within them; whereas the bad man is godless. And yet of this word—godless or ungodly—there are two senses, one in which it is the opposite of the term "godly," the other denoting the man who ignores the divine altogether: in this latter sense, as they note, the term does not apply to every bad man. The good, it is added, are also worshippers of God; for they have acquaintance with the rites of the gods, and piety is the knowledge of how to serve the gods. Further, they will sacrifice to the gods and they keep themselves pure; for they avoid all acts that are offences against the gods, and the gods think highly of them: for they are holy and just in what concerns the gods. The wise too are the only priests; for they have made sacrifices their study, as also the building of temples, purifications, and all the other matters appertaining to the gods.

The Stoics approve also of honouring parents and brothers in the second place next after the gods. They further maintain that parental affection for children is natural to the good, but not to the bad. It is one of their tenets that sins are all equal: so Chrysippus in the fourth book of his *Ethical Questions*, as well as Persaeus and Zeno. For if one truth is not more true than another, neither is one falsehood more false than another, and in the same way one deceit is not more so than another, nor sin than sin. For he who is a hundred furlongs from Canopus and he who is only one furlong away are equally not in Canopus, and so too he who commits the greater sin and he who commits the less are equally not in the path of right conduct. But Heraclides of Tarsus, who was the disciple of Antipater of Tarsus, and Athenodorus both assert that sins are not equal.

Again, the Stoics say that the wise man will take part in politics, if nothing hinders him—so, for instance, Chrysippus in the first book of his work *On Various Types of Life*—since thus he will restrain vice and promote virtue. Also (they maintain) he will marry, as Zeno says in his *Republic*, and beget children. Moreover, they say that the wise man will never form mere opinions, that is to say, he will never give assent to anything that is false; that he will also play the Cynic, Cynicism being a short cut to virtue, as Apollodorus calls it in his *Ethics;* that he will even turn cannibal under stress of circumstances. They declare that he alone is free and bad men are slaves, freedom being power of independent action, whereas slavery is privation of the same: though indeed there is also a second form of slavery consisting in subordination, and a third which implies possession of the slave as well as his subordination; the correlative of such servitude being lordship; and this too is evil. Moreover, according to them not only are the wise free, they are also kings; kingship being irresponsible rule, which none but the wise can maintain: so Chrysippus in his treatise vindicating Zeno's use of terminology. For he holds that knowledge of good and evil is a necessary attribute of the ruler, and that no bad man is acquainted with this science. Similarly the wise and good alone are fit to be magistrates, judges, or orators, whereas among the bad there is not one so qualified. Furthermore, the wise are infallible, not being liable to error. They are also without offence; for they do no hurt to others or to themselves. At the same time they are not pitiful and make no allowance for anyone; they never relax the penalties fixed by the laws, since indulgence and pity and even equitable consideration are marks of a weak mind, which affects kindness in place of chastizing. Nor do they deem punishments too severe. Again, they say that the wise man never wonders at any of the things which appear extraordinary, such as Charon's mephitic caverns, ebbings of the tide, hot springs or fiery eruptions. Nor yet, they go on to say, will the wise man live in solitude; for he is naturally made for society and action. He will, however, submit to training to augment his powers of bodily endurance.

And the wise man, they say, will offer prayers, and ask for good things from the gods: so Posidonius in the first book of his treatise *On Duties*, and Hecato in his third book *On Paradoxes*. Friendship, they declare, exists only between the wise and good, by reason of their likeness to one another. And by friendship they mean a common use of all that has to do with life, wherein we treat our friends as we should ourselves. They argue that a friend is worth having for his own sake and that it is a good thing to have many friends. But among the bad there is, they hold, no such thing as friendship, and thus no bad man has a friend. Another of their tenets is that the unwise are all mad, inasmuch as they are not wise but do what they do from that madness which is the equivalent of their folly.

Furthermore, the wise man does all things well, just as we say that Ismenias plays all airs on the flute well. Also everything belongs to the wise. For the law, they say, has conferred upon them a perfect right to all things. It is true that certain things are said to belong to the bad, just as what has been dishonestly acquired may be said, in one sense, to belong to the state, in another sense to those who are enjoying it.

They hold that the virtues involve one another, and that the possessor of one is the possessor of all, inasmuch as they have common principles, as Chrysippus says in the first book of his work *On Virtues*, Apollodorus in his *Physics according to the Early School*, and Hecato in the third book of his treatise *On Virtues*. For if a man be possessed of virtue, he is at once able to discover and to put into practice what he ought to do. Now such rules of conduct comprise rules for choosing, enduring, staying, and distributing; so that if a man does some things by intelligent choice, some things with fortitude, some things by way of just distribution, and some steadily, he is at once wise, courageous, just, and temperate. And each of the virtues has a particular subject with which it deals as, for instance, courage is concerned with things that must be endured, practical wisdom with acts to be done, acts from which one must abstain, and those which fall under neither head. Similarly each of the other virtues is concerned with its own proper sphere. To wisdom are subordinate good counsel and understanding; to temperance, good discipline and orderliness; to justice, equality and fairmindedness; to courage, constancy and vigour.

It is a tenet of theirs that between virtue and vice there is nothing intermediate, whereas according to the Peripatetics there is, namely, the state of moral improvement. For, say the Stoics, just as a stick must be either straight or crooked, so a man must be either just or unjust. Nor again are there degrees of justice and injustice; and the same rule applies to the other virtues. Further, while Chrysippus holds that virtue can be lost, Cleanthes maintains that it cannot. According to the former it may be lost in consequence of drunkenness or melancholy; the latter takes it to be inalienable owing to the certainty of our mental apprehension. And virtue in itself they hold to be worthy of choice for its own sake. At all events we are ashamed of bad conduct as if we knew that nothing is really good but the morally beautiful. Moreover, they hold that it is in itself sufficient to ensure well-being: thus Zeno, and Chrysippus in the first book of his treatise *On Virtues*, and Hecato in the second book of his treatise *On Goods:* "For if magnanimity by itself alone can raise us far above everything, and if magnanimity is but a part of virtue, then too virtue as a whole will be sufficient in itself for well-being—despising all things that seem troublesome." Panaetius, however, and Posidonius deny that virtue is self-sufficing: on the contrary, health is necessary, and some means of living and strength.

Another tenet of theirs is the perpetual exercise of virtue, as held by Cleanthes and his followers. For virtue can never be lost, and the good man is always exercising his mind, which is perfect. Again, they say that justice, as well as law and right reason, exists by nature and not by convention: so Chrysippus in his work *On the Morally Beautiful.* Neither do they think that the divergence of opinion between philosophers is any reason for abandoning the study of philosophy, since at that rate we should have to give up life altogether: so Posidonius in his *Exhortations.* Chrysippus allows that the ordinary Greek education is serviceable.

It is their doctrine that there can be no question of right as between man and the lower animals, because of their unlikeness. Thus Chrysippus in the first book of his treatise *On Justice*, and Posidonius in the first book of his *De officio.* Further, they say that the wise man will feel affection for the youths who by their countenance show a natural endowment for virtue. So Zeno in his *Republic*, Chrysippus in book i. of his work *On Modes of Life*, and Apollodorus in his *Ethics*.

Their definition of love is an effort toward friendliness due to visible beauty appearing, its sole end being friendship, not bodily enjoyment. At all events, they allege that Thrasonides, although he had his mistress in his power, abstained from her because she hated him. By which it is shown, they think, that love depends upon regard, as Chrysippus says in his treatise *Of Love*, and is not sent by the gods. And beauty they describe as the bloom or flower of virtue.

Of the three kinds of life, the contemplative, the practical, and the rational, they declare that we ought to choose the last, for that a rational being is expressly produced by nature for contemplation and for action. They tell us that the wise man will for reasonable cause make his own exit from life, on his country's behalf or for the sake of his friends, or if he suffer intolerable pain, mutilation, or incurable disease.

It is also their doctrine that amongst the wise there should be a community of wives with free choice of partners, as Zeno says in his *Republic* and Chrysippus in his treatise *On Government* [and not only they, but also Diogenes the Cynic and Plato]. Under such circumstances we shall feel paternal affection for all the children alike, and there will be an end of the jealousies arising from adultery. The best form of government they hold to be a mixture of democracy, kingship, and aristocracy (or the rule of the best).

Such, then, are the statements they make in their ethical doctrines, with much more besides, together with their proper proofs: let this, however, suffice for a statement of them in a summary and elementary form.

CHAPTER IV
THE SKEPTICAL CULMINATION

Skepticism, the earliest of the great post-Aristotelian philosophies to reach its prime, had, like Epicureanism and Stoicism, its foremovement in (the Sophists of) the time of Socrates. Against the skeptical slant of that Enlightenment, though not against its humanistic emphasis, Socrates set himself solidly, as we have seen. It was Pyrrho of Elis (365–275), a late contemporary of Aristotle, who first systematized the several distrusts that lie at the heart of the skeptical impetus, though associated with the movement successively were other eminent names, Arcesilaus (315–241), Carneades (215–130) and Sextus Empiricus (180–210 A.D.). These distrusts themselves were but the logical conclusions of the general recession from the confidence of Plato and Aristotle in the rational order of the world and in the power of mind to encompass and to profit by this order. First, there is distrust of the human senses themselves. They are uncertain, relative, and even contradictory. Then there is the distorting influence of the "Zeitgeist" upon human beliefs. Nothing seems so true that it has not somewhere been thought false, or so false that it has not somewhere been thought true. Nor is there impartial evidence that one set of cultural and historical conditions is more dependable than another. Moreover, there is no foundation for truth or any criterion; for we can judge inferences true only by the truth from which they are deduced and there is nothing to vouch for that truth as finally true. Our sensations cannot, for they are relative; and self-evidence cannot, because there is little if anything that is self-evident to everybody. "The senses are deceivers," Diogenes represents Pyrrho as saying, "and the reason disagrees with itself." Such distrusts are formulated systematically in ten so-called "tropes," of which the last adds ethical skepticism to the logical thrust. In short, the movement culminated in reaffirmation of the trinity of doubt which we have already attributed to Gorgias: (1) nothing can be known; (2) if it could be, it could not be told; (3) if it were told, it could not be understood. No wonder Pyrrho reached the point of "suspending his judgment on all points." Silence is the indicated goal—silence not only of the larynx, but that vaster silence of mind which arises from the generalized decision not to judge, not even to pass judgment against judging. Though founded prior to the other schools, this movement we remark last as representing the logical culmination of the effort of ancient mind to gain independence from the world.

. . .

DIOGENES LAERTIUS ON PYRRHO AND THE SKEPTICS

Pyrrho. Hicks's translation ("Loeb Classical Library" series).

He [Pyrrho] denied that anything was honourable or dishonourable, just or unjust. And so, universally, he held that there is nothing really existent, but custom and convention govern human action; for no single thing is in itself any more this than that.

He led a life consistent with this doctrine, going out of his way for nothing, taking no precaution, but facing all risks as they came, whether carts, precipices, dogs or what not, and, generally, leaving nothing to the arbitrament of the senses; but he was kept out of harm's way by his friends who, as Antigonus of Carystus tells us, used to follow close after him. But Aenesidemus says that it was only his philosophy that was based upon suspension of judgement, and that he did not lack foresight in his everyday acts. He lived to be nearly ninety.

. . . .

On being discovered once talking to himself, he answered, when asked the reason, that he was training to be good. In debate he was looked down upon by no one, for he could both discourse at length and also sustain a cross-examination, so that even Nausiphanes when a young man was captivated by him: at all events he used to say that we should follow Pyrrho in disposition but himself in doctrine; and he would often remark that Epicurus, greatly admiring

Pyrrho's way of life, regularly asked him for information about Pyrrho; and that he was so respected by his native city that they made him high priest, and on his account they voted that all philosophers should be exempt from taxation.

. . . .

The Sceptics . . . . were constantly engaged in overthrowing the dogmas of all schools, but enunciated none themselves; and though they would go so far as to bring forward and expound the dogmas of the others, they themselves laid down nothing definitely, not even the laying down of nothing. So much so that they even refuted their laying down of nothing, saying, for instance, "We determine nothing," since otherwise they would have been betrayed into determining; but we put forward, say they, all the theories for the purpose of indicating our unprecipitate attitude, precisely as we might have done if we had actually assented to them. Thus by the expression "We determine nothing" is indicated their state of even balance; which is similarly indicated by the other expressions, "Not more (one thing than another)," "Every saying has its corresponding opposite," and the like. But "Not more (one thing than another)" can also be taken positively, indicating that two things are alike; for example, "The pirate is no more wicked than the liar." But the Sceptics meant it not positively but negatively, as when, in refuting an argument, one says, "Neither had more existence, Scylla or the Chimaera." And "More so" itself is sometimes comparative, as when we say that "Honey is more sweet than grapes"; sometimes both positive and negative, as when we say, "Virtue profits more than it harms," for in this phrase we indicate that virtue profits and does not harm. But the Sceptics even refute the statement "Not more (one thing than another)." For, as forethought is no more existent than non-existent, so "Not more (one thing than another)" is no more existent than not. Thus, as Timon says in the *Pytho*, the statement means just absence of all determination and withholding of assent. The other statement, "Every saying, etc.," equally compels suspension of judgement; when facts disagree, but the contradictory statements have exactly the same weight, ignorance of the truth is the necessary consequence. But even this statement has its corresponding antithesis, so that after destroying others it turns round and destroys itself, like a purge which drives the substance out and then in its turn is itself eliminated and destroyed.

This the dogmatists answer by saying that they do [not merely] not deny the statement, but even plainly assert it. So they were merely using the words as servants, as it was not possible not to refute one statement by another; just as we are accustomed to say there is no such thing as space, and yet we have no alternative but to speak of space for the purpose of argument, though not of positive doctrine, and just as we say nothing comes about by necessity and yet have to speak of necessity. This was the sort of interpretation they used to give; though things appear to be such and such, they are not such in reality but only appear such. And they would say that they sought, not thoughts, since thoughts are evidently thought, but the things in which sensation plays a part.

Thus the Pyrrhonean principle, as Aenesidemus says in the introduction to his *Pyrrhonics*, is but a report on phenomena or on any kind of judgement, a report in which all things are brought to bear on one another, and in the comparison are found to present much anomaly and confusion. As to the contradictions in their doubts, they would first show the ways in which things gain credence and then by the same methods they would destroy belief in them; for they say those things gain credence which either the senses are agreed upon or which never or at least rarely change, as well as things which become habitual or are determined by law and those which please or excite wonder. They showed, then, on the basis of that which is contrary to what induces belief, that the probabilities on both sides are equal.

Perplexities arise from the agreements between appearances or judgements, and these perplexities they distinguished under ten different modes in which the subjects in question appeared to vary. The following are the ten modes laid down.

The *first* mode relates to the differences between living creatures in respect of those things which give them pleasure or pain, or are useful or harmful to them. By this it is inferred that they do not receive the same impressions from the same things, with the result that such a conflict necessarily leads to suspension of judgement. For some creatures multiply without intercourse, for example, creatures that live in fire, the Arabian phoenix and worms; others by union, such as man and the rest. Some are distinguished in one way, some in another, and for this reason they differ in their senses also, hawks for instance being most keen-sighted, and dogs having a most acute sense of smell. It is natural that if the senses, *e.g.* eyes, of animals differ, so also will the impressions produced upon them; so to the goat vine-shoots are good to eat, to man they are bitter; the quail thrives on hemlock, which is fatal to man; the pig will eat ordure, the horse will not.

The *second* mode has reference to the natures and idiosyncrasies of men; for instance, Demophon, Alexander's butler, used to get warm in the shade and shiver in the sun. Andron of Argos is reported by Aristotle to have travelled across the waterless deserts of Libya without drinking. Moreover, one man fancies the profession of medicine, another farming, and another commerce; and the same ways of life are injurious to one man but beneficial to another; from which it follows that judgement must be suspended.

The *third* mode depends on the differences between the sense-channels in different cases, for an apple gives the impression of being pale yellow in colour to the sight, sweet in taste and fragrant in smell. An object of the same shape is made to appear different by differences in the mirrors reflecting it. Thus it follows that what appears is no more such and such a thing than something different.

The *fourth* mode is that due to differences of condition and to changes in general; for instance, health, illness, sleep, waking, joy, sorrow, youth, old age, courage, fear, want, fullness, hate, love, heat, cold, to say nothing of breathing freely and having the passages obstructed. The impressions received thus appear to vary according to the nature of the conditions. Nay, even the state of madmen is not contrary to nature; for why should their state be so more than ours? Even to our view the sun has the appearance of standing still. And Theon of Tithorea used to go to bed and walk in his sleep, while Pericles' slave did the same on the housetop.

The *fifth* mode is derived from customs, laws, belief in myths, compacts between nations and dogmatic assumptions. This class includes considerations with regard to things beautiful and ugly, true and false, good and bad, with regard to the gods, and with regard to the coming into being and the passing away of the world of phenomena. Obviously the same thing is regarded by some as just and by others as unjust, or as good by some and bad by others. Persians think it not unnatural for a man to marry his daughter; to

Greeks it is unlawful. The Massagetae, according to Eudoxus in the first book of his *Voyage round the World*, have their wives in common; the Greeks have not. The Cilicians used to delight in piracy; not so the Greeks. Different people believe in different gods; some in providence, others not. In burying their dead, the Egyptians embalm them; the Romans burn them; the Paeonians throw them into lakes. As to what is true, then, let suspension of judgement be our practice.

The *sixth* mode relates to mixtures and participations, by virtue of which nothing appears pure in and by itself, but only in combination with air, light, moisture, solidity, heat, cold, movement, exhalations and other forces. For purple shows different tints in sunlight, moonlight, and lamplight; and our own complexion does not appear the same at noon and when the sun is low. Again, a rock which in air takes two men to lift is easily moved about in water, either because, being in reality heavy, it is lifted by the water or because, being light, it is made heavy by the air. Of its own inherent property we know nothing, any more than of the constituent oils in an ointment.

The *seventh* mode has reference to distances, positions, places and the occupants of the places. In this mode things which are thought to be large appear small, square things round; flat things appear to have projections, straight things to be bent, and colourless coloured. So the sun, on account of its distance, appears small, mountains when far away appear misty and smooth, but when near at hand rugged. Furthermore, the sun at its rising has a certain appearance, but has a dissimilar appearance when in mid-heaven, and the same body one appearance in a wood and another in open country. The image again varies according to the position of the object, and a dove's neck according to the way it is turned. Since, then, it is not possible to observe these things apart from places and positions, their real nature is unknowable.

The *eighth* mode is concerned with quantities and qualities of things, say heat or cold, swiftness or slowness, colourlessness or variety of colours. Thus wine taken in moderation strengthens the body, but too much of it is weakening; and so with food and other things.

The *ninth* mode has to do with perpetuity, strangeness, or rarity. Thus earthquakes are no surprise to those among whom they constantly take place; nor is the sun, for it is seen every day. This ninth mode is put eighth by Favorinus and tenth by Sextus and Aenesidemus; moreover the tenth is put eighth by Sextus and ninth by Favorinus.

The *tenth* mode rests on inter-relation, *e.g.* between light and heavy, strong and weak, greater and less, up and down. Thus that which is on the right is not so by nature, but is so understood in virtue of its position with respect to something else; for, if that change its position, the thing is no longer on the right. Similarly father and brother are relative terms, day is relative to the sun, and all things relative to our mind. Thus relative terms are in and by themselves unknowable. These, then, are the ten modes of perplexity.

But Agrippa and his school add to them five other modes, resulting respectively from disagreement, extension *ad infinitum*, relativity, hypothesis and reciprocal inference. The mode arising from disagreement proves, with regard to any inquiry whether in philosophy or in everyday life, that it is full of the utmost contentiousness and confusion. The mode which involves extension *ad infinitum* refuses to admit that what is sought to be proved is firmly established, because one thing furnishes the ground for belief in another, and so on *ad infinitum*. The mode derived from relativity declares that a thing can never be apprehended in and by itself, but only in connexion with something else. Hence all things are unknowable. The mode resulting from hypothesis arises when people suppose that you must take the most elementary of things as of themselves entitled to credence, instead of postulating them: which is useless, because some one else will adopt the contrary hypothesis. The mode arising from reciprocal inference is found whenever that which should be confirmatory of the thing requiring to be proved itself has to borrow credit from the latter, as, for example, if anyone seeking to establish the existence of pores on the ground that emanations take place should take this (the existence of pores) as proof that there are emanations.

They would deny all demonstration, criterion, sign, cause, motion, the process of learning, coming into being, or that there is anything good or bad by nature. For all demonstration, say they, is constructed out of things either already proved or indemonstrable. If out of things already proved, those things too will require some demonstration, and so on *ad infinitum;* if out of things in-demonstrable, then, whether all or some or only a single one of the steps are the subject of doubt, the whole is indemonstrable. If you think, they add, that there are some things which need no demonstration, yours must be a rare intellect, not to see that you must first have demonstration of the very fact that the things you refer to carry conviction in themselves. Nor must we prove that the elements are four from the fact that the elements are four. Besides, if we discredit particular demonstrations, we cannot accept the generalization from them. And in order that we may know that an argument constitutes a demonstration, we require a criterion; but again, in order that we may know that it is a criterion we require a demonstration; hence both the one and the other are incomprehensible, since each is referred to the other. How then are we to grasp the things which are uncertain, seeing that we know no demonstration? For what we wish to ascertain is not whether things appear to be such and such, but whether they are so in their essence.

They declared the dogmatic philosophers to be fools, observing that what is concluded *ex hypothesi* is properly described not as inquiry but assumption, and by reasoning of this kind one may even argue for impossibilities. As for those who think that we should not judge of truth from surrounding circumstances or legislate on the basis of what is found in nature, these men, they used to say, made themselves the measure of all things, and did not see that every phenomenon appears in a certain disposition and in a certain reciprocal relation to surrounding circumstances. Therefore we must affirm either that all things are true or that all things are false. For if certain things only are true <and others are false>, how are we to distinguish them? Not by the senses, where things in the field of sense are in question, since all these things appear to sense to be on an equal footing; nor by the mind, for the same reason. Yet apart from these faculties there is no other, so far as we can see, to help us to a judgement. Whoever therefore, they say, would be firmly assured about anything sensible or intelligible must first establish the received opinions about it; for some have refuted one doctrine, others another. But things must be judged either by the sensible or by the intelligible, and both are disputed. Therefore it is impossible to pronounce judgement on opinions about sensibles or intelligibles;

and if the conflict in our thoughts compels us to disbelieve every one, the standard or measure, by which it is held that all things are exactly determined, will be destroyed, and we must deem every statement of equal value. Further, say they, our partner in an inquiry into a phenomenon is either to be trusted or not. If he is, he will have nothing to reply to the man to whom it appears to be the opposite; for just as our friend who describes what appears to him is to be trusted, so is his opponent. If he is not to be trusted, he will actually be disbelieved when he describes what appears to him.

We must not assume that what convinces us is actually true. For the same thing does not convince every one, nor even the same people always. Persuasiveness sometimes depends on external circumstances, on the reputation of the speaker, on his ability as a thinker or his artfulness, on the familiarity or the pleasantness of the topic.

Again, they would destroy the criterion by reasoning of this kind. Even the criterion has either been critically determined or not. If it has not, it is definitely untrustworthy, and in its purpose of distinguishing is no more true than false. If it has, it will belong to the class of particular judgements, so that one and the same thing determines and is determined, and the criterion which has determined will have to be determined by another, that other by another, and so on *ad infinitum*. In addition to this there is disagreement as to the criterion, some holding that man is the criterion, while for some it is the senses, for others reason, for others the apprehensive presentation. Now man disagrees with man and with himself, as is shown by differences of laws and customs. The senses deceive, and reason says different things. Finally, the apprehensive presentation is judged by the mind, and the mind itself changes in various ways. Hence the criterion is unknowable, and consequently truth also.

They deny, too, that there is such a thing as a sign. If there is, they say, it must either be sensible or intelligible. Now it is not sensible, because what is sensible is a common attribute, whereas a sign is a particular thing. Again, the sensible is one of the things which exist by way of difference, while the sign belongs to the category of relative. Nor is a sign an object of thought, for objects of thought are of four kinds, apparent judgements on things apparent, non-apparent judgements on things non-apparent, non-apparent on apparent, or apparent on non-apparent; and a sign is none of these, so that there is no such thing as a sign. A sign is not "apparent on apparent," for what is apparent needs no sign; nor is it non-apparent on non-apparent, for what is revealed by something must needs appear; nor is it non-apparent on apparent, for that which is to afford the means of apprehending something else must itself be apparent; nor, lastly, is it apparent on non-apparent, because the sign, being relative, must be apprehended along with that of which it is the sign, which is not here the case. It follows that nothing uncertain can be apprehended; for it is through signs that uncertain things are said to be apprehended.

Causes, too, they destroy in this way. A cause is something relative; for it is relative to what can be caused, namely, the effect. But things which are relative are merely objects of thought and have no substantial existence. Therefore a cause can only be an object of thought; inasmuch as, if it be a cause, it must bring with it that of which it is said to be the cause, otherwise it will not be a cause. Just as a father, in the absence of that in relation to which he is called father, will not be a father, so too with a cause. But that in relation to which the cause is thought of, namely the effect, is not present; for there is no coming into being or passing away or any other process: therefore there is no such thing as cause. Furthermore, if there is a cause, either bodies are the cause of bodies, or things incorporeal of things incorporeal; but neither is the case; therefore there is no such thing as cause. Body in fact could not be the cause of body, inasmuch as both have the same nature. And if either is called a cause in so far as it is a body, the other, being a body, will become a cause. But if both be alike causes, there will be nothing to be acted upon. Nor can an incorporeal thing be the cause of an incorporeal thing, for the same reason. And a thing incorporeal cannot be the cause of a body, since nothing incorporeal creates anything corporeal. And, lastly, a body cannot be the cause of anything incorporeal, because what is produced must be of the material operated upon; but if it is not operated upon because it is incorporeal, it cannot be produced by anything whatever. Therefore there is no such thing as a cause. A corollary to this is their statement that the first principles of the universe have no real existence; for in that case something must have been there to create and act.

Furthermore there is no motion; for that which moves moves

either in the place where it is or in a place where it is not. But it cannot move in the place where it is, still less in any place where it is not. Therefore there is no such thing as motion.

They used also to deny the possibility of learning. If anything is taught, they say, either the existent is taught through its existence or the non-existent through its non-existence. But the existent is not taught through its existence, for the nature of existing things is apparent to and recognized by all; nor is the non-existent taught through the non-existent, for with the non-existent nothing is ever done, so that it cannot be taught to anyone.

Nor, say they, is there any coming into being. For that which is does not come into being, since it *is;* nor yet that which is not, for it has no substantial existence, and that which is neither substantial nor existent cannot have had the chance of coming into being either.

There is nothing good or bad by nature, for if there is anything good or bad by nature, it must be good or bad for all persons alike, just as snow is cold to all. But there is no good or bad which is such to all persons in common; therefore there is no such thing as good or bad by nature. For either all that is thought good by anyone whatever must be called good, or not all. Certainly all cannot be so called; since one and the same thing is thought good by one person and bad by another; for instance, Epicurus thought pleasure good and Antisthenes thought it bad; thus on our supposition it will follow that the same thing is both good and bad. But if we say that not all that anyone thinks good is good, we shall have to judge the different opinions; and this is impossible because of the equal validity of opposing arguments. Therefore the good by nature is unknowable.

The whole of their mode of inference can be gathered from their extant treatises. Pyrrho himself, indeed, left no writings, but his associates Timon, Aenesidemus, Numenius and Nausiphanes did; and others as well.

The dogmatists answer them by declaring that the Sceptics themselves do apprehend and dogmatize; for when they are thought to be refuting their hardest they do apprehend, for at the very same time they are asseverating and dogmatizing. Thus even when they declare that they determine nothing, and that to every argument there is an opposite argument, they are actually determining these very points and dogmatizing. The others reply, "We confess to human weaknesses; for we recognize that it is day and that we are alive, and many other apparent facts in life; but with regard to the things about which our opponents argue so positively, claiming to have definitely apprehended them, we suspend our judgement because they are not certain, and confine knowledge to our impressions. For we admit that we see, and we recognize that we think this or that, but how we see or how we think we know not. And we say in conversation that a certain thing appears white, but we are not positive that it really is white. As to our 'We determine nothing' and the like, we use the expressions in an undogmatic sense, for they are not like the assertion that the world is spherical. Indeed the latter statement is not certain, but the others are mere admissions. Thus in saying 'We determine nothing,' we are *not* determining even that."

Again, the dogmatic philosophers maintain that the Sceptics do away with life itself, in that they reject all that life consists in. The others say this is false, for they do not deny that we see; they only say that they do not know how we see. "We admit the apparent fact," say they, "without admitting that it really is what it appears to be." We also perceive that fire burns; as to whether it is its nature to burn, we suspend our judgement. We see that a man moves, and that he perishes; how it happens we do not know. We merely object to accepting the unknown substance behind phenomena. When we say a picture has projections, we are describing what is apparent; but if we say that it has no projections, we are then speaking, not of what is apparent, but of something else. This is what makes Timon say in his *Python* that he has not gone outside what is customary. And again in the *Conceits* he says:

> But the apparent is omnipotent wherever it goes;

and in his work *On the Senses*, "I do not lay it down that honey is sweet, but I admit that it appears to be so."

Aenesidemus too in the first book of his *Pyrrhonean Discourses* says that Pyrrho determines nothing dogmatically, because of the possibility of contradiction, but guides himself by apparent facts. Aenesidemus says the same in his works *Against Wisdom* and *On Inquiry*. Furthermore Zeuxis, the friend of Aenesidemus, in his work *On Two-sided Arguments*, Antiochus of Laodicea, and Apellas in his *Agrippa* all hold to phenomena alone. Therefore the apparent is the Sceptic's criterion, as indeed Aenesidemus says; and so does Epicurus. Democritus, however, denied that any apparent fact could be a criterion, indeed he denied the very existence of the apparent. Against this criterion of appearances the dogmatic philosophers urge that, when the same appearances produce in us different impressions, *e.g.* a round or square tower, the Sceptic, unless he gives the preference to one or other, will be unable to take any course; if on the other hand, say they, he follows either view, he is then no longer allowing equal value to all apparent facts. The Sceptics reply that, when different impressions are produced, they must both be said to appear; for things which are apparent are so called because they appear. The end to be realized they hold to be suspension of judgement, which brings with it tranquillity like its shadow: so Timon and Aenesidemus declare. For in matters which are for us to decide we shall neither choose this nor shrink from that; and things which are not for us to decide but happen of necessity, such as hunger, thirst and pain, we cannot escape, for they are not to be removed by force of reason. And when the dogmatists argue that he may thus live in such a frame of mind that he would not shrink from killing and eating his own father if ordered to do so, the Sceptic replies that he will be able so to live as to suspend his judgement in cases where it is a question of arriving at the truth, but not in matters of life and the taking of precautions. Accordingly we may choose a thing or shrink from a thing by habit and may observe rules and customs. According to some authorities the end proposed by the Sceptics is insensibility; according to others, gentleness.

CHAPTER V

THE GREEK AND ROMAN CAREER OF
THE ATHENIAN SCHOOLS

The two classical schools, Plato's Academy and Aristotle's Lyceum, together with the later schools, the Stoic Porch and the Epicurean Gardens, had singly and more or less jointly a long existence and influence. Their history is, in fact, the story and fate of Grecian philosophy for a long transition period. Skepticism, though not a school in quite the same sense, had a great influence upon, as well as outside of, these organized schools. The Academy passed through three stages after Plato—the Older, the Middle, and the New Academy—and can be traced in one form or another to the embezzlement of its funds by the Emperor Justinian as late as the sixth century of the Christian Era. There are gaps in our knowledge of its heads, though we know that successively after Plato came his nephew, Speusippus, Xenocrates, Polemo, and Crates. Then the Academy went skeptical, then eclectic. The Lyceum was carried on to the third century of our era, being most ably directed by Theophrastus, Aristotle's immediate successor and savior of all the Athenian schools when in 306 an effort was made to abolish them. It, like the other schools, goes progressively eclectic, and at last is lost in a vague neo-Platonism. The Epicurean school at Athens was maintained after the death of Epicurus by Hermachus and other successors who are hardly more than names to us. By the beginning of our epoch, it appears that the life of this Grecian school was dispersed in local brotherhoods, while through Lucretius and others its influence was spread at Rome. The Stoic influence was to last in definite form much longer than the Porch at Athens—for almost five hundred years in fact. Through the first period after Zeno's death, under the successive leadership of Cleanthes and Chrysippus, it passed into closer connection with the influence of Plato and Aristotle until the beginning of our era, spreading to Rome meantime, and then for two hundred years with Cicero, Seneca, Epictetus, and Marcus Aurelius as its Roman voices became the official philosophy of life of the Empire. Diogenes Laertius has left us, as we have just seen, a rather full account of the tradition, if not the facts, of the founders of the three later schools, and Cicero in his "Academica," to which we turn, gives us a picture of their later coincidences and discrepancies.

. . .

CICERO ON THE INTERRELATION OF THE SCHOOLS

Academica. Being Book i, the revised portion of a much longer manuscript. We have some five times as much of the work as is here quoted, though there are gaps as the fragmentary ending of this selection will indicate. Rackham's translation ("Loeb Classical Library" series). The translator's main marginal leads I have elevated into subheadings to make the reading easier.—T. V. S.

I. INTRODUCTION: SCENE OF THE DIALOGUE

My friend Atticus was staying with me lately at my country-place at Cumae, when a message came to us from Marcus Varro's house that he had arrived from Rome on the evening of the day before, and if not fatigued from the journey intended to come straight on to us. On hearing this, we thought that no obstacle must intervene to delay our seeing a person united to us by identity of studies as well as by old friendship; so we hastily set out to go to him, and were only a short distance from his country-house when we saw him coming towards us in person. We gave our Varro a friend's embrace, and after a fairly long interval we escorted him back to his own house. Here there was first a little conversation, and that arising out of my asking whether Rome happened to have been doing anything new; and then Atticus said, "Do pray drop those subjects, about which we can neither ask questions nor hear the answers without distress; inquire of him instead whether he himself has done anything new. For Varro's Muses have kept silent for a longer time than they used, but all the same my belief is that your friend is not taking a holiday but is hiding what he writes." "Oh no, certainly not," said Varro, "for I think that to put in writing what one wants to be kept hidden is sheer recklessness; but I have got a big task in hand, and have had for a long time: I have begun on a work dedicated to our friend here himself"—meaning me—"which is a big thing I can assure you, and which is getting a good deal of touching up and polishing at my hands." At this I said, "As to that work of yours, Varro, I have been waiting for it a long time now, but all the same I don't venture to demand it; for I have heard (since we cannot hide anything of that kind) from our friend Libo, an enthusiastic student as you know, that you are not leaving it off, but are giving it increased attention, and never lay it out of your hands. However, there is a question that it has never occurred to me to put to you before the present moment, but now, after I have embarked on the task of placing upon record the doctrines that I have learnt in common with you, and of expounding in Latin literary form the famous old system of philosophy that took its rise from Socrates, I do put the question why, though you write a great deal, you pass over this class of subject, especially when you yourself are distinguished in it, and also when this interest and this whole subject far outstrip all other interests and other sciences?"

II. VARRO WOULD LEAVE PHILOSOPHICAL AUTHORSHIP TO GREEKS

"The question that you ask," rejoined Varro, "is one which I have often pondered and considered deeply. And so I will not beat about the bush in my reply, but will say what at once occurs to me, because I have, as I said, thought much and long upon the very point that you raise. For as I saw that philosophy had been most carefully expounded in Greek treatises, I judged that any persons from our nation that felt an interest in the subject, if they were learned in the teachings of the Greeks, would sooner read Greek writings than ours, and if on the other hand they shrank from the sciences and systems of the Greeks, they would not care even for philosophy, which cannot be understood without Greek learning: and therefore I was unwilling to write what the unlearned would not be able to understand and the learned would not take the trouble to read. But you are aware (for you have passed through the same course of study yourself) that we Academics cannot be like Amafinius or Rabirius, who discuss matters that lie open to the view in ordinary language, without employing any technicality and entirely dispensing with definition and division and neat syllogistic proof, and who in fact believe that no science of rhetoric or logic exists. But we for our part while obeying the rules of the logicians and of the orators also as if they were laws, for our school considers each of these faculties a merit, are compelled to employ novel terms as well, for which the learned, as I said, will prefer to go to the Greeks, while the unlearned will not accept them even from us, so that all our toil will be undertaken in vain. Then as for natural philosophy, if I accepted the system of Epicurus, that is of Democritus, I could write about it as lucidly as Amafinius; for when once you have abolished causation, in the sense of efficient causes, what is there remarkable in talking about the accidental collision of minute bodies—that is his name for atoms? The natural science of my school you know; being a system that combines the efficient force and the matter which is fashioned and shaped by the efficient force, it must also bring in geometry;[1] but what terminology, pray, will anybody have to use in explaining geometry, or whom will he be able to bring to understand it? Even this department of ethics and the subject of moral choice and avoidance that school handles quite simply, for it frankly identifies the good of man with the good of cattle, but what a vast amount of what minute precision the teachers of our school display is not unknown to you. For if one is a follower of Zeno, it is a great task to make anybody understand the meaning of the real and simple good that is inseparable from morality, because Epicurus entirely denies that he can even guess what sort of a thing good is without pleasures that excite the sense; but if we should follow the lead of the Old Academy, the school that I as you know approve, how acutely we shall have to expound that system! How subtly, how profoundly even, we shall have to argue against the Stoics! Accordingly for my own part I adopt the great pursuit of philosophy in its entirety both (so far as I am able) as a guiding principle of life and as an intellectual pleasure, and I agree with the dictum of Plato that no greater and better gift has been bestowed by the gods upon mankind. But my friends who possess an interest in this study I send to Greece, that is, I bid them go to the Greeks, so that they may draw from the fountain-heads rather than seek out mere rivulets; while doctrines which nobody had been teaching up till now, and for which there was nobody available from whom those interested could learn them, I have done as much as lay

---

[1] I.e. (with arithmetic), the whole of mathematics so far as then discovered.

in my power (for I have no great admiration for any of my own achievements) to make them known to our fellow-countrymen; for these doctrines could not be obtained from the Greeks, nor from the Latins either since the demise of our countryman Lucius Aelius. And nevertheless in those old writers of our country whom in my imitation (it is not a translation) of Menippus I treated with a certain amount of ridicule, there is a copious admixture of elements derived from the inmost depths of philosophy, and many utterances in good logical form; and though in my funeral orations these were more easily intelligible to less learned readers if they were tempted to peruse them by a certain attractiveness of style, when we come to the prefaces to my *Antiquities*, in these my aim was, if only I attained it, to write for philosophers."

III. CICERO DEFENDS LATIN PHILOSOPHY

"What you say, Varro, is true," I rejoined, "for we were wandering and straying about like visitors in our own city, and your books led us, so to speak, right home, and enabled us at last to realize who and where we were. You have revealed the age of our native city, the chronology of its history, the laws of its religion and its priesthood, its civil and its military institutions, the topography of its districts and its sites, the terminology, classification and moral and rational basis of all our religious and secular institutions, and you have likewise shed a flood of light upon our poets and generally on Latin literature and the Latin language, and you have yourself composed graceful poetry of various styles in almost every metre, and have sketched an outline of philosophy in many departments that is enough to stimulate the student though not enough to complete his instruction. But though it is true that the case you bring forward has some probability, as accomplished students on the one hand will prefer to read the Greek writings, and on the other hand people who do not know those will not read these either, still, tell me now—do you quite prove your point? The truth rather is that both those who cannot read the Greek books will read these and those who can read the Greek will not overlook the works of their own nation. For what reason is there why accomplished Grecians should read Latin poets and not read Latin philosophers? Is it because they get pleasure from Ennius, Pacuvius, Accius and many others, who have reproduced not the words but the meaning of the Greek poets? How much more pleasure will they get from philosophers, if these imitate Plato, Aristotle and Theophrastus in the same way as those poets imitated Aeschylus, Sophocles and Euripides? At all events I see that any of our orators that have imitated Hyperides or Demosthenes are praised. But for my own part (for I will speak frankly), so long as I was held entangled and fettered by the multifarious duties of ambition, office, litigation, political interests and even some political responsibility, I used to keep these studies within close bounds, and relied merely on reading, when I had the opportunity, to revive them and prevent their fading away; but now that I have been smitten by a grievously heavy blow[2] of fortune and also released from taking part in the government of the country, I seek from philosophy a cure for my grief and I deem this to be the most honourable mode of amusing my leisure. For this occupation is the one most suited to my age; or it is the one more in harmony than any other with such praiseworthy achievements as I can claim; or else it is the most useful means of educating our fellow-citizens also; or if these things are not the case, I see no other occupation that is within our power. At all events our friend Brutus, who is eminent for every kind of distinction, is so successful an exponent of philosophy in a Latin dress that one could not feel the least need for Greek writings on the same subjects, and indeed he is an adherent of the same doctrine as yourself, as for a considerable time he heard the lectures of Aristus[3] at Athens, whose brother Antiochus you attended. Pray therefore devote yourself to this field of literature also."

IV. VARRO FOLLOWING ANTIOCHUS DEFENDS OLD ACADEMY AGAINST NEW; CICERO SIDING WITH PHILO MAINTAINS THAT THEY AGREE

"I will deal with your point," he rejoined, "although I shall require your assistance. But what is this news that I hear[4] about yourself?"

"What about, exactly?" said I. "That you have abandoned the Old Academy, and are dealing with the New." "What then?" I said. "Is our friend Antiochus to have had more liberty to return

---

[2] The death of his daughter Tullia.

[3] Succeeded Antiochus as head of the Old Academy.   [4] I.e., from Atticus.

from the new school to the old, than we are to have to move out of the old one into the new? Why, there is no question that the newest theories are always most correct and free from error; although Philo, Antiochus's master, a great man as you yourself judge him, makes an assertion in his books which we used also to hear from his own lips,—he says that there are not two Academies, and proves that those who thought so were mistaken." "What you say is true," said he, "but I think that you are not unacquainted with what Antiochus wrote to combat those statements of Philo." "On the contrary, I should like you, if you do not mind, to recapitulate the arguments to which you refer, and also the whole theory of the Old Academy, with which I have been out of touch for a long while now; and at the same time," I said, "let us if you please sit down for our talk." "Let us sit down by all means," he said, "for I am in rather weak health. But let us see whether Atticus would like me to undertake the same task that I see you want me to." "To be sure I should," said Atticus, "for what could I like better than to recall to memory the doctrines that I heard long ago from Antiochus, and at the same time to see if they can be satisfactorily expressed in Latin?" After these remarks we took our seats in full view of one another.

Then Varro began as follows: "It is my view, and it is universally agreed, that Socrates was the first person who summoned philosophy away from mysteries veiled in concealment by nature herself, upon which all philosophers before him had been engaged, and led it to the subject of ordinary life, in order to investigate the virtues and vices, and good and evil generally, and to realize that heavenly matters are either remote from our knowledge or else, however fully known, have nothing to do with the good life. The method of discussion pursued by Socrates in almost all the dialogues so diversely and so fully recorded by his hearers is to affirm nothing himself but to refute others, to assert that he knows nothing except the fact of his own ignorance, and that he surpassed all other people in that they think they know things that they do not know but he himself thinks he knows nothing, and that he believed this to have been the reason why Apollo declared him to be the wisest of all men,[5] because all wisdom consists solely in not thinking that you

[5] Plato, *Apology* 21A.

know what you do not know. He used to say this regularly, and remained firm in this opinion, yet nevertheless the whole of his discourses were spent in praising virtue and in exhorting mankind to the zealous pursuit of virtue, as can be gathered from the books of members of the Socratic school, and particularly from those of Plato. But originating with Plato, a thinker of manifold variety and fertility, there was established a philosophy that, though it had two appellations, was really a single uniform system, that of the Academic and the Peripatetic schools, which while agreeing in doctrine differed in name; for Plato left his sister's son Speusippus as 'heir' to his system, but two pupils of outstanding zeal and learning, Xenocrates, a native of Calchedon, and Aristotle, a native of Stagira; and accordingly the associates of Aristotle were called the Peripatetics, because they used to debate while walking in the Lyceum, while the others, because they carried on Plato's practice of assembling and conversing in the Academy, which is another gymnasium, got their appellation from the name of the place. But both schools drew plentiful supplies from Plato's abundance, and both framed a definitely formulated rule of doctrine, and this fully and copiously set forth, whereas they abandoned the famous Socratic custom of discussing everything in a doubting manner and without the admission of any positive statement. Thus was produced something that Socrates had been in the habit of reprobating entirely, a definite science of philosophy, with a regular arrangement of subjects and a formulated system of doctrine. At the outset it is true this was a single system with two names, as I said, for there was no difference between the Peripatetics and the Old Academy of those days. Aristotle excelled, as I at all events think, in a certain copiousness of intellect, but both schools drew from the same source, and both made the same classification of things as desirable and to be avoided.

V. ANTIOCHUS'S ETHICS: GOODS ARE MENTAL, BODILY AND EXTERNAL

"But what am I about?" he said, "am I quite all there, who teach these things to you? Even if it is not a case of the proverbial pig teaching Minerva, anyway whoever teaches Minerva is doing a silly thing." "Do pray go on, Varro," rejoined Atticus, "for I love our literature and our fellow-countrymen profoundly, and I delight in the doctrines of your school when set forth in Latin and as you are setting them forth." "What do you suppose that I feel about it," said I, "seeing that I have already offered myself as an exponent of philosophy to our nation?" "Well then, let us proceed," said he, "as we are agreed. There already existed, then, a threefold scheme of philosophy inherited from Plato: one division dealt with conduct and morals, the second with the secrets of nature, the third with dialectic and with judgement of truth and falsehood, correctness and incorrectness, consistency and inconsistency, in rhetorical discourse. And for the first of these sections, the one dealing with the right conduct of life, they[6] went for a starting-point to nature, and declared that her orders must be followed, and that the chief good which is the ultimate aim of all things is to be sought in nature and in nature only; and they laid it down that to have attained complete accordance with nature in mind, body and estate is the limit of things desirable and the End of goods. Among goods of the body they laid it down that some resided in the whole frame and others in the parts: health, strength and beauty were goods of the whole, goods of the parts were sound senses and the particular excellences of the parts severally, for instance speed in the feet, power in the hands, clearness in the voice, and also an even and distinct articulation of sounds as a quality of the tongue. Goodness of the mind consisted in the qualities conducive to the comprehension of virtue; these they divided into gifts of nature and features of the moral character—quickness of apprehension and memory they assigned to nature, each of them being a mental and intellectual property, while to the moral character they deemed to belong the interests or 'habit' which they moulded partly by diligent practice and partly by reason, practice and reason being the domain of philosophy itself. In this philosophy a commencement not carried to completion is called 'progress' towards virtue, but the completed course is virtue, which is the 'consummation' of nature, and is the most supremely excellent of all the faculties of the mind as they define them. This then is their account of the mind. To 'estate'—that was the third division—they said belonged certain properties that influenced the exercise of virtue. For virtue is displayed in connexion with the goods of the mind and those of the body, and with some that are the attributes not so much of nature as of happiness. Man

[6] I.e., the original Academy.

they deemed to be, so to say, a 'part' of the state and of the human race as a whole, and they held that a man was conjoined with his fellow-men by the 'partnership of humanity.' And this being their treatment of the supreme good as bestowed by nature, all other goods they considered to be factors contributing either to its increase or to its protection, for instance wealth, resources, fame, influence. Thus they introduced a triple classification of goods.

VI. VIRTUE AND CONDUCT

"And this corresponds with the three classes of goods which most people think to be intended by the Peripatetics. This is indeed correct, for this classification is theirs, but it is a mistake if people suppose that the Academics quoted above and the Peripatetics were different schools. This theory was common to both, and both held that the end of goods was to acquire either all or the greatest of the things that are by nature primary, and are intrinsically worthy of desire; and the greatest of these are the ones which have their being in the mind itself and in virtue itself. Accordingly the whole of the great philosophy of antiquity held that happiness lies in virtue alone, yet that happiness is not supreme without the addition of the goods of the body and all the other goods suitable for the employment of virtue that were specified above. From this scheme they used also to arrive at a first principle of conduct in life and of duty itself, which principle lay in safeguarding the things that nature prescribed. Hence sprang the duty of avoiding idleness and of disregarding pleasures, leading on to the undergoing of many great toils and pains for the sake of the right and noble, and of the objects in harmony with the plan marked out by nature, from which sprang friendship, and also justice and fairness; and these they rated higher than pleasures and an abundance of the good things of life. This then was their system of ethics, the plan and outline of the department that I placed first.

"The subject of nature (for that came next) they dealt with by the method of dividing nature into two principles,[7] the one the active, and the other the 'passive,' on which the active operated and out of which an entity was created. The active principle they deemed to constitute force, the one acted on, a sort of 'material'; yet

[7] Apparently Antiochus with Plato identified matter and space.

they held that each of the two was present in the combination of both, for matter could not have formed a concrete whole by itself with no force to hold it together, nor yet force without some matter (for nothing exists that is not necessarily somewhere). But when they got to the product of both force and matter, they called this 'body,' and, if I may use the term, 'quality'—as we are dealing with unusual subjects you will of course allow us occasionally to employ words never heard before, as do the Greeks themselves, who have now been handling these topics for a long time."

VII. ANTIOCHUS'S PHYSICS: ENTITIES ARE MATTER INFORMED BY FORCE

"To be sure we will," said Atticus; "indeed you shall be permitted to employ even Greek words if Latin ones happen to fail you." "That is certainly kind of you, but I will do my best to talk Latin, except in the case of words of the sort now in question, so as to employ the term 'philosophy' or 'rhetoric' or 'physics'[8] or 'dialectic,'[9] which like many others are now habitually used as Latin words. I have therefore given the name of 'qualities' to the things that the Greeks call *poiotētes;* even among the Greeks it is not a word in ordinary use, but belongs to the philosophers, and this is the case with many terms. But the dialecticians' vocabulary is none of it the popular language, they use words of their own; and indeed this is a feature shared by almost all the sciences: either new names have to be coined for new things, or names taken from other things have to be used metaphorically. This being the practice of the Greeks, who have now been engaged in these studies for so many generations, how much more ought it to be allowed to us, who are now attempting to handle these subjects for the first time!" "Indeed, Varro," said I, "I think you will actually be doing a service to your fellow-countrymen if you not only enlarge their store of facts, as you have done, but of words also." "Then on your authority we will venture to employ new words, if we have to. Well then, those qualities are of two sorts, primary and derivative. Things of primary quality are homogeneous and simple; those derived from them

[8] *I.e.,* the whole of natural science of which physics in the modern sense is a part.

[9] *I.e.,* logic (including both formal logic and epistemology or the theory of knowledge.)

are varied and 'multiform.' Accordingly air (this word also we now use as Latin) and fire and water and earth are primary; while their derivatives are the species of living creatures and of the things that grow out of the earth. Therefore those things are termed first principles and (to translate from the Greek) elements; and among them air and fire have motive and efficient force, and the remaining divisions, I mean water and earth, receptive and 'passive' capacity. Aristotle deemed that there existed a certain fifth sort of element, in a class by itself and unlike the four that I have mentioned above, which was the source of the stars and of thinking minds. But they hold that underlying all things is a substance called 'matter,' entirely formless and devoid of all 'quality' (for let us make this word more familiar and manageable by handling), and that out of it all things have been formed and produced, so that this matter can in its totality receive all things and undergo every sort of transformation throughout every part of it, and in fact even suffer dissolution, not into nothingness but into its own parts, which are capable of infinite section and division, since there exists nothing whatever in the nature of things that is an absolute least, incapable of division; but that all things that are in motion move by means of interspaces,[10] these likewise being infinitely divisible. And since the force that we have called 'quality'[11] moves in this manner and since it thus vibrates to and fro, they think that the whole of matter also is itself in a state of complete change throughout, and is made into the things which they term 'qualified,' out of which in the concrete whole of substance, a continuum united with all its parts, has been produced one world, outside of which there is no portion of matter and no body, while all the things that are in the world are parts of it, held together by a sentient being, in which perfect reason, is immanent, and which is immutable and eternal since nothing stronger exists to cause it to perish; and this force they say is the soul of the world, and is also perfect intelligence and wisdom, which they entitle God, and is a sort of 'providence' knowing the things that fall

[10] *I.e.*, spaces of void or vacuum that are between the solids and enable them to move.

[11] The Stoics asserted that everything real has two components, the active and the passive, force and matter, and they expressed the former as quality; but they emphasized their materialism by sometimes speaking of the qualifying force as a current of air.

within its province, governing especially the heavenly bodies, and then those things on earth that concern mankind; and this force they also sometimes call Necessity, because nothing can happen otherwise than has been ordained by it under a 'fated and unchangeable concatenation of everlasting order'; although they sometimes also term it Fortune, because many of its operations are unforeseen and unexpected by us on account of their obscurity and our ignorance of causes.

VIII. ANTIOCHUS'S LOGIC

"Then the third part of philosophy, consisting in reason and in discussion, was treated by them both as follows. The criterion of truth arose indeed from the senses, yet was not in the senses: the judge of things was, they held, the mind—they thought that it alone deserves credence, because it alone perceives that which is eternally simple and uniform and true to its own quality. This thing they call the *Idea*, a name already given it by Plato; we can correctly term it *form*. All the senses on the other hand they deemed to be dull and sluggish, and entirely unperceptive of all the things supposed to fall within the province of the senses, which were either so small as to be imperceptible by sense, or in such a violent state of motion that no single thing was ever stationary, nor even remained the same thing, because all things were in continual ebb and flow; accordingly all this portion of things they called the object of opinion. Knowledge on the other hand they deemed to exist nowhere except in the notions and reasonings of the mind; and consequently they approved the method of defining *things*, and applied this 'real definition' to all the subjects that they discussed. They also gave approval to derivation of words, that is, the statement of the reason why each class of things bears the name that it does—the subject termed by them etymology and then they used derivations as 'tokens' or so to say marks of things, as guides for arriving at proofs or conclusions as to anything of which they desired an explanation; and under this head was imparted their whole doctrine of Dialectic, that is, speech cast in the form of logical argument; to this as a 'counterpart' was added the faculty of Rhetoric, which sets out a continuous speech adapted to the purpose of persuasion.

"This was their primary system, inherited from Plato; and if you wish I will expound the modifications of it that have reached me."

"Of course we wish it," said I, "if I may reply for Atticus as well."
"And you reply correctly," said Atticus, "for he is giving a brilliant
exposition of the doctrine of the Peripatetics and the Old Academy."

IX. DEPARTURES FROM THE OLD DOCTRINE

"Aristotle was the first to undermine the Forms of which I spoke
a little while before, which had been so marvellously embodied in
the system of Plato, who spoke of them as containing an element of
divinity. Theophrastus, who has a charming style and also a certain
conspicuous uprightness and nobility of character, in a way made
an even more violent breach in the authority of the old doctrine;
for he robbed virtue of her beauty and weakened her strength by
denying that the happy life is placed in her alone. As for his pupil
Strato, although he had a penetrating intellect nevertheless he
must be kept altogether separate from that school; he abandoned
the most essential part of philosophy, which consists in ethics, to
devote himself entirely to research in natural science, and even in
this he differed very widely from his friends. On the other hand
Speusippus and Xenocrates, the first inheritors of the system and
authority of Plato, and after them Polemo and Crates, and also
Crantor, gathered in the one fold of the Academy, were assiduous
defenders of the doctrines that they had received from their
predecessors. Finally, Polemo had had diligent pupils in Zeno and
Arcesilas, but Zeno, who was Arcesilas's senior in age and an extremely subtle dialectician and very acute thinker, instituted a reform of the system. This remodelled doctrine also I will expound, if
you approve, as it used to be expounded by Antiochus." "I do approve," said I, "and Pomponius, as you see, indicates his agreement."

X. ZENO'S ETHICS CLASSIFICATION: OF VALUES

"Well, Zeno was by no means the man ever to hamstring virtue,
as Theophrastus had done, but on the contrary to make it his practice to place all the constituents of happiness in virtue alone, and
to include nothing else in the category of Good, entitling virtue 'the
noble,' which denoted a sort of uniform, unique and solitary good.
All other things, he said, were neither good nor bad, but nevertheless some of them were in accordance with nature and others con-

trary to nature; also among these he counted another interposed or 'intermediate' class of things. He taught that things in accordance with nature were to be chosen and estimated as having a certain value, and their opposites the opposite, while things that were neither he left in the 'intermediate' class. These he declared to possess no motive force whatever, but among things to be chosen some were to be deemed of more value and others of less:[12] the more valuable he termed 'preferred,' the less valuable, 'rejected.' And just as with these he had made an alteration of terminology rather than of substance, so between a right action and a sin he placed appropriate action and action violating propriety as things intermediate, classing only actions rightly done as goods and actions wrongly done, that is sins, as evils, whereas the observance or neglect of appropriate acts he deemed intermediate, as I said. And whereas his predecessors said that not all virtue resides in the reason, but that certain virtues are perfected by nature or by habit, he placed all the virtues in reason; and whereas they thought that the kinds of virtues that I have stated above can be classed apart, he argued that this is absolutely impossible, and that not merely the exercise of virtue, as his predecessors held, but the mere state of virtue is in itself a splendid thing, although no body possesses virtue without continuously exercising it. Also whereas they did not remove emotion out of humanity altogether, and said that sorrow and desire and fear and delight were natural, but curbed them and narrowed their range, Zeno held that the wise man was devoid of all these 'diseases'; and whereas the older generation said that these emotions were natural and non-rational, and placed desire and reason in different regions of the mind, he did not agree with these doctrines either, for he thought that even the emotions were voluntary and were experienced owing to a judgement of opinion, and he held that the mother of all the emotions was a sort of intemperance and lack of moderation. These more or less were his ethical doctrines.

XI. ZENO'S PHYSICS AND LOGIC

"His views as to the natural substances were as follows. First, in dealing with the four recognized primary elements he did not add

---

[12] *I.e.*, of minus value, in grades of undesirability: this inaccuracy occurs in the Greek authorities.

this fifth substance which his predecessors deemed to be the source of sensation and of intellect; for he laid it down that the natural substance that was the parent of all things, even of the senses and the mind, was itself fire. He also differed from the same thinkers in holding that an incorporeal substance, such as Xenocrates and the older thinkers also had pronounced the mind to be, was incapable of any activity, whereas anything capable of acting, or being acted upon in any way could not be incorporeal. In the third department of philosophy he made a number of changes. Here first of all he made some new pronouncements about sensation itself, which he held to be a combination[13] of a sort of impact offered from outside (which he called *phantasia* and we may call a presentation, and let us retain this term at all events, for we shall have to employ it several times in the remainder of my discourse),—well, to these presentations received by the senses he joins the act of mental assent which he makes out to reside within us and to be a voluntary act. He held that not all presentations are trustworthy but only those that have a 'manifestation,' peculiar to themselves, of the objects presented; and a trustworthy presentation, being perceived as such by its own intrinsic nature, he termed 'graspable'—will you endure these coinages?" "Indeed we will," said Atticus, "for how else could you express *'catalēpton'*?" "But after it had been received and accepted as true, he termed it a 'grasp,' resembling objects gripped in the hand—and in fact he had derived the actual term from manual prehension, nobody before having used the word in such a sense, and he also used a number of new terms (for his doctrines were new). Well, a thing grasped by sensation he called itself a sensation, and a sensation so firmly grasped as to be irremovable by reasoning he termed knowledge, but a sensation not so grasped he termed ignorance, and this was the source also of opinion, an unstable impression akin to falsehood and ignorance. But as a stage between knowledge and ignorance he placed that 'grasp' of which I have spoken, and he reckoned it neither as a right nor as a wrong impression, but said that it was only 'credible.' On the strength of this he deemed the senses also trustworthy, because, as I said above, he held that a grasp achieved by the senses was both true and trustworthy, not because it grasped all the properties of the thing, but because

---

[13] *I.e.*, a combination of external impression or presentation and internal assent; but the sentence is interrupted by parentheses.

it let go nothing that was capable of being its object, and because nature had bestowed as it were a 'measuring-rod' of knowledge and a first principle of itself from which subsequently notions of things could be impressed upon the mind, out of which not first principles only but certain broader roads to the discovery of reasoned truth were opened up. On the other hand error, rashness, ignorance, opinion, suspicion, and in a word all the things alien to firm and steady assent, Zeno set apart from virtue and wisdom. And it is on these points more or less that all Zeno's departure and disagreement from the doctrine of his predecessors turned."

XII. CICERO REPLIES FOR PHILO'S 'PROBABILITY = PLATONISM'

When he had said this, I remarked: "You have certainly given a short and very lucid exposition of the theory both of the Old Academy and of the Stoics; though I think it to be true, as our friend Antiochus used to hold, that the Stoic theory should be deemed a correction of the Old Academy rather than actually a new system." "It is now your rôle," rejoined Varro, "as a seceder from the theory of the older period and a supporter of the innovations of Arcesilas, to explain the nature and the reason of the rupture that took place, so as to enable us to see whether the secession was fully justified." "It was entirely with Zeno, so we have been told," I replied, "that Arcesilas set on foot his battle, not from obstinacy or desire for victory, as it seems to me at all events, but because of the obscurity of the facts that had led Socrates to a confession of ignorance, as also previously his predecessors Democritus, Anaxagoras, Empedocles, and almost all the old philosophers, who utterly denied all possibility of cognition or perception or knowledge, and maintained that the senses are limited, the mind feeble, the span of life short, and that truth (in Democritus's phrase) is sunk in an abyss, opinion and custom are all-prevailing, no place is left for truth, all things successively are wrapped in darkness. Accordingly Arcesilas said that there is nothing that can be known, not even that residuum of knowledge that Socrates had left himself—the truth of this very dictum:[14] so hidden in obscurity did he believe that everything lies, nor is there anything that can be perceived or understood, and for these reasons, he said, no one must make any posi-

---

[14] We do not even know that nothing can be known.

tive statement or affirmation or give the approval of his assent to any proposition, and a man must always restrain his rashness and hold it back from every slip, as it would be glaring rashness to give assent either to a falsehood or to something not certainly known, and nothing is more disgraceful than for assent and approval to outstrip knowledge and perception. His practice was consistent with this theory—he led most of his hearers to accept it by arguing against the opinions of all men, so that when equally weighty reasons were found on opposite sides on the same subject, it was easier to withhold assent from either side. They call this school the New Academy,—to me it seems old, at all events if we count Plato a member of the Old Academy, in whose books nothing is stated positively and there is much arguing both *pro* and *contra*, all things are inquired into and no certain statement is made; but nevertheless let the Academy that you expounded be named the Old and this one the New; and right down to Carneades, who was fourth in succession from Arcesilas, it continued to remain true to the same theory of Arcesilas. Carneades however was acquainted with every department of philosophy, and as I have learnt from his actual hearers, and especially from the Epicurean Zeno, who though disagreeing very much with Carneades, nevertheless had an exceptional admiration for him, he possessed an incredible facility. . . . .''

Much as Rome drew upon its conquered territories for slaves and commodities, so it turned to its more civilized dependencies first for philosophy and then for religion. Philosophy is a manifestation if not a rationalization of culture. The schools, as we have seen, flourished at Athens while the political glory of the city-state was passing. Epicureanism furnished an aesthetic adornment for empire-builders, and is appropriately reflected in Latin poetry by Lucretius and, less didactically, by Horace. But Stoicism could furnish a theoretical basis for the practical cosmopolitanism of empire; it could dignify the individual lives of types no closer together than the famous slave, Epictetus, and the famous emperor, Aurelius; and it could furnish a rationalized escape through ataraxy or suicide when life became too much for either governors or governed. There was less rôle for skepticism among administrative Romans. Neo-Platonism, in a limited influence at Rome and in the empire, was a dim foretaste of the more austere way of life which early Christianity was to be. Roman patricians early sent their sons to Athenian schools—which one did not greatly matter—to be educated, as southern planters in colonial days sent their sons to England. Then schools arose in Rome itself to carry on the influence first felt at Athens. Men like Polybius, the Greek historian, as a political hostage in Rome, gave vogue to Greek culture and ideas. Cicero carried back to Rome from a sojourn in various schools at Athens and at Rhodes acquaintance with all major doctrines, interpreting to his countrymen perhaps better than more profound men could have a sort of modified Stoicism. Horace, too, journeyed to Athens to become a man of the world, and a singer of Rome's greatness. Seneca further disseminated the spirit of Stoicism. In short, Roman culture was up to the Christian conquest of it chiefly such echoes of Greek intellectual life as empire-builders liked to hear, could assimilate and repeat, and did upon occasion nobly practice.

CHAPTER VI

ROMAN STOICISM: COSMOPOLITANISM AND CONSOLATION

The theory of Stoicism underwent little modification in its Roman adherents. Its individualism was so applied as both to describe and to exemplify a sturdy type of self-contained character when the circumstances called for self-sufficiency. But with the empire as foreground, the Romans particularly developed the cosmopolitanism which at Athens was obvious as an implication but remained dormant in early Stoicism. Polybius (ca. 204–122), as a Greek hostage, saw Roman constitutional development as a natural outworking of tendencies inherent in their temperament and in the rational cosmos. Cicero (106–43) was the only native Roman who wrote extensively on political philosophy, and as such he became the medium through which the Stoic conception of natural law permeated medieval political theory by way of the Church Fathers. Seneca (ca. 4 B.C.–65 A.D.) justified philosophy as a way of life and an unfailing source of consolation. Epictetus (first century A.D., exact date unknown), a crippled slave, preached the fulfilment of duties determined by one's station, made adherence to the ideal of a universal society more noble than participation in civic affairs, and dignified the life of mind and the virtue of a magnanimous acceptance of whatever befalls, assured that the universe is rational and therefore that things cannot happen amiss. Marcus Aurelius (121–180 A.D.), Roman emperor, preached in tone genuinely religious the overmastering providence of divine reason, to which evil itself somehow ministers, and the quest for happiness only in co-operation with divine purpose. To renounce self and to pursue the common good is to find the true and only worthy self. In general, it may be said that, apart from recommending a noble ideal of self-sufficiency of which suicide could easily be, and sometimes actually was, made an implication, Roman Stoicism found in the "ius naturale" the rational meaning common to divergent customs and laws in the empire ("ius gentium"), and made available for later theory and practice (cf. Grotius) the valuable notion of differential rationality (desirability) of social and political concord.

.   .   .

POLYBIUS

Polybius was a Greek, taken to Rome as a hostage for refusing to assist the Romans against Perseus (167 B.C.) but given access to materials and personages so that he might continue his historical work.

His significance in the history of philosophy is as a connecting link between the classical Greek theory of state-evolution and state-degradation, on the one side, and Roman practice and history, on the other. He applies the Greek theory to explain the Roman fact. Through him Plato in particular comes mildly to life as an observer of a later scene.

What is left of Book vi of his histories is devoted to Rome. Though I have here only about one-fifth of the book, this fifth comprises practically all the theoretical part. The remainder deals largely with Roman military practice. Omissions from the fragments are indicated, and the heading and subheadings are mine.—T. V. S.

ON THE PHILOSOPHY OF THE ROMAN CONSTITUTION[1]

I. THE LESSON OF HISTORY AND THE MORAL OF STATES

What chiefly attracts and chiefly benefits students of history is just this—the study of causes and the consequent power of choosing what is best in each case. Now the chief cause of success or the reverse in all matters is the form of a state's constitution; for springing from this, as from a fountain-head, all designs and plans of action not only originate, but reach their consummation.

.   .   .   .

In my opinion there are two fundamental things in every state, by virtue of which its principle and constitution is either desirable or the reverse. I mean customs and laws. What is desirable in these makes men's private lives righteous and well ordered and the general character of the state gentle and just, while what is to be avoided has the opposite effect. So just as when we observe the

[1] *The Histories of Polybius*, Book vi. Paton's translation ("Loeb Classical Library" series).

laws and customs of a people to be good, we have no hesitation in pronouncing that the citizens and the state will consequently be good also, thus when we notice that men are covetous in their private lives and that their public actions are unjust, we are plainly justified in saying that their laws, their particular customs, and the state as a whole are bad. . . . .

II. FORMS OF STATES COMPARED

In the case of those Greek states which have often risen to greatness and have often experienced a complete change of fortune, it is an easy matter both to describe their past and to pronounce as to their future. For there is no difficulty in reporting the known facts, and it is not hard to foretell the future by inference from the past. But about the Roman state it is neither at all easy to explain the present situation owing to the complicated character of the constitution, nor to foretell the future owing to our ignorance of the peculiar features of public and private life at Rome in the past. Particular attention and study are therefore required if one wishes to attain a clear general view of the distinctive qualities of their constitution.

Most of those whose object it has been to instruct us methodically concerning such matters, distinguish three kinds of constitutions, which they call kingship, aristocracy, and democracy. Now we should, I think, be quite justified in asking them to enlighten us as to whether they represent these three to be the sole varieties or rather to be the best; for in either case my opinion is that they are wrong. For *it is evident that we must regard as the best constitution a combination of all these three varieties,*[2] since we have had proof

[2] My italics, to indicate what Polybius thought to be the secret of power of Rome. Lycurgus, in the estimation of Polybius, had shown the way to excellence; Rome followed. "For the purpose of remaining in secure possession of their own territory and maintaining their freedom," says Polybius, "the legislation of Lycurgus is amply sufficient, and to those who maintain this to be the object of political constitutions we must admit that there is not and never was any system or constitution superior to that of Lycurgus. But if anyone is ambitious of greater things, and esteems it finer and more glorious than that to be the leader of many men and to rule and lord it over many and have the eyes of all the world turned to him, it must be admitted that from this point of view the Laconian constitution is defective, while that of Rome is superior and better framed for the attainment of power, as is indeed evident from the actual course of events. For when the Lacedaemonians endeavoured to obtain supremacy in Greece, they very soon ran the risk of losing their own

of this not only theoretically but by actual experience, Lycurgus having been the first to draw up a constitution—that of Sparta—on this principle. Nor on the other hand can we admit that these are the only three varieties; for we have witnessed monarchical and tyrannical governments, which while they differ very widely from kingship, yet bear a certain resemblance to it, this being the reason why monarchs in general falsely assume and use, as far as they can, the regal title. There have also been several oligarchical constitutions which seem to bear some likeness to aristocratic ones, though the divergence is, generally, as wide as possible. The same holds good about democracies. The truth of what I say is evident from the following considerations. It is by no means every monarchy which we can call straight off a kingship, but only that which is voluntarily accepted by the subjects and where they are governed rather by an appeal to their reason than by fear and force. Nor again can we style every oligarchy an aristocracy, but only that where the government is in the hands of a selected body of the justest and wisest men. Similarly that is no true democracy in which the whole crowd of citizens is free to do whatever they wish or purpose, but when, in a community where it is traditional and customary to reverence the gods, to honour our parents, to respect our elders, and to obey the laws, the will of the greater number prevails, this is to be called a democracy. We would therefore assert that there are six kinds of governments, the three above mentioned which are in everyone's mouth and the three which are naturally allied to them, I mean monarchy, oligarchy, and mob-rule. Now the first of these to come into being is monarchy, its growth being

liberty; whereas the Romans, who had aimed merely at the subjection of Italy, in a short time brought the whole world under their sway . . . ." (*ibid.* vi. 50).

Again Polybius says: "To me it seems that as far as regards the maintenance of concord among the citizens, the security of the Laconian territory and the preservation of the freedom of Sparta, the legislation of Lycurgus and the foresight he exhibited were so admirable that one is forced to regard his institutions as of divine rather than human origin" (*ibid.* 48).

And balancing the accounts between Sparta and Rome, Polybius says: "Lycurgus then, foreseeing, by a process of reasoning, whence and how events naturally happen, constructed his constitution untaught by adversity, but the Romans while they have arrived at the same final result as regards their form of government, have not reached it by any process of reasoning, but by the discipline of many struggles and troubles, and always choosing the best by the light of the experience gained in disaster have thus reached the same result as Lycurgus, that is to say, the best of all existing constitutions" (*ibid.* 10.)—T. V. S.

natural and unaided; and next arises kingship derived from monarchy by the aid of art and by the correction of defects. Monarchy first changes into its vicious allied form, tyranny; and next, the abolishment of both gives birth to aristocracy. Aristocracy by its very nature degenerates into oligarchy; and when the commons inflamed by anger take vengeance on this government for its unjust rule, democracy comes into being; and in due course the licence and lawlessness of this form of government produces mob-rule to complete the series. The truth of what I have just said will be quite clear to anyone who pays due attention to such beginnings, origins, and changes as are in each case natural. For he alone who has seen how each form naturally arises and develops, will be able to see when, how, and where the growth, perfection, change, and end of each are likely to occur again. And it is to the Roman constitution above all that this method, I think, may be successfully applied, since from the outset its formation and growth have been due to natural causes. . . . .

III. THE NATURAL BALANCE ACHIEVED BY ROME

The three kinds of government that I spoke of above all shared in the control of the Roman state. And such fairness and propriety in all respects was shown in the use of these three elements for drawing up the constitution and in its subsequent administration that it was impossible even for a native to pronounce with certainty whether the whole system was aristocratic, democratic, or monarchical. This was indeed only natural. For if one fixed one's eyes on the power of the consuls, the constitution seemed completely monarchical and royal; if on that of the senate it seemed again to be aristocratic; and when one looked at the power of the masses, it seemed clearly to be a democracy. . . . .

I will now explain how each of the three parts is enabled, if they wish, to counteract or co operate with the others. The consul, when he leaves with his army, ... appears indeed to have absolute authority in all matters necessary for carrying out his purpose; but in fact he requires the support of the people and the senate, and is not able to bring his operations to a conclusion without them. For it is obvious that the legions require constant supplies, and without the consent of the senate, neither corn, clothing, nor pay can be provided; so that the commander's plans come to nothing, if the senate chooses to be deliberately negligent and obstructive. It also depends on the senate whether or not a general can carry out completely his conceptions and designs, since it has the right of either superseding him when his year's term of office has expired or of retaining him in command. Again it is in its power to celebrate with pomp and to magnify the successes of a general or on the other hand to obscure and belittle them. For the processions they call triumphs, in which the generals bring the actual spectacle of their achievements before the eyes of their fellow-citizens, cannot be properly organized and sometimes even cannot be held at all, unless the senate consents and provides the requisite funds. As for the people it is most indispensable for the consuls to conciliate them, however far away from home they may be; for . . . . it is the people which ratifies or annuls terms of peace and treaties, and what is most important, on laying down office the consuls are obliged to account for their actions to the people. So that in no respect is it safe for the consuls to neglect keeping in favour with both the senate and the people.

The senate again, which possesses such great power, is obliged in the first place to pay attention to the commons in public affairs and respect the wishes of the people, and it cannot carry out inquiries into the most grave and important offences against the state, punishable with death, and their correction, unless the *senatus consultum* is confirmed by the people. The same is the case in matters which directly affect the senate itself. For if anyone introduces a law meant to deprive the senate of some of its traditional authority, or to abolish the precedence and other distinctions of the senators or even to curtail them of their private fortunes, it is the people alone which has the power of passing or rejecting any such measure. And what is most important is that if a single one of the tribunes interposes, the senate is unable to decide finally about any matter, and cannot even meet and hold sittings; and here it is to be observed that the tribunes are always obliged to act as the people decree and to pay every attention to their wishes. Therefore for all these reasons the senate is afraid of the masses and must pay due attention to the popular will.

Similarly, again, the people must be submissive to the senate and respect its members both in public and in private. Through the whole of Italy a vast number of contracts, which it would not be easy to enumerate, are given out by the censors for the construction and repair of public buildings, and besides this there are many things which are farmed, such as navigable rivers, harbours, gardens, mines, lands, in fact everything that forms part of the Roman dominion. Now all these matters are undertaken by the people, and one may almost say that everyone is interested in these contracts and the work they involve. For certain people are the actual purchasers from the censors of the contracts, others are the partners of these first, others stand surety for them, others pledge their fortunes to the state for this purpose. Now in all these matters the senate is supreme. It can grant extension of time; it can relieve the contractor if any accident occurs; and if the work proves to be absolutely impossible to carry out it can liberate him from his contract. There are in fact many ways in which the senate can either benefit or injure those who manage public property, as all these matters are referred to it. What is even more important is that the judges in most civil trials, whether public or private, are appointed from its members, where the action involves large interests. So that all citizens being at the mercy of the senate, and looking forward with alarm to the uncertainty of litigation, are very shy of obstructing or resisting its decisions. Similarly everyone is reluctant to oppose the projects of the consuls as all are generally and individually under their authority when in the field.

Such being the power that each part has of hampering the others or co-operating with them, their union is adequate to all emergencies, so that it is impossible to find a better political system than this. For whenever the menace of some common danger from abroad compels them to act in concord and support each other, so great does the strength of the state become, that nothing which is requisite can be neglected, as all are zealously competing in devising means of meeting the need of the hour, nor can any decision arrived at fail to be executed promptly, as all are co operating both in public and in private to the accomplishment of the task they have set themselves; and consequently this peculiar form of constitution possesses an irresistible power of attaining every object upon which it is resolved. When again they are freed from external menace, and reap the harvest of good fortune and affluence which is the result of their success, and in the enjoyment of this prosperity are corrupted by flattery and idleness and wax insolent and overbear-

ing, as indeed happens often enough, it is then especially that we see
the state providing itself a remedy for the evil from which it suffers.
For when one part having grown out of proportion to the others
aims at supremacy and tends to become too predominant, it is evident that, as for the reasons above given none of the three is absolute, but the purpose of the one can be counterworked and thwarted
by the others, none of them will excessively outgrow the others or
treat them with contempt. All in fact remains *in statu quo*, on the
one hand, because any aggressive impulse is sure to be checked and
from the outset each estate stands in dread of being interfered with
by the others. . . . .

IV. THE ROMAN VS. GREEK CONSTITUTIONS

One may say that nearly all authors have handed down to us the
reputation for excellence enjoyed by the constitutions of Sparta,
Crete, Mantinea, and Carthage. Some make mention also of those
of Athens and Thebes. I leave these last two aside; for I am myself
convinced that the constitutions of Athens and Thebes need not be
dealt with at length, considering that these states neither grew
by a normal process, nor did they remain for long in their most
flourishing state, nor were the changes they underwent immaterial;
but after a sudden effulgence so to speak, the work of chance and
circumstance, while still apparently prosperous and with every
prospect of a bright future, they experienced a complete reverse
of fortune. For the Thebans, striking at the Lacedaemonians
through their mistaken policy and the hatred their allies bore them,
owing to the admirable qualities of one or at most two men, who
had detected these weaknesses, gained in Greece a reputation for
superiority. Indeed, that the successes of the Thebans at that time
were due not to the form of their constitution, but to the high qualities of their leading men, was made manifest to all by Fortune immediately afterwards. For the success of Thebes grew, attained its
height, and ceased with the lives of Epaminondas and Pelopidas;
and therefore we must regard the temporary splendour of that state
as due not to its constitution, but to its men. We must hold very
much the same opinion about the Athenian constitution. For
Athens also, though she perhaps enjoyed more frequent periods of
success, after her most glorious one of all which was coeval with the
excellent administration of Themistocles, rapidly experienced a

complete reverse of fortune owing to the inconstancy of her nature. For the Athenian populace always more or less resembles a ship without a commander. In such a ship when fear of the billows or the danger of a storm induces the mariners to be sensible and to attend to the orders of the skipper, they do their duty admirably. But when they grow over-confident and begin to entertain contempt for their superiors and to quarrel with each other, as they are no longer all of the same way of thinking, then with some of them determined to continue the voyage, and others putting pressure on the skipper to anchor, with some letting out the sheets and other preventing them and ordering the sails to be taken in, not only does the spectacle strike anyone who watches it as disgraceful owing to their disagreement and contention, but the position of affairs is a source of actual danger to the rest of those on board; so that often after escaping from the perils of the widest seas and fiercest storms they are shipwrecked in harbour and when close to the shore. This is what has more than once befallen the Athenian state. After having averted the greatest and most terrible dangers owing to the high qualities of the people and their leaders, it has come to grief at times by sheer heedlessness and unreasonableness in seasons of unclouded tranquillity. Therefore I need say no more about this constitution or that of Thebes, states in which everything is managed by the uncurbed impulse of a mob in the one case exceptionally headstrong and ill-tempered and in the other brought up in an atmosphere of violence and passion. . . . .

V. ROMAN RELIGION AS AN INSTRUMENT OF STATECRAFT

But the quality in which the Roman commonwealth is most distinctly superior is in my opinion the nature of their religious convictions. I believe that it is the very thing which among other peoples is an object of reproach, I mean superstition, which maintains the cohesion of the Roman State. These matters are clothed in such pomp and introduced to such an extent into their public and private life that nothing could exceed it, a fact which will surprise many. My own opinion at least is that they have adopted this course for the sake of the common people. It is a course which perhaps would not have been necessary had it been possible to form a state composed of wise men, but as every multitude is fickle, full of lawless desires, unreasoned passion, and violent anger, the multitude must be held in by invisible terrors and suchlike pageantry. For this reason I think, not that the ancients acted rashly and at haphazard in introducing among the people notions concerning the gods and beliefs in the terrors of hell, but that the moderns are most rash and foolish in banishing such beliefs. The consequence is that among the Greeks, apart from other things, members of the government, if they are entrusted with no more than a talent, though they have ten copyists and as many seals and twice as many witnesses, cannot keep their faith; whereas among the Romans those who as magistrates and legates are dealing with large sums of money maintain correct conduct just because they have pledged their faith by oath. Whereas elsewhere it is a rare thing to find a man who keeps his hands off public money, and whose record is clean in this respect, among the Romans one rarely comes across a man who has been detected in such conduct.

VI. ROME LIKE ALL ELSE SUBJECT TO DECAY

That all existing things are subject to decay and change is a truth that scarcely needs proof; for the course of nature is sufficient to force this conviction on us. There being two agencies by which every kind of state is liable to decay, the one external and the other a growth of the state itself, we can lay down no fixed rule about the former, but the latter is a regular process. I have already stated what kind of state is the first to come into being, and what the next, and how the one is transformed into the other; so that those who are capable of connecting the opening propositions of this inquiry with its conclusion will now be able to foretell the future unaided. And what will happen is, I think, evident. When a state has weathered many great perils and subsequently attains to supremacy and uncontested sovereignty, it is evident that under the influence of long established prosperity, life will become more extravagant and the citizens more fierce in their rivalry regarding office and other objects than they ought to be. As these defects go on increasing, the beginning of the change for the worse will be due to love of office and the disgrace entailed by obscurity, as well as to extravagance and purse-proud display; and for this change the populace will be responsible when on the one hand, they are puffed up by the flattery of others who aspire to office. For now, stirred to fury and swayed by passion in all their counsels, they will no longer consent to obey or even to be the equals of the ruling caste, but will demand the lion's share for themselves. When this happens, the state will change its name to the finest sounding of all, freedom and democracy, but will change its nature to the worst thing of all, mob-rule.

CICERO

Justifies His Interest in Philosophy[3]

I observe . . . . that a great deal of talk has been current about the large number of books that I have produced within a short space of time, and that such comment has not been all of one kind; some people have been curious as to the cause of this sudden outburst of philosophical interest on my part, while others have been eager to learn what positive opinions I hold on the various questions. Many also, as I have noticed, are surprised at my choosing to espouse a philosophy that in their view robs the world of daylight and floods it with darkness as of night; and they wonder at my coming forward so unexpectedly as the champion of a derelict system and one that has long been given up.

As a matter of fact however I am no new convert to the study of philosophy. From my earliest youth I have devoted no small amount of time and energy to it, and I pursued it most keenly at the very periods when I least appeared to be doing so, witness the philosophical maxims of which my speeches are full, and my intimacy with the learned men who have always graced my household, as well as those eminent professors, Diodotus, Philo, Antiochus and Posidonius, who were my instructors. Moreover, if it be true that all the doctrines of philosophy have a practical bearing, I may claim that in my public and private conduct alike I have practised the precepts taught by reason and by theory.

IV. If again anyone asks what motive has induced me so late in the day to commit these precepts to writing, there is nothing that I can explain more easily. I was languishing in idle retirement, and the state of public affairs was such that an autocratic form of government had become inevitable. In these circumstances, in the first place I thought that to expound philosophy to my fellow-country-

[3] From the early part of Cicero's ambitious treatise, *On the Nature of the Gods*, Book i, secs. iii–v. Rackham's translation ("Loeb Classical Library" series).

men was actually my duty in the interests of the commonwealth, since in my judgement it would greatly contribute to the honour and glory of the state to have thoughts so important and so lofty enshrined in Latin literature also; and I am the less inclined to repent of my undertaking because I can clearly perceive what a number of my readers have been stimulated not only to study but to become authors themselves. A great many accomplished students of Greek learning were unable to share their acquisitions with their fellow-citizens, on the ground that they doubted the possibility of conveying in Latin the teachings they had received from the Greeks. In the matter of style however I believe that we have made such progress that even in richness of vocabulary the Greeks do not surpass us. Another thing that urged me to this occupation was the dejection of spirit occasioned by the heavy and crushing blow[4] that had been dealt me by fortune. Had I been able to find any more effective relief from my sorrow, I should not have had recourse to this particular form of consolation; but the best way open to me of enjoying even this consolation to the full extent was to devote myself not only to reading books but also to composing a treatise on the whole of philosophy. Now the readiest mode of imparting a knowledge of the subject in all its departments and branches is to write an exposition of the various methods in their entirety; since it is a striking characteristic of philosophy that its topics all hang together and form a consecutive system; one is seen to be linked to another, and all to be mutually connected and attached.

V. Those however who seek to learn my personal opinion on the various questions show an unreasonable degree of curiosity. In discussion it is not so much weight of authority as force of argument that should be demanded. Indeed the authority of those who profess to teach is often a positive hindrance to those who desire to learn; they cease to employ their own judgement, and take what they perceive to be the verdict of their chosen master as settling the question. In fact I am not disposed to approve the practice traditionally ascribed to the Pythagoreans, who, when questioned as to the grounds of any assertion that they advanced in debate, are said to have been accustomed to reply 'He himself said so,' 'he

---

[4] The death of his daughter in 45 B.C.

himself' being Pythagoras. So potent was an opinion already decided, making authority prevail unsupported by reason.

To those again who are surprised at my choice of a system to which to give my allegiance, I think that a sufficient answer has been given in the four books of my *Academica*.[5] Nor is it the case that I have come forward as the champion of a lost cause and of a position now abandoned. When men die, their doctrines do not perish with them, though perhaps they suffer from the loss of their authoritative exponent. Take for example the philosophical method referred to, that of a purely negative dialectic which refrains from pronouncing any positive judgement. This, after being originated by Socrates, revived by Arcesilas, and reinforced by Carneades, has flourished right down to our own period; though I understand that in Greece itself it is now almost bereft of adherents. But this I ascribe not to the fault of the Academy but to the dullness of mankind. If it is a considerable matter to understand any one of the systems of philosophy singly, how much harder is it to master them all! Yet this is the task that confronts those whose principle is to discover the truth by the method of arguing both for and against all the schools. In an undertaking so extensive and so arduous, I do not profess to have attained success, though I do claim to have attempted it. At the same time it would be impossible for the adherents of this method to dispense altogether with any standard of guidance. This matter it is true I have discussed elsewhere more thoroughly; but some people are so dull and slow of apprehension that they appear to require repeated explanations. Our position is not that we hold that nothing is true, but that we assert that all true sensations are associated with false ones so closely resembling them that they contain no infallible mark to guide our judgement and assent.[6] From this followed the corollary, that many sensations are *probable*, that is, though not amounting to a full perception they are yet possessed of a certain distinctness and clearness, and so can serve to direct the conduct of the wise man.

[5] The first book of the extant portion of this work we have quoted at the end of the Greek period.—T. V. S.

[6] The Stoics on the contrary held that true sensations are distinguished from false ones by an infallible mark and command our instinctive assent to their truth.

On the Ideal Constitution[7]

XXI. . . . . LAELIUS. . . . . I desired this [a discussion of state-craft], not only because it was proper that an eminent statesman rather than anyone else should discuss the State, but also because I recollected that you used to converse very frequently with Panaetius on this subject in company with Polybius—two Greeks who were perhaps the best versed of them all in politics—and that you assembled many arguments to prove that the form of government handed down to us by our ancestors is by far the best of all. Now since you are better prepared than the rest of us to undertake this discussion, you will do us all a favour, if I may speak for the company, by presenting your ideas on the State.

XXII. SCIPIO. I cannot, indeed, assert that any other subject claims more of my interest and careful thought, Laelius, than the one which you now assign to me. Furthermore, since I have noticed that the thoughts and efforts of every craftsman, if he is proficient, are directed to no other end than the improvement of his skill in his own craft, should not I, seeing that the guardianship and adminis-tration of the State have been handed down to me by my parents and ancestors as my sole task, have to confess that I am more slothful than any craftsman, if I have devoted less labour to the supreme craft than they to their humble tasks? But I am not satis-fied with the works dealing with this subject which the greatest and wisest men of Greece have left us; nor on the other hand am I bold enough to rate my opinion above theirs. Therefore I ask you to listen to me as to one who is neither entirely ignorant of the Greek authorities, nor, on the other hand, prefers their views, particularly on this subject, to our own, but rather as to a Roman who though provided by a father's care with a liberal education and eager for knowledge from boyhood, yet has been trained by experience and the maxims learned at home much more than by books. . . . .

XXVII. In kingships the subjects have too small a share in the administration of justice and in deliberation; and in aristocracies the masses can hardly have their share of liberty, since they are entirely excluded from deliberation for the common weal and from power; and when all the power is in the people's hands, even though they exercise it with justice and moderation, yet the resulting

[7] *The Republic*. Keyes's translation ("Loeb Classical Library" series). Only a few paragraphs from Book i, as indicated, are taken from this extended work.

equality itself is inequitable, since it allows no distinctions in rank. . . . .

XXVIII. I am now speaking of these three forms of government, not when they are confused and mingled with one another, but when they retain their appropriate character. All of them are, in the first place, subject each to the faults I have mentioned, and they suffer from other dangerous faults in addition: for before every one of them lies a slippery and precipitous path leading to a certain depraved form that is a close neighbour to it. . . . .

XXIX. . . . . A wise man should be acquainted with these changes, but it calls for great citizens and for a man of almost divine powers to foresee them when they threaten, and, while holding the reins of government, to direct their courses and keep them under his control. Therefore I consider a fourth form of government the most commendable—that form which is a well-regulated mixture of the three which I mentioned at first.

On Law, Justice, and Reason[8]

VI. . . . . The most learned men have determined to begin with Law [in seeking Justice], and it would seem that they are right, if, according to their definition, Law is the highest reason, implanted in Nature, which commands what ought to be done and forbids the opposite. This reason, when firmly fixed and fully developed in the human mind, is Law. And so they believe that Law is intelligence, whose natural function it is to command right conduct and forbid wrongdoing. They think that this quality has derived its name in Greek from the idea of granting to every man his own, and in our language I believe it has been named from the idea of choosing. For as they have attributed the idea of fairness to the word law, so we have given it that of selection, though both ideas properly belong to Law. Now if this is correct, as I think it to be in general, then the origin of justice is to be found in Law, for law is a natural force; it is the mind and reason of the intelligent man, the standard by which Justice and injustice are measured. . . . .

VII. . . . . That animal which we call man, endowed with foresight and quick intelligence, complex, keen, possessing memory, full

[8] *Laws*. Keyes's translation ("Loeb Classical Library" series). These selections are a small part of the first of the three books of the *Laws*. Marcus is speaking, but I have dropped the dialogue form for the sake of brevity and continuity.—T. V. S.

of reason and prudence, has been given a certain distinguished status by the supreme God who created him; for he is the only one among so many different kinds and varieties of living beings, who has a share in reason and thought, while all the rest are deprived of it. But what is more divine, I will not say in man only, but in all heaven and earth, than reason? And reason, when it is full grown and perfected, is rightly called wisdom. Therefore, since there is nothing better than reason, and since it exists both in man and God, the first common possession of man and God is reason. But those who have reason in common must also have right reason in common. And since right reason is Law, we must believe that men have Law also in common with the gods. Further, those who share Law must also share Justice; and those who share these are to be regarded as members of the same commonwealth. If indeed they obey the same authorities and powers, this is true in a far greater degree; but as a matter of fact they do obey this celestial system, the divine mind, and the God of transcendent power. Hence we must now conceive of this whole universe as one commonwealth of which both gods and men are members. . . . .

X. . . . . The points which are now being briefly touched upon are certainly important; but out of all the material of the philosophers' discussions, surely there comes nothing more valuable than the full realization that we are born for Justice, and that right is based, not upon men's opinions, but upon Nature. This fact will immediately be plain if you once get a clear conception of man's fellowship and union with his fellow-men. For no single thing is so like another, so exactly its counterpart, as all of us are to one another. Nay, if bad habits and false beliefs did not twist the weaker minds and turn them in whatever direction they are inclined, no one would be so like his own self as all men would be like all others. And so, however we may define man, a single definition will apply to all. This is a sufficient proof that there is no difference in kind between man and man; for if there were, one definition could not be applicable to all men; and indeed reason, which alone raises us above the level of the beasts and enables us to draw inferences, to prove and disprove, to discuss and solve problems, and to come to conclusions, is certainly common to us all, and, though varying in what it learns, at least in the capacity to learn it is invariable. For the same things are invariably perceived by the senses, and those things which stimulate the senses, stimulate them in the same way in all men; and those rudimentary beginnings of intelligence to which I have referred, which are imprinted on our minds, are imprinted on all minds alike; and speech, the mind's interpreter, though differing in the choice of words, agrees in the sentiments expressed. In fact, there is no human being of any race who, if he finds a guide, cannot attain to virtue.

In Final Praise of the Immutable Law[9]

XXII. . . . . True law is right reason in agreement with nature; it is of universal application, unchanging and everlasting; it summons to duty by its commands, and averts from wrongdoing by its prohibitions. And it does not lay its commands or prohibitions upon good men in vain, though neither have any effect on the wicked. It is a sin to try to alter this law, nor is it allowable to attempt to repeal any part of it, and it is impossible to abolish it entirely. We cannot be freed from its obligations by senate or people, and we need not look outside ourselves for an expounder or interpreter of it. And there will not be different laws at Rome and at Athens, or different laws now and in the future, but one eternal and. unchangeable law will be valid for all nations and all times, and there will be one master and rule, that is, God, over us all, for he is the author of this law, its promulgator, and its enforcing judge. Whoever is disobedient is fleeing from himself and denying his human nature, and by reason of this very fact he will suffer the worst penalties, even if he escapes what is commonly considered punishment. . . . .

SENECA

On Leisure[10]

What I have to say [on Leisure] I shall develop under two heads, showing, first, that it is possible for a man to surrender himself wholly to the contemplation of truth, to search out the art of living, and to practice it in retirement, even from his earliest years; secondly, that, when a man has now earned release from public service

[9] This final and lofty panegyric is taken from *The Republic*, Book iii, being the only fragment that remains of chap. xxii.—T. V. S.

[10] *Moral Essays*, Vol. II, Book viii: "To Serenus. On Leisure." Basore's translation ("Loeb's Classical Library" series). About half of the essay is here reproduced.—T. V. S.

and his life is almost over, it is possible that he may with perfect justice do the same thing and turn his mind to quite different activities, after the manner of the Vestal virgins, whose years are allotted to varied duties while they are learning to perform the sacred rites, and, when they have learned, they begin to teach.

I shall show, too, that the Stoics also accept this doctrine, not because I have made it my rule to set up nothing contrary to the teaching of Zeno or Chrysippus, but because the matter itself suffers me to adopt their opinion; for if a man always follows the opinion of one person, his place is not in the senate, but in a faction.[11] Would that all things were now understood, that truth were uncovered and revealed, and that we never altered our mandates! As it is, we are in search of truth in company with the very men that teach it.

The two sects, the Epicureans and the Stoics, are at variance, as in most things, in this matter also; they both direct us to leisure, but by different roads. Epicurus says: "The wise man will not engage in public affairs except in an emergency." Zeno says: "He will engage in public affairs unless something prevents him." The one seeks leisure by fixed purpose, the other for a special cause; but the term "cause" has here broad application. If the state is too corrupt to be helped, if it is wholly dominated by evils, the wise man will not struggle to purpose, nor spend himself when nothing is gained. If he is lacking in influence or power and the state is unwilling to accept his services, if he is hampered by ill health, he will not enter upon a course for which he knows he is unfitted, just as he would not launch upon the sea a battered ship, just as he would not enlist for a service in the army if he were disabled. Consequently, it is also possible that a man whose fortunes are still unharmed may establish himself in a safe retreat before he experiences any of the storms of life, and thenceforth devote himself to the liberal studies and demand uninterrupted leisure to cultivate the virtues, which even those who are most retired are able to practise. It is of course required of a man that he should benefit his fellow-men—many if he can; if not, a few; if not a few, those who are nearest; if not these, himself. For when he renders himself useful to others, he engages in public affairs. Just as the man that chooses to become worse injures not only himself but all those whom, if he had become better,

---

[11] Cf. Senator Borah's place in contemporary opinion.—T. V. S.

he might have benefited, so whoever wins the approval of himself benefits others by the very fact that he prepares what will prove beneficial to them.

Let us grasp the idea that there are two commonwealths—the one, a vast and truly common state, which embraces alike gods and men, in which we look neither to this corner of earth nor to that, but measure the bounds of our citizenship by the path of the sun; the other, the one to which we have been assigned by the accident of birth. This will be the commonwealth of the Athenians or of the Carthaginians, or of any other city that belongs, not to all, but to some particular race of men. Some yield service to both commonwealths at the same time—to the greater and to the lesser—some only to the lesser, some only to the greater. This greater commonwealth we are able to serve even in leisure—nay, I am inclined to think, even better in leisure. . . . .

And with what thought does the wise man retire into leisure? In the knowledge that there also he will be doing something that will benefit posterity. Our school at any rate is ready to say that both Zeno and Chrysippus accomplished greater things than if they had led armies, held public office, and framed laws. The laws they framed were not for one state only, but for the whole human race. Why, therefore, should such leisure as this not be fitting for the good man, who by means of it may govern the ages to come, and speak, not to the ears of the few, but to the ears of all men of all nations, both those who now are and those who shall be? In brief, I ask you whether Cleanthes and Chrysippus and Zeno lived in accordance with their teachings. Undoubtedly you will reply that they lived just as they taught that men ought to live. And yet no one of them governed a state. You reply: "They had neither the fortune nor the rank which ordinarily admit one to the management of public affairs." But, nevertheless, they did not lead a life of sloth; they found a way to make their own repose a greater help to mankind than all the pother and sweat of others. Therefore, though they played no public part, they none the less have been thought to have played a great part.

Moreover, there are three kinds of life, and it is a common question as to which of them is best. One is devoted to pleasure, a second to contemplation, a third to action. Having first put away our strife and having put away the hatred which we have relentlessly declared against those who pursue ends different from ours, let us see how all these, under different names, come to the same thing. For he who sanctions pleasure is not without contemplation, nor he who surrenders to contemplation without pleasure, nor is he whose life is devoted to action without contemplation. But you say: "Whether something is a chief aim or is merely attached to some other chief aim makes a very great difference." Yes, grant that there is a huge difference, nevertheless the one does not exist without the other. That man is not given to contemplation without action, nor this one to action without contemplation, nor does that third one—concerning whom we have agreed to form a bad opinion —give sanction to idle pleasure, but to the pleasure that he renders stable for himself by his reason; thus even this pleasure-loving sect is itself committed to action. Clearly is it committed to action! since Epicurus himself declares that he will at times withdraw from pleasure, will even seek pain if he foresees that he will either repent of pleasure, or will be able to substitute a lesser pain for one that is greater. And what is my purpose in stating these things? To make it clear that contemplation is favoured by all. Some men make it their aim; for us it is a roadstead, but not the harbour.

Add, further, that on the authority of Chrysippus a man has a right to live a life of leisure; I do not mean, that he may tolerate leisure, but that he may choose it. Our school refuses to allow the wise man to attach himself to any sort of state. But what difference does it make in what manner the wise man arrives at leisure— whether because no state is available to him or because he is not available to the state—if he is nowhere to find a state? Besides, no state will ever be available to the fastidious searcher. I ask you to what state should the wise man attach himself? To that of the Athenians, in which Socrates was sentenced to death, from which Aristotle fled to avoid being sentenced? in which all the virtues are crushed by envy? Surely you will say that no wise man will wish to attach himself to this state. Shall the wise man, then, attach himself to the state of the Carthaginians, in which faction is always rife and all the best men find "freedom" their foe, in which justice and goodness have supreme contempt, and enemies are treated with inhuman cruelty and fellow-citizens like enemies? From this state also will he flee. If I should attempt to enumerate them one by one, I should not find a single one which could tolerate the wise man or which the wise man could tolerate. But if that state which we dream of can nowhere be found, leisure begins to be a necessity for all of us, because the one thing that might have been preferred to leisure nowhere exists. If anyone says that the best life of all is to sail the sea, and then adds that I must not sail upon a sea where shipwrecks are a common occurrence and there are often storms that sweep the helmsman in an adverse direction, I conclude that this man, although he lauds navigation, really forbids me to launch my ship.[12]

On Self-Control[13]

The question has often been raised whether it is better to have moderate emotions, or none at all. Philosophers of our school reject the emotions; the Peripatetics keep them in check. I, however, do not understand how any half-way disease can be either wholesome or helpful. Do not fear; I am not robbing you of any privileges which you are unwilling to lose! I shall be kindly and indulgent towards the objects for which you strive—those which you hold to be necessary to our existence, or useful, or pleasant; I shall simply strip away the vice. For after I have issued my prohibition against the desires, I shall still allow you to wish that you may do the same things fearlessly and with greater accuracy of judgment, and to feel even the pleasures more than before; and how can these pleasures help coming more readily to your call, if you are their lord rather than their slave!

"But," you object, "it is natural for me to suffer when I am bereaved of a friend; grant some privileges to tears which have the right to flow! It is also natural to be affected by men's opinions and to be cast down when they are unfavourable; so why should you not allow me such an honourable aversion to bad opinion?"

There is no vice which lacks some plea; there is no vice that at the start is not modest and easily entreated; but afterwards the trouble spreads more widely. If you allow it to begin, you cannot make sure of its ceasing. Every emotion at the start is weak. Afterwards, it rouses itself and gains strength by progress; it is more easy to forestall it than to forego it. Who does not admit that all

[12] The essay is apparently incomplete.

[13] *Moral Essays*, III, 332–36, Letter CXVI. Gunmere's translation ("Loeb Classical Library" series).

the emotions flow as it were from a certain natural source? We are endowed by Nature with an interest in our own well-being; but this very interest, when overindulged, becomes a vice. Nature has intermingled pleasure with necessary things—not in order that we should seek pleasure, but in order that the addition of pleasure may make the indispensable means of existence attractive to our eyes. Should it claim rights its own, it is luxury.

Let us therefore resist these faults when they are demanding entrance, because, as I have said, it is easier to deny them admittance than to make them depart. And if you cry: "One should be allowed a certain amount of grieving, and a certain amount of fear," I reply that the "certain amount" can be too long-drawn-out, and that it will refuse to stop short when you so desire. The wise man can safely control himself without becoming over-anxious; he can halt his tears and his pleasures at will; but in our case, because it is not easy to retrace our steps, it is best not to push ahead at all. I think that Panaetius gave a very neat answer to a certain youth who asked him whether the wise man should become a lover: "As to the wise man, we shall see later; but you and I, who are as yet far removed from wisdom, should not trust ourselves to fall into a state that is disordered, uncontrolled, enslaved to another, contemptible to itself. If our love be not spurned, we are excited by its kindness; if it be scorned, we are kindled by our pride. An easily-won love hurts us as much as one which is difficult to win; we are captured by that which is compliant, and we struggle with that which is hard. Therefore, knowing our weakness, let us remain quiet. Let us not expose this unstable spirit to the temptations of drink, or beauty, or flattery, or anything that coaxes and allures."

Now that which Panaetius replied to the question about love may be applied, I believe, to all the emotions. In so far as we are able, let us step back from slippery places; even on dry ground it is hard enough to take a sturdy stand. At this point, I know, you will confront me with that common complaint against the Stoics: "Your promises are too great, and your counsels too hard. We are mere manikins, unable to deny ourselves everything. We shall sorrow, but not to any great extent; we shall feel desires, but in moderation; we shall give way to anger, but we shall be appeased." And do you know why we have not the power to attain this Stoic ideal? It is because we refuse to believe in our power. Nay, of a surety, there is something else which plays a part: it is because we are in love with our vices; we uphold them and prefer to make excuses for them rather than shake them off. We mortals have been endowed with sufficient strength by nature, if only we use this strength, if only we concentrate our powers and rouse them all to help us or at least not to hinder us. The real reason for failure is unwillingness, the pretended reason, inability. Farewell.

To Helvia His Mother on Consolation[14]

Often, my best of mothers, I have felt the impulse to send you consolation,[15] and as often I have checked it. The motives that urged me to be so bold were many. In the first place, I thought that I should lay aside all my troubles when, even though I could not stop your weeping, I had meanwhile at least wiped away your tears; again, I felt sure that I should have more power to raise you up, if I had first arisen from my own grief; besides, I was afraid that Fortune, though vanquished by me, might still vanquish someone dear to me. And so, placing my hand over my own gash, I was trying as best I could to creep forward to bind up your wounds. On the other hand, there were reasons which made me delay as regards my purpose. I knew that I ought not to intrude upon your grief while its violence was fresh, lest my very condolences should irritate and inflame it; for in bodily ills also nothing is more harmful than an untimely use of medicine. I was waiting, therefore, until your grief should of itself subdue its violence, and its soreness, soothed by time to tolerate remedies, should submit to being touched and handled. Moreover, although I unrolled all the works that the most famous writers had composed for the purpose of repressing and controlling sorrow,[16] not one instance did I find of a man who had offered consolation to his dear ones when he himself was bewailed by them; thus, in a novel situation I faltered, and I feared that my words might supply, not consolation, but aggravation. And be-

[14] *Ibid.*, Vol. II, Book xii. Basore's translation ("Loeb Classical Library" series). Less than one-fifth of the essay is here reproduced. In its entirety it constitutes a treatise on motherhood as well as an essay on consolation.—T. V. S.

[15] Writing in philosophic serenity from his place of exile, Seneca seeks to allay his mother's grief at the mishap that has befallen him. After her widowhood she seems to have lived with her father in Spain, but had apparently visited Rome shortly before her son's banishment.

[16] Cf. the "form" telegrams of consolation of our time.—T. V. S.

sides, a man who was lifting his head from the very bier to comfort his dear ones—what need he would have of words that were new and not drawn from the common and everyday forms of condolence! But the very greatness of every grief that passes bounds must necessarily snatch away the power of choosing words, since often it chokes even the voice itself. Yet I shall try as best I can, not because I have confidence in my eloquence, but because the mere fact that I myself am able to act as comforter may amount to most effective comfort. You who could refuse me nothing, will surely not, I hope, refuse me—although all sorrow is stubborn—your consent to my setting bounds to your grieving. . . . .

I have determined to conquer your grief, not to dupe it. And too I shall conquer it, I think, if, in the first place, I show that there is nothing in my condition that could cause anyone to call me wretched, still less cause those also to whom I am related to be wretched on my account; and, secondly, if I turn next to you, and prove that your fortune also, which depends wholly upon mine, is not a painful one.

First of all, I shall proceed to prove what your love is eager to hear—that I am suffering no ill. If I can, I shall make it clear that those very circumstances, which your love fancies weigh me down, are not intolerable; but if it will be impossible for you to believe this, I, at any rate, shall be better pleased with myself if I show that I am happy under circumstances that usually make others wretched. You are not asked to believe the report of others about me; that you may not be at all disturbed by ungrounded suppositions, I myself inform you that I am not unhappy. That you may be the more assured, I will add, too, that I cannot even be made unhappy.

We are born under conditions that would be favourable if only we did not abandon them. Nature intended that we should need no great equipment for living happily; each one of us is able to make his own happiness. External things are of slight importance, and can have no great influence in either direction. Prosperity does not exalt the wise man, nor does adversity cast him down; for he has always endeavoured to rely entirely upon himself. What, then? Do I say that I am a wise man? By no means; for if I could make that claim, I should thereby not only deny that I am unhappy, but should also declare that I am the most fortunate of all men and had been brought into nearness with God. As it is, fleeing to that which is able to lighten all sorrows, I have surrendered myself to wise men and, not yet being strong enough to give aid to myself, I have taken refuge in the camp of others [i.e. the Stoic school]—of those, clearly, who can easily defend themselves and their followers. They have ordered me to stand every watching, like a soldier placed on guard, and to anticipate all the attempts and all the assaults of Fortune long before she strikes. Her attack falls heavy only when it is sudden; he easily withstands her who always expects her. For the arrival too of the enemy lays low only those whom it catches off guard; but those who have made ready for the coming war before it arrives, fully formed and ready armed, easily sustain the first impact, which is always the most violent. Never have I trusted Fortune, even when she seemed to be offering peace; the blessings she most fondly bestowed upon me—money, office, and influence— I stored all of them in a place from which she could take them back without disturbing me. Between them and me I have kept a wide space; and so she has merely taken them, not torn them, from me. No man is crushed by hostile Fortune who is not first deceived by her smiles. Those who love her gifts as if they were their very own and lasting, who desire to be esteemed on account of them, grovel and mourn when the false and fickle delights forsake their empty, childish minds, that are ignorant of every stable pleasure; but he who is not puffed up by happy fortune does not collapse when it is reversed. The man of long-tested constancy, when faced with either condition, keeps his mind unconquered; for in the very midst of prosperity he proves his strength to meet adversity. . . . .

Since you have no reason, my dearest mother, to be forced to endless tears on my account, it follows that you are goaded to them by reasons of your own. . . . .

I know well that this is a matter that is not in our own power, and that no emotion is submissive, least of all that which is born from sorrow; for it is wild and stubbornly resists every remedy. Sometimes we will to crush it and to swallow down our cries, yet tears pour down our faces even when we have framed the countenance to deceive. Sometimes we occupy the mind with public games or the bouts of gladiators, but amid the very spectacles that divert the mind it is crushed by some slight reminder of its loss. Therefore it is better to subdue our sorrow than to cheat it; for when it has

withdrawn and has been beguiled by pleasures or engrossments, it rises up again, and from its very rest gathers new strength for its fury. But the grief that has submitted to reason is allayed for ever. And so I am not going to point you to the expedients that I know many have used, suggesting that you distract or cheer your mind by travel, whether to distant or pleasant places, that you employ much time in diligent examination of your accounts and in the management of your estate, that you should always be involved in some new tasks. All such things avail for a brief space only, and are not the remedies but the hindrances of sorrow; but I would rather end it than beguile it. And so I guide you to that in which all who fly from Fortune must take refuge—to philosophic studies. They will heal your wound, they will uproot all your sadness. Even if you had not been acquainted with them before, you would need to use them now; but, so far as the old-fashioned strictness of my father permitted you, though you have not indeed fully grasped all the liberal arts, still you have had some dealings with them. Would that my father, truly the best of men, had surrendered less to the practice of his forefathers, and had been willing to have you acquire a thorough knowledge of the teachings of philosophy instead of a mere smattering! In that case you would now have, not to devise, but merely to display, your protection against Fortune. But he did not suffer you to pursue your studies because of those women who do not employ learning as a means to wisdom, but equip themselves with it for the purpose of display. Yet, thanks to your acquiring mind, you imbibed more than might have been expected in the time you had; the foundations of all systematic knowledge have been laid. Do you return now to these studies; they will render you safe. They will comfort you, they will cheer you; if in earnest they gain entrance to your mind, nevermore will sorrow enter there, nevermore anxiety, nevermore the useless distress of futile suffering. To none of these will your heart be open; for to all other weaknesses it has long been closed. Philosophy is your most unfailing safeguard, and she alone can rescue you from the power of Fortune.
. . . .

But because, though you have done everything, your thoughts must necessarily revert at times to me, and it must be that under the circumstances no one of your children engages your mind so often—not that the others are less dear, but that it is nature to lay the hand more often on the part that hurts—hear now how you must think of me. I am as happy and cheerful as when circumstances were best. Indeed, they are now best, since my mind, free from all other engrossments, has leisure for its own tasks, and now finds joy in lighter studies, now, being eager for the truth, mounts to the consideration of its own nature and the nature of the universe. It seeks knowledge, first, of the lands where they lie, then of the laws that govern the encompassing sea with its alternations of ebb and flow. Then it takes ken of all the expanse, charged with terrors, that lies between heaven and earth—this nearer space, disturbed by thunder, lightning, blasts of winds, and the downfall of rain and snow and hail. Finally, having traversed the lower spaces, it bursts through to the heights above, and there enjoys the noblest spectacle of things divine, and, mindful of its own immortality, it proceeds to all that has been and will ever be throughout the ages of all time.

EPICTETUS
(60?–120?)

These selections are from George Long's translations, and are arranged by the editor with subheadings, the first six headings being from the *Discourses of Epictetus*, the last five being from his *Encheiridion* (or *Manual*).—T.V.S.

THE BEGINNING OF WISDOM

The beginning of philosophy, to him at least who enters on it in the right way and by the door, is a consciousness of his own weakness and inability about necessary things; for we come into the world with no natural notion of a right-angled triangle, or of a diesis (a quarter tone), or of a half-tone; but we learn each of these things by a certain transmission according to art; and for this reason those who do not know them do not think that they know them. But as to good and evil, and beautiful and ugly, and becoming and unbecoming, and happiness and misfortune, and proper and improper, and what we ought to do and what we ought not to do, who ever came into the world without having an innate idea of them? Wherefore we all use these names, and we endeavor to fit the preconceptions to the several cases (things) thus: he has done well; he has not done well; he has done as he ought, not as he ought; he has been unfortunate, he has been fortunate; he is unjust, he is just; who does not use these names? who among us defers the use of them till he has learned them, as he defers the use of the words about lines (geometrical figures) or sounds? And the cause of this is that we come into the world already taught as it were by nature some things on this matter, and proceeding from these we have added to them self-conceit. For why, a man says, do I not know the beautiful and the ugly? Have I not the notion of it? You have. Do I not adapt it to particulars? You do. Do I not then adapt it properly? In that lies the whole question; and conceit is added here; for beginning from these things which are admitted men proceed to that which is matter of dispute by means of unsuitable adaptation; for if they possessed this power of adaptation in addition to those things, what would hinder them from being perfect? But now since you think that you properly adapt the preconceptions to the particulars, tell me whence you derive this (assume that you do). Because I think so. But it does not seem so to another, and he thinks that he also makes a proper adaptation; or does he not think so? He does think so. Is it possible then that both of you can properly apply the preconceptions to things about which you have contrary opinions? It is not possible. Can you then show us anything better towards adapting the preconceptions beyond your thinking that you do? Does the madman do any other things than the things which seem to him right? Is then this criterion sufficient for him also? It is not sufficient. Come then to something which is superior to seeming. What is this?

Observe, this is the beginning of philosophy, a perception of the disagreement of men with one another, and an inquiry into the cause of the disagreement, and a condemnation and distrust of that which only "seems," and a certain investigation of that which "seems" whether it "seems" rightly, and a discovery of some rule, as we have discovered a balance in the determination of weights, and a carpenter's rule (or square) in the case of straight and crooked things—this is the beginning of philosophy.

Marks of Improvement

He who is making progress, having learned from philosophers that desire means the desire of good things, and aversion means aversion from bad things; having learned too that happiness and tranquillity are not attainable by man otherwise than by not failing to obtain what he desires, and not falling into that which he would avoid; such a man takes from himself desire altogether and confers it, but he employs his aversion only on things which are dependent on his will. For if he attempts to avoid anything independent of his will, he knows that sometimes he will fall in with something which he wishes to avoid, and he will be unhappy. Now if virtue promises good fortune and tranquillity and happiness, certainly also the progress towards virtue is progress towards each of these things. For it is always true that to whatever point the perfecting of anything leads us, progress is an approach towards this point.

How then do we admit that virtue is such as I have said, and yet seek progress in other things and make a display of it? What is the product of virtue? Tranquillity. Who then makes improvement? Is it he who has read many books of Chrysippus? But does virtue consist in having understood Chrysippus? If this is so, progress is clearly nothing else than knowing a great deal of Chrysippus. But now we admit that virtue produces one thing, and we declare that approaching near to it is another thing, namely, progress or improvement. Such a person, says one, is already able to read Chrysippus by himself. Indeed, sir, you are making great progress. What kind of progress? But why do you mock the man? Why do you draw him away from the perception of his own misfortunes? Will you not show him the effect of virtue that he may learn where to look for improvement? Seek it there, wretch, where your work lies. And where is your work? In desire and in aversion, that you may not be disappointed in your desire, and that you may not fall into that which you would avoid; in your pursuit and avoiding, that you commit no error; in assent and suspension of assent, that you be not deceived. The first things, and the most necessary are those which I have named. But if with trembling and lamentation you seek not to fall into that which you avoid, tell me how you are improving.

The Rôle of the Rational

To the rational animal only is the irrational intolerable; but that which is rational is tolerable. Blows are not naturally intolerable. How is that? See how the Lacedaemonians endure whipping when they have learned that whipping is consistent with reason. To hang yourself is not intolerable. When then you have the opinion that it is rational, you go and hang yourself. In short, if we observe, we shall find that the animal man is pained by nothing so much as by that which is irrational; and, on the contrary, attracted to nothing so much as to that which is rational.

On Providence

From everything, which is or happens in the world, it is easy to praise Providence, if a man possesses these two qualities: the faculty of seeing what belongs and happens to all persons and things, and a grateful disposition. If he does not possess these two qualities, one man will not see the use of things which are and which happen: another will not be thankful for them, even if he does know them. If God had made colors, but had not made the faculty of seeing them, what would have been their use? None at all. On the other hand, if he had made the faculty of vision, but had not made objects such as to fall under the faculty, what in that case also would have been the use of it? None at all. Well, suppose that he had made both, but had not made light? In that case, also, they would have been of no use. Who is it then who has fitted this to that and that to this?

On Certain Uses of Piety

I indeed think that the old man ought to be sitting here, not to contrive how you may have no mean thoughts nor mean and ignoble talk about yourselves, but to take care that there be not among us any young men of such a mind, that when they have recognized their kinship to God, and that we are fettered by these bonds, the body, I mean, and its possessions, and whatever else on account of them is necessary to us for the economy and commerce of life, they should intend to throw off these things as if they were burdens painful and intolerable, and to depart to their kinsman. But this is the labor that your teacher and instructor ought to be employed upon, if he really were what he should be. You should come to him and say: Epictetus, we can no longer endure being bound to this poor body, and feeding it, and giving it drink and rest, and cleaning it, and for the sake of the body complying with the wishes of these and of those. Are not these things indifferent and nothing to us; and is not death no evil? And are we not in a manner kinsmen of God, and did we not come from him? Allow us to depart to the place from which we came; allow us to be released at last from these bonds by which we are bound and weighed down. Here there are robbers and thieves and courts of justice, and those who are named tyrants, and think that they have some power over us by means of the body and its possessions. Permit us to show them that they have no power over any man.

And I on my part would say: Friends, wait for God: when he shall give the signal and release you from this service, then go to him; but for the present endure to dwell in this place where he has put you. Short indeed is this time of your dwelling here, and easy to bear for those who are so disposed; for what tyrant, or what thief, or what court of justice are formidable to those who have thus considered as things of no value the body and the possessions of the body? Wait then, do not depart without a reason.

On Seeing Things as They Are

When you make any charge against Providence, consider, and you will learn that the thing has happened according to reason. Yes, but the unjust man has the advantage. In what? In money. Yes, for he is superior to you in this, that he flatters, is free from shame, and is watchful. What is the wonder? But see if he has the advantage over you in being faithful, in being modest; for you will not find it to be so; but wherein you are superior, there you will find that you have the advantage. I once said to a man who was vexed because Philostorgus was fortunate: Would you choose to lie with Sura? May it never happen, he replied, that this day should come. Why then are you vexed, if he receives something in return for that which he sells; or how can you consider him happy who acquires those things by such means as you abominate; or what wrong does Providence, if he gives the better things to the better men? Is it not better to be modest than to be rich? He admitted this. Why are you vexed then, man, when you possess the better thing? Remember then always and have in readiness the truth, that this is a law of nature, that the superior has an advantage over the inferior in that in which he is superior; and you will never be vexed.

But my wife treats me badly. Well, if any man asks you what this is, say, my wife treats me badly. Is there then nothing more?

Nothing. My father gives me nothing. [What is this? My father gives me nothing. Is there nothing else then? Nothing]; but to say that this is an evil is something which must be added to it externally, and falsely added. For this reason we must not get rid of poverty, but of the opinion about poverty, and then we shall be happy.

Philosophy Looks Within

Philosophy does not propose to secure for a man any external thing. If it did (or if it were not, as I say), philosophy would be allowing something which is not within its province. For as the carpenter's material is wood, and that of the statuary is copper, so the matter of the art of living is each man's life. When then is my brother's? That again belongs to his own art; but with respect to yours, it is one of the external things, like a piece of land, like health, like reputation. But philosophy promises none of these. In every circumstance I will maintain, she says, the governing part conformable to nature.

On Things That Are within Our Power

Of things some are in our power, and others are not. In our power are opinion, movement towards a thing, desire, aversion, turning from a thing; and in a word, whatever are our acts. Not in our power are the body, property, reputation, offices (magisterial power), and in a word, whatever are not our own acts. And the things in our power are by nature free, not subject to restraint or hindrance; but the things not in our power are weak, slavish, subject to restraint, in the power of others. Remember then, that if you think the things which are by nature slavish to be free, and the things which are in the power of others to be your own, you will be hindered, you will lament, you will be disturbed, you will blame both gods and men; but if you think that only which is your own to be your own, and if you think that what is another's, as it really is, belongs to another, no man will ever compel you, no man will hinder you, you will never blame any man, you will accuse no man, you will do nothing involuntarily (against your will), no man will harm you, you will have no enemy, for you will not suffer any harm.

If then you desire (aim at) such great things remember that you must not (attempt to) lay hold of them with a small effort; but you must leave alone some things entirely, and postpone others for the present. But if you wish for these things also (such great things), and power (office) and wealth, perhaps you will not gain even these very things (power and wealth) because you aim also at those former things (such great things); certainly you will fail in those things through which alone happiness and freedom are secured. Straightway then practise saying to every harsh appearance: You are an appearance, and in no manner what you appear to be. Then examine it by the rules which you possess, and by this first and chiefly, whether it relates to the things which are not in our power; and if it relates to anything which is not in our power, be ready to say that it does not concern you.

Take No Thought of Things

If you intend to improve, throw away such thoughts as these: if I neglect my affairs, I shall not have the means of living: unless I chastise my slave, he will be bad. For it is better to die of hunger and so to be released from grief and fear than to live in abundance with perturbation; and it is better for your slave to be bad than for you to be unhappy. Begin then from little things. Is the oil spilled? Is a little wine stolen? Say on the occasion, at such price is sold freedom from perturbation; at such price is sold tranquillity, but nothing is got for nothing. And when you call your slave, consider that it is possible that he does not hear; and if he does hear, that he will do nothing which you wish. But matters are not so well with him, but altogether well with you, that it should be in his power for you to be not disturbed.

Avoid Ostentation

On no occasion call yourself a philosopher, and do not speak much among the uninstructed about theorems (philosophical rules, precepts); but do that which follows from them. For example, at a banquet do not say how a man ought to eat, but eat as you ought to eat. For remember that in this way Socrates also altogether avoided ostentation. Persons used to come to him and ask to be recommended by him to philosophers, and he used to take them to philosophers, so easily did he submit to being overlooked. Accordingly, if any conversation should arise among uninstructed persons about any theorem, generally be silent; for there is great danger that you will immediately vomit up what you have not digested. And when a man shall say to you that you know nothing, and you are not vexed, then be sure that you have begun the work (of philosophy). For even sheep do not vomit up their grass and show to the shepherds how much they have eaten; but when they have internally digested the pasture, they produce externally wool and milk. Do you also show not your theorems to the uninstructed, but show the acts which come from their digestion.

Fortify Your Minds with These Maxims

In everything (circumstance) we should hold these maxims ready to hand:

> Lead me, O Zeus, and thou, O Destiny,
> The way that I am bid by you to go:
> To follow I am ready. If I choose not,
> I make myself a wretch, and still must follow.
>
> But whoso nobly yields unto necessity,
> We hold him wise, and skill'd in things divine.

And the third also: O Crito, if so it pleases the gods, so let it be; Anytus and Meletus are able indeed to kill me, but they cannot harm me.

MARCUS AURELIUS ANTONINUS
(121–180 A.D.)

These selections are all from the *Meditations* (George Long's translation). Book ii is included entire. The heading is mine, but no subheadings are added because of the weak continuity from paragraph to paragraph; the student may best read the paragraphs as aphorisms strung together.—T. V. S.

On the Conduct of Life

II. Begin the morning by saying to thyself, I shall meet with the busybody, the ungrateful, arrogant, deceitful, envious, unsocial. All these things happen to them by reason of their ignorance of what is good and evil. But I who have seen the nature of the good that it is beautiful, and of the bad that it is ugly, and the nature of him who does wrong, that it is akin to me, not [only] of the same blood or seed, but that it participates in [the same] intelligence and [the same] portion of the divinity, I can neither be injured by any of them, for no one can fix on me what is ugly, nor can I be angry with my kinsman, nor hate him. For we are made for co-operation, like feet, like hands, like eyelids, like the rows of the upper and lower teeth. To act against one another then is contrary to nature; and it is acting against one another to be vexed and to turn away.

2. Whatever this is that I am, it is a little flesh and breath, and the ruling part. Throw away thy books; no longer distract thyself: it is not allowed; but as if thou wast now dying, despise the flesh; it is blood and bones and a network, a contexture of nerves, veins and arteries. See the breath also, what kind of a thing it is; air, and not always the same, but every moment sent out and again sucked in. The third then is the ruling part: consider thus: Thou art an old man; no longer let this be a slave, no longer be pulled by the strings like a puppet to unsocial movements, no longer be either dissatisfied with thy present lot, or shrink from the future.

3. All that is from the gods is full of providence. That which is from fortune is not separated from nature or without an interweaving and involution with the things which are ordered by Providence. From thence all things flow; and there is besides necessity, and that which is for the advantage of the whole universe, of which thou art a part. But that is good for every part of nature which the nature of the whole brings, and what serves to maintain this nature. Now the universe is preserved, as by the changes of the elements so by the changes of things compounded of the elements. Let these principles be enough for thee; let them always be fixed opinions. But cast away the thirst after books, that thou mayest not die murmuring, but cheerfully, truly, and from thy heart thankful to the gods.

4. Remember how long thou hast been putting off these things, and how often thou hast received an opportunity from the gods, and yet dost not use it. Thou must now at last perceive of what universe thou art a part, and of what administrator of the universe thy existence is an efflux, and that a limit of time is fixed for thee, which if thou dost not use for clearing away the clouds from thy mind, it will go and thou wilt go, and it will never return.

5. Every moment think steadily as a Roman and a man to do what thou hast in hand with perfect and simple dignity, and feeling of affection, and freedom, and justice; and to give thyself relief from all other thoughts. And thou wilt give thyself relief, if thou doest every act of thy life as if it were the last, laying aside all carelessness

and passionate aversion from the commands of reason, and all hypocrisy, and self-love, and discontent with the portion which has been given to thee. Thou seest how few the things are, the which if a man lays hold of, he is able to live a life which flows in quiet, and is like the existence of the gods; for the gods on their part will require nothing more from him who observes these things.

6. Do wrong to thyself, do wrong to thyself, my soul; but thou wilt no longer have the opportunity of honoring thyself. Every man's life is sufficient. But thine is nearly finished, though thy soul reverences not itself, but places thy felicity in the souls of others.

7. Do the things external which fall upon thee distract thee? Give thyself time to learn something new and good, and cease to be whirled around. But then thou must also avoid being carried about the other way. For those too are triflers who have wearied themselves in life by their activity, and yet have no object to which to direct every movement, and, in a word, all their thoughts.

8. Through not observing what is in the mind of another a man has seldom been seen to be unhappy; but those who do not observe the movements of their own minds must of necessity be unhappy.

9. This thou must always bear in mind, what is the nature of the whole, and what is my nature, and how this is related to that, and what kind of a part it is of what kind of a whole; and that there is no one who hinders thee from always doing and saying the things which are according to the nature of which thou art a part.

10. Theophrastus, in his comparison of bad acts—such a comparison as one would make in accordance with the common notions of mankind—says, like a true philosopher, that the offenses which are committed through desire are more blameable than those which are committed through anger. For he who is excited by anger seems to turn away from reason with a certain pain and unconscious contraction; but he who offends through desire, being overpowered by pleasure, seems to be in a manner more intemperate and more womanish in his offenses. Rightly then, and in a way worthy of philosophy, he said that the offense which is committed with pleasure is more blameable than that which is committed with pain; and on the whole the one is more like a person who has been first wronged and through pain is compelled to be angry; but the other is moved by his own impulse to do wrong, being carried toward doing something by desire.

11. Since it is possible that thou mayest depart from life this very moment, regulate every act and thought accordingly. But to go away from among men, if there are gods, is not a thing to be afraid of, for the gods will not involve thee in evil; but if indeed they do not exist, or if they have no concern about human affairs, what is it to me to live in a universe devoid of gods or devoid of providence? But in truth they do exist, and they do care for human things, and they have put all the means in man's power to enable him not to fall into real evils. And as to the rest, if there was anything evil, they would have provided for this also, that it should be altogether in a man's power not to fall into it. Now, that which does not make a man worse, how can it make a man's life worse? But neither through ignorance, nor having the knowledge, but not the power to guard against or correct these things, is it possible that the nature of the universe has overlooked them; nor is it possible that it has made so great a mistake, either through want of power or want of skill, that good and evil should happen indiscriminately to the good and the bad. But death certainly, and life, honor and dishonor, pain and pleasure, all these things equally happen to good men and bad, being things which make us neither better nor worse. Therefore they are neither good nor evil.

12. How quickly all these things disappear, in the universe the bodies themselves, but in time the remembrance of them; what is the nature of all sensible things, and particularly those which attract with the bait of pleasure or terrify by pain, or are noised abroad by vapory fame; how worthless, and contemptible, and sordid and perishable, and dead they are—all this it is the part of the intellectual faculty to observe. To observe too who these are whose opinions and voices give reputation; what death is, and the fact that, if a man looks at it in itself, and by the abstractive power of reflection resolves into their parts all the things which present themselves to the imagination in it, he will then consider it to be nothing else than an operation of nature; and if any one is afraid of an operation of nature he is a child. This, however, is not only an operation of nature, but it is also a thing which conduces to the purposes of nature. To observe, too, how man comes near to the deity, and by what part of him, and when this part of man is so disposed.

13. Nothing is more wretched than a man who traverses everything in a round, and pries into the things beneath the earth, as the

poet says, and seeks by conjecture what is in the minds of his neighbors, without perceiving that it is sufficient to attend to the demon within him, and to reverence it sincerely. And reverence of the demon consists in keeping it pure from passion and thoughtlessness, and dissatisfaction with what comes from gods and men. For the things from the gods merit veneration for their excellence; and the things from men should be dear to us by reason of kinship; and sometimes even, in a manner, they move our pity by reason of men's ignorance of good and bad; this defect being not less than that which deprives us of the power of distinguishing things that are white and black.

14. Though thou shouldest be going to live three thousand years, and as many times ten thousand years, still remember that no man loses any other life than this which he now lives, nor lives any other than this which he now loses. The longest and shortest are thus brought to the same. For the present is the same to all, though that which perishes is not the same; and so that which is lost appears to be a mere moment. For a man cannot lose either the past or the future: for what a man has not, how can any one take this from him? These two things then thou must bear in mind: the one, that all things from eternity are of like forms and come round in a circle, and that it makes no difference whether a man shall see the same things during a hundred years or two hundred, or an infinite time; and the second, that the longest liver and he who will die soonest lose just the same. For the present is the only thing of which a man can be deprived, if it is true that this is the only thing which he has, and that a man cannot lose a thing if he has it not.

15. Remember that all is opinion. For what was said by the Cynic Monimus is manifest: and manifest too is the use of what was said, if a man receives what may be got out of it as far as it is true.

16. The soul of man does violence to itself, first of all, when it becomes an abscess and, as it were, a tumor on the universe, so far as it can. For to be vexed at anything which happens is a separation of ourselves from nature, in some part of which the natures of all other things are contained. In the next place, the soul does violence to itself when it turns away from any man, or even moves toward him with the intention of injuring, such as are the souls of those who are angry. In the third place, the soul does violence to

itself when it is overpowered by pleasure or by pain. Fourthly, when it plays a part, and does or says anything insincerely and untruly. Fifthly, when it allows any act of its own and any movement to be without an aim, and does anything thoughtlessly and without considering what it is, it being right that even the smallest things be done with reference to an end; and the end of rational animals is to follow the reason and the law of the most ancient city and polity.

17. Of human life the time is a point, and the substance is in a flux, and the perception dull, and the composition of the whole body subject to putrefaction, and the soul a whirl, and fortune hard to divine, and fame a thing devoid of judgment. And, to say all in a word, everything which belongs to the body is a stream, and what belongs to the soul is a dream and vapor, and life is a warfare and a stranger's sojourn, and after-fame is oblivion. What, then, is that which is able to conduct a man? One thing, and only one— philosophy. But this consists in keeping the demon within a man free from violence and unharmed, superior to pains and pleasures, doing nothing without a purpose, nor yet falsely and with hypocrisy, not feeling the need of another man's doing or not doing anything; and besides, accepting all that happens, and all that is allotted, as coming from thence, wherever it is, from whence he himself came; and, finally, waiting for death with a cheerful mind, as being nothing else than a dissolution of the elements of which every living being is compounded. But if there is no harm to the elements themselves in each continually changing into another, why should a man have any apprehension about the change and dissolution of all the elements? For it is according to nature, and nothing is evil which is according to nature.

This in Carnuntum.[17]

VII. 11. To the rational animal the same act is according to nature and according to reason.

55. Do not look around thee to discover other men's ruling principles, but look straight to this, to what nature leads thee, both the universal nature through the things which happen to thee, and

[17] Carnuntum was a town of Pannonia, on the south side of the Danube, about thirty miles east of Vindobona (Vienna). Orosius (vii. 15) and Eutropius (viii. 13) say that Antoninus remained three years at Carnuntum during his war with the Marcomanni.

thy own nature through the acts which must be done by thee. But every being ought to do that which is according to its constitution; and all other things have been constituted for the sake of rational beings, just as among irrational things the inferior for the sake of the superior, but the rational for the sake of one another.

The prime principle then in man's constitution is the social. And the second is not to yield to the persuasions of the body, for it is the peculiar office of the rational and intelligent motion to circumscribe itself, and never to be overpowered, either by the motion of the senses or of the appetites, for both are animal; but the intelligent motion claims superiority and does not permit itself to be overpowered by the others. And with good reason, for it is formed by nature to use all of them. The third thing in the rational constitution is freedom from error and deception. Let then the ruling principle holding fast to these things go straight on, and it has what is its own.

VIII. 47. If thou art pained by any external thing, it is not this thing that disturbs thee, but thy own judgment about it. And it is in thy power to wipe out this judgment now. But if anything in thy own disposition gives thee pain, who hinders thee from correcting thy opinion? And even if thou art pained because thou art not doing some particular thing which seems to thee to be right, why dost thou not rather act than complain? But some insuperable obstacle is in the way? Do not be grieved then, for the cause of its not being done depends not on thee. But it is not worth while to live, if this cannot be done. Take thy departure then from life contentedly, just as he dies who is in full activity, and well pleased too with the things which are obstacles.

58. He who fears death either fears the loss of sensation or a different kind of sensation. But if thou shalt have no sensation, neither wilt thou feel any harm; and if thou shalt acquire another kind of sensation, thou wilt be a different kind of living being, and thou wilt not cease to live.

IX. 3. Do not despise death, but be well content with it, since this too is one of those things which nature wills. For such as it is to be young and to grow old, and to increase and to reach maturity, and to have teeth and beard and gray hairs, and to beget, and to be pregnant, and to bring forth, and all the other natural operations which the seasons of thy life bring, such also is dissolution. This, then, is consistent with the character of a reflecting man, to be neither careless nor impatient nor contemptuous with respect to death, but to wait for it as one of the operations of nature. As thou now waitest for the time when the child shall come out of thy wife's womb, so be ready for the time when thy soul shall fall out of this envelope. But if thou requirest also a vulgar kind of comfort which shall reach thy heart, thou wilt be made best reconciled to death by observing the objects from which thou art going to be removed, and the morals of those with whom thy soul will no longer be mingled. For it is no way right to be offended with man, but it is thy duty to care for them and to bear with them gently; and yet to remember that thy departure will be not from men who have the same principles as thyself. For this is the only thing, if there be any, which could draw us the contrary way and attach us to life, to be permitted to live with those who have the same principles as ourselves. But now thou seest how great is the trouble arising from the discordance of those who live together, so that thou mayest say, Come quick, O death, lest perchance I, too, should forget myself.

28. The periodic movements of the universe are the same, up and down from age to age. And either the universal intelligence puts itself in motion for every separate effect, and if this is so, be thou content with that which is the result of its activity; or it puts itself in motion once, and everything else comes by way of sequence in a manner; or indivisible elements are the origin of all things. In a word, if there is a god, all is well; and if chance rules, do not thou also be governed by it.

40. Either the gods have no power or they have power. If, then, they have no power, why dost thou pray to them? But if they have power, why dost thou not pray for them to give thee the faculty of not fearing any of the things which thou fearest, or of not desiring any of the things which thou desirest, or not being pained at any thing, rather than pray that any of these things should not happen or happen? for certainly if they can co-operate with men, they can co-operate for these purposes. But perhaps thou wilt say, the gods have placed them in thy power. Well, then, is it not better to use what is in thy power like a free man than to desire in a slavish and abject way what is not in thy power? And who has told thee that the gods do not aid us even in the things which are in our power?

Begin, then, to pray for such things and thou wilt see. One man prays thus: How shall I be able to lie with that woman? Do thou pray thus: How shall I not desire to lie with her? Another prays thus: How shall I be released from this? Another prays: How shall I not desire to be released? Another thus: How shall I not lose my little son? Thou thus: How shall I not be afraid to lose him? In fine, turn thy prayers this way, and see what comes.

XI. 19. There are four principal aberrations of the superior faculty against which thou shouldst be constantly on thy guard, and when thou hast detected them, thou shouldst wipe them out and say on each occasion thus: this thought is not necessary: this tends to destroy social union: this which thou art going to do comes not from the real thoughts; for thou shouldst consider it among the most absurd of things for a man not to speak from his real thoughts. But the fourth is when thou shalt reproach thyself for anything, for this is an evidence of the diviner part within thee being overpowered and yielding to the less honourable and to the perishable part, the body, and to its gross pleasures.

XII. 4. I have often wondered how it is that every man loves himself more than all the rest of men, but yet sets less value on his own opinion of himself than on the opinion of others. If then a god or a wise teacher should present himself to a man and bid him to think of nothing and design nothing which he would not express as soon as he conceived it, he could not endure it even for a single day. So much more respect have we to what our neighbors shall think of us than to what we shall think of ourselves.

5. How can it be that the gods, after having arranged all things well and benevolently for mankind, have overlooked this alone, that some men and very good men, and men who, as we may say, have had most communion with the divinity, and through pious acts and religious observances have been most intimate with the divinity, when they have once died should never exist again, but should be completely extinguished?

But if this is so, be assured that if it ought to have been otherwise, the gods would have done it. For if it were just, it would also be possible; and if it were according to nature, nature would have had it so. But because it is not so, if in fact it is not so, be thou convinced that it ought not to have been so; for thou seest even of thyself that in this inquiry thou art disputing with the deity; and we should not thus dispute with the gods, unless they were most excellent and most just, but if this is so, they would not have allowed anything in the ordering of the universe to be neglected unjustly and irrationally.

14. Either there is a fatal necessity and invincible order, or a kind providence, or a confusion without a purpose and without a director. If then there is an invincible necessity, why dost thou resist? But if there is a providence which allows itself to be propitiated, make thyself worthy of the help of the divinity. But if there is a confusion without a governor, be content that in such a tempest thou hast in thyself a certain ruling intelligence. And even if the tempest carry thee away, let it carry away the poor flesh, the poor breath, everything else; for the intelligence at least it will not carry away.

24. . . . . Thou must neither blame chance nor accuse providence. . . . .

26. When thou art troubled about anything, thou hast forgotten this, that all things happen according to the universal nature; and forgotten this, that a man's wrongful act is nothing to thee; and further thou hast forgotten this, that everything which happens, always happened so and will happen so, and now happens so everywhere; forgotten this, too, how close is the kinship between a man and the whole human race, for it is a community, not of a little blood or seed, but of intelligence. . . . .

CHAPTER VII

LUCRETIUS AND AESTHETIC NATURALISM

Lucretius (96[?]–55 B.C.) became the major voice to Rome, and for that matter to the world, of the atomistic physics which had culminated in Democritus and the hedonistic ethics which had culminated in Epicurus. These he blended and presented not as science but as art, not for pure knowledge but for satisfactory living. Living in and writing for a more or less religious period, Lucretius set out, on the negative side, to emancipate men from superstition. Here the atomistic physics served him well. But for death and the fear of what might come after death, religion could become positive and make a genuine contribution to life. The first task of the liberator, therefore, is to destroy the bases of fear and thus to undermine superstition. Atomism made it possible to deny immortality, since at death the atomic complexes that compose us are dissipated. Nothing bad can happen to us when we are no more. Since, then, there is nothing to fear, we may enjoy life while we have it. Moreover, the gods are not interested in us; they have more important concern than with our little and transient glows. We may, however, be interested in them. They set us a high and lasting example of how better to live out our brief span. The second task of the liberator is to show how to appropriate both the gods and the earth for positive ends. Let us live like the gods—detachedly, observantly, serenely. Science, thought Lucretius, can give us objects to appropriate and a method of using our minds which guarantees us a constant and gentle satisfaction. If pleasure is too much to expect from the world, absence of pain is sufficient to make life worth while. This we may will with a freedom that beginning with the separate atoms comes to full fruition in the power of man's mind to be its own master. "True piety," declares Lucretius, "is this: to look on all things with a master eye and mind at peace." A

246

theory of knowledge to fit these facts and a mantle of poetic beauty to make contemplation of them itself a gentle but great good— these are the final contributions of Lucretius to the art of life.

. . .

ON THE NATURE OF THINGS

Acknowledgments are made to the memory of John Mason Good, who in 1805 gave this metrical translation of Lucretius to the world. The analysis is taken, with acknowledgments to George Bell & Sons, London, from the John Selby Watson prose translation of the poem.

There are six books to the poem, of approximately the same length. We are able to publish here only one. We have chosen the first, as turning to poetic account the atomistic physics that has played so large a rôle in ancient (and modern) speculation.—T. V. S.

BOOK I

ARGUMENT

Lucretius invokes Venus as the great cause of production (vss. 1-44). He then dedicates his work to Memmius; praises Epicurus, whose doctrine he follows; vindicates his subject from the charge of impiety; exposes the emptiness of the religious system of his day, and the fictions of the poets; and introduces, not without allusion to the difficulties to be overcome, the great arguments of which he proposes to treat (vss. 45-159). Entering upon his subject, he shows, first, that nothing can proceed from nothing, and that nothing can return to nothing (vss. 160-265). Second, that there are certain minute corpuscles, which, though imperceptible to our senses, are conceivable in our minds, and from which all things originate (vss. 266-329). Third, that there is vacuum or empty space (vss. 330-430). Fourth, that there is nothing in the universe but body and space, and that all other things which are said to be are only adjuncts or events, properties or accidents of body and space (vss. 431-83). He then proceeds to demonstrate that the primary corpuscles, or elements of things, are perfectly solid, indivisible, and eternal (vss. 484-635). He refutes those who had held other opinions, as Heraclitus, who said that fire was the origin of things; and others, who had maintained the same of air, water, and earth (vss. 636-712). He attacks Empedocles, who said that the universe was compounded of the four elements, and Anaxagoras, who advocated the *homoeomeria* (vss. 713-919). He then contends that the universe is boundless, that atoms are infinite in number, and that space must be unlimited (vss. 920-1050). Last, he refutes those who think that there is a center of things, to which heavy bodies tend downward, and light bodies upward; and concludes with a praise of philosophy, which assists mankind to penetrate the mysteries of nature.

PARENT of ROME! by gods and men beloved,
Benignant VENUS! thou, the sail-clad main
And fruitful earth, as round the seasons roll,

With life who swellest, for by thee all live,
And, living, hail the cheerful light of day:—
Thee, goddess, at thy glad approach, the winds,
The tempests fly: dedalian Earth to thee
Pours forth her sweetest flow'rets: Ocean laughs,
And the blue heavens in cloudless splendour decked.
For, when the Spring first opes her frolic eye,
And genial zephyrs long locked up respire,
Thee, goddess, then, th' aerial birds confess,
To rapture stung through every shivering plume:
Thee, the wild herds; hence, o'er the joyous glebe
Bounding at large; or, with undaunted chest,
Stemming the torrent tides. Through all that lives
So, by thy charms, thy blandishments o'erpowered,
Springs the warm wish thy footsteps to pursue:
Till through the seas, the mountains, and the floods,
The verdant meads, and woodlands filled with song,
Spurred by desire each palpitating tribe
Hastes, at thy shrine, to plant the future race.
   Since, then, with universal sway thou rul'st,
And thou alone; nor aught without thee springs,
Aught gay or lovely; thee I woo to guide
Aright my flowing song, that aims to paint
To MEMMIUS' view the ESSENCES OF THINGS:
MEMMIUS, my friend, by thee, from earliest youth,
O goddess! led, and trained to every grace.
Then, O, vouchsafe thy favour, power divine!
And with immortal eloquence inspire.
Quell, too, the fury of the hostile world,
And lull to peace, that all the strain may hear.
For peace is thine: on thy soft bosom he,
The warlike field who sways, almighty MARS,
Struck by triumphant Love's eternal wound,
Reclines full frequent: with uplifted gaze
On thee he feeds his longing, lingering eyes,
And all his soul hangs quivering from thy lips.
O! while thine arms in fond embraces clasp
His panting members, sovereign of the heart!
Ope thy bland voice, and intercede for ROME.

For, while th' unsheathed sword is brandished, vain
And all unequal is the poet's song;
And vain th' attempt to claim his patron's ear.
  Son of the MEMMII! thou, benignant, too,
Freed from all cares, with vacant ear attend;
Nor turn, contemptuous, ere the truths I sing,
For thee first harmonized, are full perceived.
Lo! to thy view I spread the rise of things;
Unfold th' immortals, and their blest abodes:
How Nature all creates, sustains, matures,
And how, at length, dissolves; what forms the mass,
Termed by the learned, Matter, Seeds of Things,
And generative Atoms, or, at times,
Atoms primordial, as hence all proceeds.
  Far, far from mortals, and their vain concerns,
In peace perpetual dwell th' immortal gods:
Each self-dependent, and from human wants
Estranged for ever. There, nor pain pervades,
Nor danger threatens; every passion sleeps;
Vice no revenge, no rapture virtue prompts.
  Not thus mankind. Them long the tyrant power
Of SUPERSTITION swayed, uplifting proud
Her head to heaven, and with horrific limbs
Brooding o'er earth; till he, the man of Greece,
Auspicious rose, who first the combat dared,
And broke in twain the monster's iron rod.
No thunder him, no fell revenge pursued
Of heaven incensed, or deities in arms.
Urged rather, hence, with more determined soul,
To burst through Nature's portals, from the crowd
With jealous caution closed; the flaming walls
Of heaven to scale, and dart his dauntless eye,
Till the vast whole beneath him stood displayed.
Hence taught he us, triumphant, what might spring,
And what forbear: what powers inherent lurk,
And where their bounds and issues. And, hence, we,
Triumphant too, o'er SUPERSTITION rise,
Contemn her terrors, and unfold the heavens.

Nor deem the truths PHILOSOPHY reveals
Corrupt the mind, or prompt to impious deeds.
No: SUPERSTITION may, and nought so soon,
But Wisdom never. SUPERSTITION 'twas
Urged the fell GRECIAN chiefs, with virgin blood,
To stain the virgin altar. Barbarous deed!
And fatal to their laurels! AULIS saw,
For there DIANA reigns, th' unholy rite.
Around she looked; the pride of GRECIAN maids,
The lovely IPHIGENIA, round she looked,—
Her lavish tresses, spurning still the bond
Of sacred fillet, flaunting o'er her cheeks,—
And sought, in vain, protection. She surveyed
Near her, her sad, sad sire; th' officious priests
Repentant half, and hiding their keen steel,
And crowds of gazers weeping as they viewed.
Dumb with alarm, with supplicating knee,
And lifted eye, she sought compassion still;
Fruitless and unavailing: vain her youth,
Her innocence, and beauty; vain the boast
Of regal birth; and vain that first herself
Lisped the dear name of Father, eldest born.
Forced from her suppliant posture, straight she viewed
The altar full prepared: not there to blend
Connubial vows, and light the bridal torch;
But, at the moment when mature in charms,
While Hymen called aloud, to fall, e'en then,
A father's victim, and the price to pay
Of GRECIAN navies, favoured thus with gales.—
Such are the crimes that SUPERSTITION prompts!
    And dost thou still resist us? trusting still
The fearful tale by priests and poets told?—
I, too, could feign such fables; and combine
As true to fact, and of as potent spell,
To freeze thy blood, and harrow every nerve.—
Nor wrong th' attempt. Were mortal man assured
Eternal death would close this life of woe,
And nought remain of curse beyond the grave,
E'en then religion half its force would lose;

Vice no alarm, and virtue feel no hope.
But, whilst the converse frights him, man will dread
Eternal pain, and flee from impious deeds.
Yet doubtful is the doctrine, and unknown
Whether, co-eval with th' external frame,
The soul first lives, when lives the body first,
Or boasts a date anterior: whether doomed
To common ruin, and one common grave,
Or through the gloomy shades, the lakes, the caves,
Of EREBUS to wander: or, perchance,
As ENNIUS taught, immortal bard, whose brows
Unfading laurels bound, and still whose verse
All Rome recites, entranced—perchance condemned
The various tribes of brutes, with ray divine,
To animate and quicken: though the bard,
In deathless melody, has elsewhere sung
Of ACHERUSIAN temples, where, nor soul
Nor body dwells, but images of men,
Mysterious shaped; in wondrous measure wan.
Here HOMER's spectre roamed, of endless fame
Possest: his briny tears the bard surveyed,
And drank the dulcet precepts from his lips.
    Such are the various creeds of men. And hence
The philosophic sage is called t' explain,
Not the mere phases of the heavens alone,
The sun's bright path, the moon's perpetual change,
And powers of earth productive, but to point,
In terms appropriate, the dissevering lines
'Twixt mind and brutal life; and prove precise
Whence spring those shadowy forms, which, e'en in hours
Wakeful and calm, but chief when dreams molest,
Or dire disease, we see, or think we see,
Though the dank grave have long their bones inhumed.
    Yet not unknown to me how hard the task
Such deep obscurities of GREECE t' unfold
In LATIN numbers; to combine new terms,
And strive with all our poverty of tongue.—
But such thy virtue, and the friendship pure
My bosom bears, that arduous task I dare;

And yield the sleepless night, in hope to cull
Some happy phrase, some well-selected verse
Meet for the subject; to dispel each shade,
And bid the mystic doctrine hail the day.
For shades there are, and terrors of the soul,
The day can ne'er disperse, though blazing strong
With all the sun's bright javelins. These alone
To Nature yield, and Reason; and, combined,
This is the precept they for ever teach,
That NOUGHT FROM NOUGHT BY POWER DIVINE HAS RISEN.
But the blind fear, the superstition vain
Of mortals uninformed, when spring, perchance,
In heaven above, or earth's sublunar scene,
Events to them impervious, instant deem
Some power supernal present, and employed.—
Admit this truth, that NOUGHT FROM NOTHING SPRINGS,
And all is clear. Developed, then, we trace,
Through Nature's boundless realm, the rise of things,
Their modes, and powers innate; nor need from heaven
Some god's descent to rule each rising fact.
    Could things from nought proceed, then whence the use
Of generative atoms, binding strong
Kinds to their kinds perpetual? Man himself
Might spring from ocean; from promiscuous earth
The finny race, or feathery tribes of heaven:
Prone down the skies the bellowing herds might bound,
Or frisk from cloud to cloud: while flocks, and beasts
Fierce and most savage, undefined in birth,
The field or forest might alike display.
Each tree, inconstant to our hopes, would bend
With foreign fruit: and all things all things yield.
Whence but from elemental seeds that act
With truth, and power precise, can causes spring
Powerful and true themselves? But grant such seeds,
And all, as now, through Nature's wide domain,
In time predicted, and predicted place,
Must meet the day concordant; must assume
The form innately stampt, and prove alone
Why all from all things never can proceed.

Whence does the balmy rose possess the spring?
The yellow grain the summer? or, the vine
With purple clusters, cheer th' autumnal hours?
Whence, true to time, if such primordial seeds
Act not harmonious, can aught here surveyed,
Aught in its season, rear its tender form,
And the glad earth protrude it to the day?
But, if from nought things rise, then each alike,
In every spot, at every varying month,
Must spring discordant; void of primal seeds
To check all union till th' allotted hour.

Nor space for growth would then be needful: all
Springing from nought, and still from nought supplied.
The puny babe would start abrupt to man;
And trees umbrageous, crowned with fruit mature,
Burst, instant, from the greensward. But such facts
Each day opposes; and, opposing, proves
That all things gradual swell from seeds defined,
Of race and rank observant, and intent
T' evince th' appropriate matter whence they thrive.

But matter thus appropriate, or e'en space
For growth mature, form not the whole required.
The timely shower from heaven must add benign
Its influence too, ere yet the teeming earth
Emit her joyous produce; or, the ranks
Of man and reptile, thence alone sustained,
May spring to life, and propagate their kinds.
Say rather, then, in much that meets the view,
That various powers combine, concordant all,
Common and elemental, as in words
Such elemental letters,—than contend,
That void of genial atoms, aught exists.

Why formed not Nature man with ample powers
To fathom, with his feet, th' unbottomed main?
To root up mountains with his mighty hands?
Or live o'er lapsing ages victor still?
Why, but because primordial matter, fixt
And limited in act, to all is dealt
Of things created, whence their forms expand.

And hence again we learn, and prove express,
Nought springs from nought, and that, from seeds precise,
Whate'er is formed must meet th' ethereal day.

Mark how the cultured soil the soil excels
Uncultured, richer in autumnal fruits.
Here, too, the latent principle of things,
Freed by the plough, the fertile glebe that turns
And subjugates the sod, exert their power,
And swell the harvest: else, spontaneous, all
Would still ascend by labour unimproved.

And as from nought the genial seeds of things
Can never rise, so Nature that dissolves
Their varying forms, to nought can ne'er reduce.

Were things destructible throughout, then all
Abrupt would perish, passing from the sight;
Nor foreign force be wanting to disjoin
Their vital parts, or break th' essential bond.
But since, from seeds eternal all things rise,
Till force like this prevail, with sudden stroke
Crushing the living substance, or within
Deep entering each interstice, to dissolve
All active, Nature no destruction views.

Were time the total to destroy of all
By age decayed,—say whence could VENUS' self
The ranks renew of animated life?
Or, if renewed, whence earth's dedalian power
Draw the meet foods to nurture, and mature?
Whence springs and rivers, with perpetual course,
The deep supply? or, ether feed the stars?
Whate'er could perish, ever-during time,
And rolling ages, must have long destroy'd.
But if, through rolling ages, and the lapse
Of ever-during time, still firm at base,
Material things have stood, then must that base
Exist immortal, and the fates defy.

Thus, too, the same efficient force applied
Alike must all things rupture, if, within,
No substance dwelled eternal to maintain
In close, and closer, links their varying bonds.

E'en the least touch,—for every cause alike
Must break their textures, equal in effect,
If no imperishable power opposed,—
E'en touch were then irrevocable death.
But since, with varying strength, the seeds within
Adhere, of form precise, and prove express
Their origin eternal,—free from ill,
And undivided must those forms endure,
Till some superior force the compact cleave.
Thus things to nought dissolve not; but, subdued,
Alone return to elemental seeds.

When, on the bosom of maternal EARTH,
His showers redundant genial ETHER pours,
The dulcet drops seem lost: but harvests rise,
Jocund and lovely; and, with foliage fresh,
Smiles every tree, and bends beneath its fruit.
Hence man and beast are nourished; hence o'erflow
Our joyous streets with crowds of frolic youth;
And with fresh songs th' umbrageous groves resound.
Hence the herds fatten, and repose at ease,
O'er the gay meadows, their unwieldy forms;
While from each full-distended udder drops
The candid milk spontaneous; and hence, too,
With tottering footsteps, o'er the tender grass,
Gambol their wanton young, each little heart
Quivering beneath the genuine nectar quaffed.

So nought can perish, that the sight surveys,
With utter death; but Nature still renews
Each from the other, nor can form afresh
One substance, till another be destroyed.

But come, my friend, and, since the muse has sung
Things cannot spring from, or return to nought,
Lest thou should'st urge, still sceptic, that no eye
Their generative atoms e'er has traced;
Mark in what scenes thyself must own, perforce,
Still atoms dwell, though viewless still to sense.

And, first, th' excited wind torments the deep;
Wrecks the tough bark, and tears the shivering clouds:
Now, with wide whirlwind, prostrating alike

O'er the waste champaign, trees, and bending blade;
And now, perchance, with forest-rending force,
Rocking the mighty mountains on their base.
So vast its fury!—But that fury flows
Alone from viewless atoms, that, combined,
Thus form the fierce tornado, raging wild
O'er heaven, and earth, and ocean's dread domain.
As when a river, down its verdant banks
Soft-gliding, sudden from the mountains round
Swells with the rushing rain—the placid stream
All limit loses, and, with furious force,
In its resistless tide, bears down, at once,
Shrubs, shattered trees, and bridges, weak alike
Before the tumbling torrent: such its power!—
Loud roars the raging flood, and triumphs still,
O'er rocks, and mounds, and all that else contends.
So roars th' enraged wind: so, like a flood,
Where'er it aims, before its mighty tide,
Sweeps all created things: or round, and round,
In its vast vortex curls their tortured forms.—
Though viewless, then, the matter thus that acts,
Still there is matter: and, to Reason's ken,
Conspicuous as the visual texture traced
In the wild wave that emulates its strength.

   Next, what keen eye e'er followed, in their course,
The light-winged ODOURS? or developed clear
The mystic forms of cold, or heat intense?
Or sound through ether fleeting?—yet, though far
From human sight removed, by all confessed
Alike material; since alike the sense
They touch impulsive; and since nought can touch
But matter; or, in turn, be touched itself.

   Thus, too, the garment that along the shore,
Lashed by the main, imbibes the briny dew,
Dries in the sunbeam: but, alike unseen,
Falls the moist ether, or again flies off
Entire, abhorrent of the red-eyed noon.
So fine the attenuated spray that floats
In the pure breeze; so fugitive to sight.

A thousand proofs spring up. The ring that decks
The fair one's finger, by revolving years,
Wastes imperceptibly. The dropping shower
Scoops the rough rock. The plough's attempered share
Decays: and the thick pressure of the crowd,
Incessant passing, wears the stone-paved street.
E'en the gigantic forms of solid brass,
Placed at our portals, from the frequent touch
Of devotees and strangers, now display
The right hand lessened of its proper bulk.—
All lose, we view, by friction, their extent;
But, in what time, what particles they lose,
This envious Nature from our view conceals.

Thus, too, both Time and Nature give to things
A gradual growth: but never yet the sight
That gradual growth explored; nor marked their fall,
Still gradual too, by age, or sure decay:
Nor traced what portions of incumbent rock,
Loaded with brine, the caustic wave dissolves.—
So fine the particles that form the world.

Yet not corporeal is the whole produced
By Nature. In created things exists,
Search where thou wilt, an INCORPOREAL VOID.
This mark, and half philosophy is thine.
Doubtful no longer shalt thou wander: taught
Th' entire of things, and by our verse convinced.
And know this VOID is SPACE UNTOUCHED and PURE.

Were SPACE like this vouchsafed not, nought could move:
Corporeal forms would still resist, and strive
With forms corporeal, nor consent to yield;
While the great progress of creation ceased.
But what more clear in earth or heaven sublime,
Or the vast ocean, than, in various modes,
That various matter moves? which, but for SPACE,
'Twere vain t' expect: and vainer yet to look
For procreative power, educing still
Kinds from their kinds through all revolving time.

True, things are solid deemed: but know that those
Deemed so the most are rare and unconjoined.

From rocks, and caves, translucent lymph distils,
And, from the tough bark, drops the healing balm.
The genial meal, with mystic power, pervades
Each avenue of life; and the grove swells,
And yields its various fruit, sustained alone
From the pure food propelled through root and branch.
Sound pierces marble; through reclusest walls
The bosom-tale transmits: and the keen frost
E'en to the marrow winds its sinuous way.—
Destroy all vacuum, then, close every pore,
And, if thou canst, for such events account.
　　Say, why of equal bulk, in equal scale,
Are things oft found unequal in their poise?
O'er the light wool the grosser lead prevails
With giant force. But were th' amount alike
Of matter each contained, alike the weight
Would prove perpetual: for, from matter sole,
Flows weight, and moment, ever prone to earth:
While vacant space nor weight nor moment knows.
Where things surpoise, then, though of equal bulk,
There MATTER most resides: but where ascends
The beam sublime, the rising substance holds
A smaller share, and larger leaves the VOID.
　　Hence draws the sage his creed: in all produced
Finds vacuum still, and calls that vacuum SPACE.
　　But some there are such doctrines who deny:
And urge in proof, deceptive, that the wave
Not through imagined pores admits the race
With glitt'ring scales—but yields at once, and opes
The liquid path; and occupies, in turn,
The space behind the aureat fish deserts.
Thus, too, that all things act: the spot possessed
Exchanging sole, while each continues full.
Believe them not. If nought of space the wave
Give to its gilded tenants, how, resolve,
Feel they the power t' advance? and if t' advance
They know not, how can, next, the wave thus yield?—
Or matter ne'er can move, then, or within
Some VOID must mix through all its varying forms,

Whence springs alone the power of motion first.

When force mechanic severs, and, abrupt,
Drives two broad bodies distant, quick between
Flows the light air, and fills the vacuum formed.
But ne'er so rapid can the light air flow
As to forbid all void; since, step by step,
It still must rush till the whole space be closed.
Nor credit those who urge such bodies sole
Can part because the liquid air, compress'd
To closer texture, gives the needed space.
Such feeble reas'ners, in opposing VOID,
A double VOID confess: for, first, perforce,
A void they own, where void was none before,
Betwixt the substance severed; and bring next
A proof surmountless that the air itself
Thronged with a prior void: else how, to bounds
Of closer texture, could it e'er contract?

A thousand facts crowd round me: to the same
Converging all. But ample these, I ween,
Though but the footsteps of the mighty whole,
To fix thy faith, and guide thee to the rest.
For as the hound, when once the tainted dew
His nostrils taste, pursues the vagrant fox
O'er hills, and dales, and drags him from his lair;
So may'st thou trace from fact associate fact,
Through every maze, through every doubtful shade,
Till Truth's bright form, at length, thy labours crown.

Nor tardy be the toil, for much remains.
So oft, O MEMMIUS! from the sacred fount
By wisdom fed, so largely have I drank,
And such the dulcet doctrines yet untold,
That age may first unman us, and break down
The purple gates of life, ere the bold muse
Exhaust the boundless subject. Haste we, then,
Each pulse is precious, haste we to proceed.

Know, then, th' ENTIRE OF NATURE sole consists
Of SPACE and BODY: this the substance moved,
And that the area of its motive power.
That there is BODY, every sense we boast

Demonstrates strong: and, if we trust not sense,
Source of all science, then the mind itself,
Perplexed and hopeless, must still wander on
In reasoning lost, to every doubt a prey.
And were not SPACE, were vacuum not allow'd,
In nought could bodies, then, their powers display
Of various action: each compressing each
To motion fatal, as already sung.

Nor is there aught such vacant SPACE besides,
And MATTER close-embodied, can be traced
A substance forming discrepant from each.
Search where thou wilt, whate'er occurs to view,
Of bulk minute, or large, though e'en its form
Change with the hour, if tangible it prove,
This stamps it MATTER, and forbids all doubt.
But if intangible, throughout if still
To matter pervious, act where'er it may,
'Tis then void SPACE, and can be nought besides.

All things, moreo'er, a substance must evince
Acting, or suffering act; or, form the sphere
In which to act or suffer. But to act,
Or suffer action, must be MATTER's sole;
While SPACE alone that needed sphere admits.

Nought, then, 'twixt SPACE and MATTER can subsist
Of INTERMEDIATE SUBSTANCE: nought be traced
By keenest efforts of th' external sense,
Or by the meditating mind deduced.
All else we meet with or conceive but these
Are mere CONJUNCTIONS, or EVENTS attached.
And know the learned by CONJUNCTIONS name
Those powers in each perpetual that inhere,
And ne'er can part till VOID or MATTER cease.
Thus heat to fire, fluidity to streams,
Weight to the rock, to all of MATTER touch,
And want of touch to SPACE. While Discord, Peace,
Oppression, Freedom, Poverty, and Wealth,
And aught that else, of matter, and of space
Lives independent, though engendered hence,
Are termed, and justly, by the wise EVENTS.

E'en TIME, that measures all things, of itself
Exists not; from the mind alone produced,
As, link by link, contemplating minute,
Things present, past, or future: for, of TIME,
From these disjoined, in motion, or at rest
Tranquil and still, what mortal can conceive?

Thus spring EVENTS to birth. The rape renowned
Of beauteous HELEN, or the fall of TROY,
Though deemed existences, yet of themselves
Existed never: on material things,
On place and persons acting, or coerced,
Alone dependent. These revolving years
Have long th' irrevocable doom assigned:
And rape and conquest, as EVENTS that claimed
From these existence, now exist no more.—

Had ne'er been formed the matter, or the space,
Whose power conjunctive gave those scenes to be;
No fire had e'er, from lovely HELEN's eyes,
Glanced through the bosom of the TROJAN youth,
And kindled the fierce flames of storied war:
No giant horse the fell ACHAIAN throngs
Poured forth at night, subverting PRIAM's realm.
Mark, then, how different FACTS exist and blend
From VOID or MATTER; and how justly termed
Of place and body the derived EVENTS.

Know, too, that bodies, in their frame consist,
Part, of primordial atoms uncombined,
And part combined and blending: these alone
Pervious and rare; while those so solid formed
No force create can sever, or dissolve.

Nor deem such solids doubtful: though so deemed
By sages oft, who plausibly object
That sound, that thunder, that the voice itself
Breaks through domestic walls: that rigid steel
Admits the blaze, and whitens: vitreous rocks
Melt in the fierce volcano: gold and brass
Forego their icy hardness, and alike
Yield in the fiery conflict, and dissolve:
That e'en the silver chalice, fill'd with lymph

Fervid or cold, unlocks its secret pores,
And warms, at once, or chills th' embracing hand.
Hence deem they matter pervious all, and void
Of solid substance. But attend, benign,
And, since right reason, and the frame of things
Demand the verse, the muse shall briefly prove
The seeds, the principles of matter all
Both solid, and eternal, whence alone
Springs the stupendous fabric of the world.

Of SPACE, of MATTER, as already sung,
Th' ENTIRE of things consists, by nature formed
Distinct and adverse; and existing pure
Each uncontrolled of each. Where matter dwells
Void space can ne'er be found, nor matter found,
Search where thou wilt, where space resides and reigns.
As space is vacant then, material seeds
Must solid prove, perforce, and free from void.

Thus, too, as vacuum dwells in all produced,
Some solid substance must that vacuum bound:
Nor aught of vacuum can created things
Be proved to enclose, if solids not exist,
Whose power alone can such enclosures form.
But solids must be matter; the prime seeds
Of all surveyed, harmonious in their act,
And undecayed when all decays around.

Were there no space, th' ENTIRE OF THINGS would prove
One boundless solid: and were nought conceived
Of viewless seeds, close filling, void of space,
Each spot possest, all then were vacuum blank.
Thus each from each, from matter space exists
Distinct and clear: since never all is void,
Nor ever full; but this from that preserved
By countless atoms acting though unseen.
These, as already sung, no powers can pierce:
O'er blows external, o'er each vain attempt
Of penetrative solvents, or aught else
Philosophy reveals, triumphant still.
For nought can break, of vacuum all devoid,
Or melt, or moulder, or within admit

Vapour, or cold, or power of pungent heat,
By which dissolves this fabric of the world.
'Tis vacuum lays the base: as this exists,
Augments, or lessens, things alone decay.
What then is solid, and from vacuum free,
Must undecayed, and still eternal live.

Were matter not eternal, ages since
All had returned to nothing whence it sprang,
And from that nothing all again revived.
But since from nothing nought can ever rise,
As proved above, nor aught to nothing shrink,
Seeds there must be of ever-during date,
To which, perpetual, things dissolve, or whence
Flows the fresh pabulum that all repairs.
But seeds thus simple must be solid too;
Else unpreserved through countless ages past,
And useless to recruit th' exhausted world.

Else friction, too, had injured: each by each
Through myriad years abraded, and reduced,
Till nought conceptible had lived to rear,
Each in its time, the progenies of earth:
For all is wasted easier than renewed.
And hence, had all been thus disturbed, dissolved,
And frittered through the long anterior lapse
Of countless ages, future time in vain
Would strive the ruined fragments to repair.
But what more obvious than that bounds exist
To matter decompounding, primal seeds
To forms defined coercing; since again
All springs to birth, harmonious, kinds from kinds,
True to their times, and perfect in their powers?

Yet, though the principles of matter thus
Prove firm and solid, its component forms,
As air, earth, vapour, or translucent stream,
May still be soft and pliant, as combined,
E'en from their birth, with less, or larger void.
But had those principles themselves been reared
Pliant and soft, then whence the sturdy steel,
The close-compacted flint, or aught besides,

Of equal texture, traced through Nature's realm?
Thus simple solids must be still confest;
And all be soft, or rigid, as of these
In more or less concentrate mode composed.

   To all has Nature given a bound precise
Of being and perfection; and promulged,
To every varying rank, her varying laws;
Urging to this, from that restraining firm.
Nought suffers change: the feathery tribes of heaven
Bear, on their glossy plumes, through every class,
The same fixt hues that first those classes stamped.
Hence matter too, through all its primal seeds,
Is proved immutable: for if, o'ercome
By aught of foreign force, those seeds could change,
All would be doubtful; nor the mind conceive
What might exist, or what might never live:
Nor why, decide, such variance in their powers,
And final terms of life, or instinct strong,
Through every age, still urging every race
To each pursuit, each action of their sires.

   Know, too, each seed, each substance is composed
Of points extreme no sense can e'er detect:
Points that, perforce, minutest of themselves,
To parts can ne'er divide: nor self-educed,
Nor, but as formed, existing, else destroyed.
Parts such can hold not: each the first, pure part,
Itself, of other substance: which, when joined
Alone by kindred parts, in order due,
Forms, from such junction, the prime seeds of things.
But e'en such parts, though by the mind as parts
Conceived, disjoined can ne'er exist; and thence
Adhere by firm, indissoluble bond.

   Thus seeds are simple solids, formed compact
Of points extreme, that never can recede:
Not lab'ring jointly to produce some end,
But potent from simplicity alone,
And hence eternal: equally unprone
To waste or sever; and by nature kept
To feed the suffering fabric of the world.

Did no such points exist, extreme and least,
Each smallest atom would be, then, combined
Of parts all infinite; for every part
Parts still would boast, dividing without end.
And, say, what difference could there, then, subsist
Twixt large and small? for though th' ENTIRE OF THINGS
Should infinitely be deemed, each smallest speck
Still parts as infinite would hold embraced.
But since at this the reasoning mind revolts,
Then must it own, o'erpowered, that points exist
Least by their nature, and of parts devoid:
And solid, hence, and of eternal date.

Hence seeds arise, the last, least parts conceived
Of actual being: the extremest points
To which creative Nature all resolves.
Which, if not least, if still of parts possest,
Could ne'er, with close exactitude, renew
The universal frame: all, all would rise
Of weight diverse, and ever varying form,
Casual in tie, in motion undefined.

Yet should we grant that matter, without end,
For ever wastes; e'en then, from earliest time,
Some matter must have triumphed undecayed,
Cohering still: but what can thus cohere,
What brave the unnumbered repercussions felt
Through ages now evolved, can ne'er decay:
Alike the future conquering as the past.

Hence those who deem the fabric of the world
Educed from FIRE, itself the source of all,
Far wander from the truth. Thus deemed the sage,
Chief of his sect, and fearless in the fight,
Famed HERACLITUS; by the learn'd esteemed
Of doubtful phrase, mysterious; but revered
By crowds of GRECIANS, flimsy, and untaught.
For such th' obscure applaud; delighted most
With systems dark, and most believing true
The silver sounds that charm th' enchanted ear.
But whence, I ask, if all from FIRE proceed
Unmixed and simple, spring created things

So various in their natures? Urge not here
That fire condenses now, and now expands;
For if the same, divided or entire,
Its parts condensed a heat can only prove
More fierce; and less when rarefied, and thin.
Still all is FIRE. Nor canst thou e'er conceive
From fire that aught can spring but fire itself.
Much less, in fire made dense alone, or rare,
Trace the vast variance of created things.
Dense, too, and rare a vacuum must imply,
As urged already; yet full well convinced
What straits surround them if a void exist,
Such sages doubt, but, doubting, still deny:
Fearful of danger, yet averse from truth.
Such, too, reflect not that from things create,
Should void withdraw, the whole at once were dense,
One solid substance all, and unempowered
Aught from itself t' eject, as light, and smoke
Flies from the purple flame; evincing clear
Its parts unsolid, and commixt with void.
But should it still, perchance, be urged, that fires
Perish by junction, and their substance change,
Then must that changing substance waste to nought;
And thus from nought th' ENTIRE of nature spring.
For what once changes, by the change alone
Subverts immediate its anterior life.
But still, victorious, something must exist,
Or all to nought would perish; and, in turn,
From nought regerminate to growth mature.
    Yet though, most certain, things there are exist
That never change, the seeds of all surveyed,
Whose presence, absence, or arrangement new
That ALL new-models, certain 'tis, alike,
Those seeds can ne'er be FIRE. For what avails
Such absence, presence, or arrangement new
Of igneous matter, if the whole throughout
Alike be igneous? Change howe'er it may,
Through every variance all must still be flame.—
Ask'st thou whence fire proceeds then? As I deem,

From certain seeds to certain motions urged,
Or forms, or combinations; which, when changed,
Change too their nature; and, though yielding fire,
Not fire resembling, or aught else perceived
By human sense, or tangible to touch.

To hold, moreo'er, as HERACLITUS held,
That all is fire, and nought besides exists
Through Nature's boundless fabric, is to rave.
T' oppose the mental sense, erroneous oft,
To sense external, whence all knowledge flows,
And whence himself first traced that flame exists.
To sense he trusts, when sense discloses fire,
And yet distrusts in things disclosed as clear.
Can there, in man, be conduct more absurd!—
Where shall we turn us? Where, if thus we fly
Those senses chief that sever true from false?—

Why, rather, too, should all that else exists
Be thus denied, and fire alone maintained,
Than fire denied, and all maintained besides?
Tenets alike preposterous and wild.
Hence those, in FIRE, who trace the rise of things,
And nought but FIRE; for those for AIR who strive
As source of all; or those the dimpling STREAM
Who fondly fancy; or the ponderous EARTH,
For each has armed its champions in its turn,
Alike wide wander from unerring truth.

Nor wanders less the sage who AIR with FIRE
Would fain commix, or limpid STREAM with EARTH;
Or those the whole who join, FIRE, ETHER, EARTH,
And pregnant SHOWERS, and thence the world deduce.
Thus sung EMPEDOCLES, in honest fame
First of his sect; whom AGRIGENTUM bore
In cloud-capt SICILY. Its sinuous shores
Th' IONIAN main, with hoarse, unwearied weave,
Surrounds, and sprinkles with its briny dew:
And, from the fair ÆOLIAN fields, divides
With narrow frith that spurns the impetuous surge.
Here vast CHARYBDIS raves: here ÆTNA rears
His infant thunders, his dread jaws unlocks,

And heaven and earth with fiery ruin threats.
Here many a wonder, many a scene sublime,
As on he journeys, checks the traveller's steps;
And shows, at once, a land in harvests rich,
And rich in sages of illustrious fame.
But nought so wonderous, so illustrious nought,
So fair, so pure, so lovely, can it boast,
EMPEDOCLES, as thou! whose song divine,
By all rehearsed, so clears each mystic lore,
That scarce mankind believed thee born of man.
Yet e'en EMPEDOCLES, and those above,
Already sung, of far inferior fame,
Though doctrines frequent from their bosoms flowed
Like inspiration, sager and more true
Than e'er the PYTHIAN maid, with laurels crowned,
Spoke from the .ripod at APOLLO's shrine;
E'en these mistook the principles of things,
And greatly wandered in attempt so great.
And, first, they deemed that motion might exist
From VOID exempt: that things might still be rare,
Still soften, as earth, ether, fire, or fruits,
Or e'en the ranks of animated life,
Though VOID commixed not with their varying frames.
Then, too, they held no final term ordained
To comminuting atoms: which, through time,
Still crumbled on, and never could be least.
Though from such points as sense itself surveys,
Extreme and least, conjecture we may form
Of points extreme, impalpable to sight,
Least in themselves, that never can divide.
   With them, moreo'er, the seeds of things were formed
Soft, and unsolid: but whate'er is soft,
Whate'er unsolid, as at first they spring
From other substance, must perforce decay.
So all to nought would perish, and again
From nought regerminate to growth mature:
Doctrines the muse already has disproved.
Such seeds, too, must be foes; created each
To each adverse; and hence can never meet

But sure perdition waits: or, chance, they part,
Disperst abrupt, as, in contending storms,
Wind, rain, and thunder scatter, and are lost.
　But, from such four-fold foes, could all things spring,
And, sprung, to such dissolve—why rather term
Those jarring powers the primal seeds of things,
Than things of them? since, in alternate course,
Each flows from each: th' alternate form is seized,
Th' alternate nature, through perennial time.
Yet could'st thou deem such powers adverse might blend,
And earth with fire, with ether lymph commix,
And still retain their natures unimpaired;
Whilst thus retained, no living form could rise
Traced through creation, animate, or void,
As springs the verdant shrub, of reasoning soul.
For each its nature, through the varying mass,
Would still evince, and earth with air commix,
In ceaseless strife,—and fire with crystal lymph.
But primal seeds, whene'er the form of things
Mutual they gender, must, perforce, assume
An unobtrusive nature, close concealed,
Lest aught superior rise, of power adverse,
And thus th' harmonious union be destroyed.
　Such sages, too, from heaven, and heaven's bright fires
Maintain that all proceeds: that fire drawn hence
Converts to ether, ether into showers,
And showers benign to earth: and hence again,
That all from earth returns: first liquid dew,
Then air, and heat conclusive; changing thus,
In ceaseless revolution, changing thus
From heaven to earth, from earth to heaven sublime:
A change primordial seeds could ne'er sustain.
So something still must, void of change, exist;
Or all would perish, all to nought return;
For what once changes, by the change alone
Subverts immediate its anterior life.
Since, then, as sung above, these all commute
Each into each, some seeds must still be owned
That ne'er can change, or all to nought would waste.

Hold rather, then, such seeds exist, endowed
With powers so curious that, as now combined,
If fire they form, combine them but anew,
Add, or deduct, give motion, or subtract,
And all is air; and changing thus, and changed,
That things from things perpetual take their rise.
  Nor urge, still sceptic, that each hour displays
All life protruded from the genial EARTH:
Fed by the balmy AIR; by heaven's OWN FIRE
Matured; and saved from pestilence and death
Alone by SHOWERS benignant: and that hence
Man, beast, and herbs alike exist, and thrive.
The fact we own: we own from solid food,
And crystal streams, man draws his daily breath,
Of nerve, of bone, of being else deprived:
But, owning, add, the compounds meet for man,
For brute, for herbage, differ in their kinds,
By different tastes discerned: and differ thus,
And only thus, as formed from various seeds,
To all things common, but in various modes
Combined, and fitted to each rising want.
Nor small of import are the modes diverse
In which those seeds approach, recede, or blend:
Since heaven, and earth, and suns, and seas immense,
Herbs, instinct, reason, all are hence derived:
The mode but changed, the matter still the same.
Thus, though the lines, these doctrines that recite,
Flow from the same fixt elemental types,
Yet line from line, in sense, in sound compared,
Egregious differs. Re-arranged alone,
Such the vast power by graphic types possest!
Start not when told, then, that the seeds of things
Boast powers superior, and can all create.
  From such mistakes, detected and exposed,
Now turn we: and in order next survey
Those doctrines first the GRECIAN schools imbibed
From sapient ANAXAGORAS, by them
Termed HOMŒOMERY; a phrase ourselves,
In tongue deficient, never can translate.

But these its institutes: that bone from bones,
Minute, and embryon, nerve from nerves arise,
And blood from blood, by countless drops increased.
Gold, too, from golden atoms, earths concrete
From earths extreme; from fiery matters fire,
And lymph from limpid dew. And thus throughout
From primal kinds that kinds perpetual spring.
Yet VOID he granted not in aught create,
Nor POINTS EXTREME that never can divide.
In both erroneous, and with those deceived
Classed in our numbers, and opposed above.

   Too feeble, too, the rudiments he chose,
If rudiments they be, that hold, at once,
The powers of things, and form the things themselves.
All toil alike, and perish void of aid:
For, when the hour of dissolution draws,
Say, which can baffle the dread fangs of death?
Can ether, lymph, or fire? can nerve, or bones?
In each the strife were vain: since all produced,
Surveyed, or viewless, impotent alike,
Must yield to fate, and perish unredeemed.
But things produced to nought can never fall,
Or fallen, regerminate, as proved above.

   Food rears the body, and its growth sustains:
But well we know its tendons, nerves, and blood,
Hence all matured, are foreign and unlike.
If, then, each food be compound, if commixt
With miniatures of all, of blood and nerve,
Of bone and veins; each food compact, or moist,
Of parts unlike must then itself consist;
Of bone, of blood, of tendon, vein, and nerve.
Thus all things spring from earth: but if in earth
All lurk enveloped, earth of forms consists
Strange, and discordant, panting for the day.
Change still the picture, and the same still flows:
In timbers, thus, if smoke, flame, ashes blend,
Then, too, those timbers hostile parts comprise.

   But, here, the ready answer, framed of yore,
By him, the founder of the system, springs:

That, though in all things all things lurk commixt,
What most prevails, what boasts the largest share,
Lies superficial, and is noticed chief.
Fruitless remark, unsolid, and untrue.
For still, at times, when crushed to dust minute
Beneath the pond'rous mill-stone's mighty orb
The crumbling corn with human blood must weep,
Or aught besides of fluid found in man,
And stain with hues obscene: and still, at times,
Each herb unfold the balmy milk so sweet,
That swells the fleecy flock, or odorous kine.
The furrowed glebe, the labouring plough beneath,
Must, too, develope, in its secret womb,
Plants, fruits, and foliage, oft dispersed, and hid:
And, to the woodman, the cleft stock disclose
With ashes smoke, and smoke commixt with fire.
These, facts deny: in things things ne'er exist;
But seeds of things, in various modes arranged,
Various themselves: whence rises all surveyed.

But should'st thou urge that oft beneath the storm,
When rubbed by many a repercussion rude,
Branch against branch, the forest's topmost height
Has blazed from tree to tree; the fact we grant:
Not, with each trunk, that native fires combine;
But that perpetual friction quick collects
Their seeds dispersed; hence gathering ten-fold force,
And flame engendering. For could fire itself
A part constituent of the forest form,
No hour could hide the mischief; every tree
Would blaze, and burn till boundless ruin reigned.

See, then, as earlier sung, how much imports
Th' arrangement, motion, magnitude, and form
Of primal seeds combined: and how the same,
Transposed but little, fuel quick convert
To flame, bright blazing up the swarthy flue:
As FLUE and FUEL, terms of different sound,
Of different sense, their letters but transposed,
Each into each converts with magic speed.

But should'st thou urge that all things still may flow
From primal seeds, and yet those seeds possess
The form, the nature of the things themselves;
The scheme falls self-destroyed.—For then, must seeds
Hold powers adverse; and laugh, and shake their sides,
While tears of anguish down their cheeks distil.
    Come, now, and mark perspicuous what remains.
Obscure the subject: but the thirst of fame
Burns all my bosom; and through every nerve
Darts the proud love of letters, and the muse.
I feel th' inspiring power; and roam resolved
Through paths PIERIAN never trod before.
Sweet are the springing founts with nectar new;
Sweet the new flowers that bloom: but sweeter still
Those flowers to pluck, and weave a roseate wreath,
The muses yet to mortals ne'er have deigned.
With joy the subject I pursue; and free
The captived mind from Superstition's yoke.
With joy th' obscure illume; in liquid verse,
Graceful, and clear, depicting all surveyed:
By reason guided. For as oft, benign,
The sapient nurse, when anxious to enforce
On the pale boy, the wormwood's bitter draught,
With luscious honey tints the goblet's edge,
Deceiving thus, while yet unused to guile,
His unsuspecting lip; till deep he drinks,
And gathers vigour from the venial cheat:
So I, since dull the subject, and the world
Abashed recoils, would fain, in honeyed phrase,
Tuned by the muses, to thine ear recite
Its vast concerns; if haply I may hope
To fix thine audience, while the flowing verse
Unfolds the nature, and the forms of things.
    Taught then, already that material seeds
Are solid, and o'er time triumphant live,
Attend, benignant, while we next decide
Their number, or if infinite; and tell,
Since VOID throughout exists, assigning space

For place and motion, if th' ENTIRE of things
Be bounded, or unfathomed, and immense.
    Th' ENTIRE of things, then, bounds can never know:
Else parts possest of farthest and extreme.
But parts can only be extreme, beyond
Where other substance springs, those parts extreme
Binding, though sense the limit ne'er can trace.
If, then, some other substance rise, the first
Forms not th' ENTIRE of things. Whate'er it be
That other substance still must part compose.
Vain too is distance: the vast whole alike
To all extends, embracing, and embraced.
    Yet grant th' ENTIRE of things of bound possest.
Say, to what point shall yon keen archer, placed
E'en on its utmost verge, his dart direct?
Shall aught obstruct it, or the path be clear?
Take which thou wilt: some substance choose, possest
Of power t' impede, and check its rapid race:
Or let it fly unconquered, nor restraint
E'en once encounter: thou must still confess
Th' ENTIRE of nature nought of limit knows.
Throughout the dart I'll chase; and when, at length,
Th' acceded bound is gained, I'll still demand
What yet obstructs it; still new proofs adduce
That the vast whole is boundless; and that flight
Still beyond flight for ever might be urged.
    Were, too, th' ENTIRE of nature thus confined,
Thus circumscribed precise, from its own weight
Long since, all matter to the extremest depth
Had sunk supine: nor aught the skies beneath,
Nor skies themselves, with countless stars adorned
And sun's unsuffering splendour, had remained.
Down, down th' accumulated mass had fallen
From earliest time, devoid of power to rise.
But nought of rest supine material seeds
Evince through nature; since no depth exists
Extreme, and fathomable where those seeds
Might fix collected in inert repose.

All, all is action: the vast whole alike
Moves in each part; and, from material seeds,
Draws, undiminished, its eternal food.
  Things, to the sense, are circumscribed by things.
Air bounds the hills, and hills the liquid air:
Earth ocean, ocean earth: but the vast whole
What fancied scene can bound? O'er its broad realm,
Immeasured, and immeasurably spread,
From age to age resplendent lightnings urge,
In vain their flight perpetual; distant, still,
And ever distant from the verge of things.
So vast the space on opening space that swells,
Through every part so infinite alike.
  Ask thy own reason. It will prove at once
Th' ENTIRE of nature never can have bounds.
VOID must perforce bound MATTER, MATTER VOID;
Thus mutual, one illimitable whole
Forming for ever. For were each of each
Free and unshackled, uncombined, and pure
In their own essence, not one short-lived hour
Could earth, or ocean, the refulgent fane
Of heaven sublime, or mortal forms, or those
The gods themselves inhabit, then subsist.
Freed from all order, disarranged, and rude,
Through boundless vacuum the drear mass of things
Would quick be borne: or, rather, nought had risen
From the crude chaos, joyless, and inert.
For never, doubtless, from result of thought,
Or mutual compact, could primordial seeds
First harmonize, or move with powers precise.
But ever changing, ever changed, and vext,
From earliest time, through ever-during space,
With ceaseless repercussion, every mode
Of motion, magnitude, and shape essayed;
At length th' unwieldy mass the form assumed
Of things created. Persevering, thus,
Through many an age, unnumbered springs the deep
Fed with perpetual tides: by the warm sun

Sustained, and cherished, earth renews her fruits,
And man, and beast survive; and ether glows
With living lights innum'rous: scenes throughout
'Twere vain t' expect, from all eternal time,
Had no primordial seeds, in stores immense,
Been ever nigh to renovate the world.
For as, of food deprived, the languid frame
Of man must perish, so th' ENTIRE OF THINGS
Must instant cease, should once primordial seeds
Their aid withhold, or deviate in their course.
Nor deem from mutual impulse, things with things
Can sole their forms preserve; th' eternal seeds
May, hence, be oft restrained, and e'en perchance,
Their flight delayed, till, from th' exhaustless store,
Fresh seeds arrive the fainting frame to feed:
But from concussion, frequent, they rebound,
Dissolve all tie, and leave to transient rest
The common matter whence each substance springs.
Hence must incalculable seeds exist
Ceaseless in act; and the vast whole derive
Alone from boundless matter impulse due.

    But fly, O MEMMIUS, fly the sect deceived,
Who teach that things, with gravitation firm,
To the vast centre of th' ENTIRE, alike,
Unerring press: the world who fain would prove
Void of external impulse, may subsist,
And nought its post desert, profound, or high,
Since of such gravitating power possest.
For canst thou deem that aught may thus sustain,
And poise itself? that aught of solid weight,
Placed at earth's utmost depth, could upwards strive
Reversed; and to the surface—(in the stream
As spreads the downwards shadow)—still adhere?
For thus such sages hold: thus man, and beast
Subsist, they teach, inverted, earth beneath:
From their firm station, down their deeper skies
As unexposed to fall, as towards the heavens
Ourselves to mount sublime: by them the sun,
When night to us unfolds his stars, surveyed;

And equal measuring, in alternate course,
With us, their months, their darkness, and their day.
Such are the specious fancies error feigns,
In idle hour, to minds perverse and vain.
Where all is infinite, what spot precise
Can e'er be central? or were centre owned,
Why towards such spot should matter rather end,
Than elsewhere more remote, and deeper still?
For vacant space, through every part alike,
Central or not, must yield to things compact,
And pond'rous, as their varying weight compels;
Nor through the boundless VOID one point exists
Where things may rest, as if of weight deprived.
No power it boasts t' uphold; but still recedes,
As Nature prompts, and opes the needed path.
Hence, by the love alone of centre struck,
Th' harmonious frame of things could ne'er be formed.
   Moreo'er such sages urge not that the whole
Strives towards the centre equal; but terrene
Alone, and fluid matters; the deep main,
The mountain cataract, and the forms produced
From earth Dedalian: while the breezy air,
And the light flame, far from such centre stray,
Through ether trembling, and, with lambent fire,
Feeding, through time, the sun's refulgent blaze;
As feeds maternal earth the myriad forms
Of herbs, and trees, and animated life,
From her own bosom nurtured, and sustained.
Thus, too, they teach that heaven, with bound sublime,
Encircles all things, lest the world's wide walls,
And all enveloped, volatile as flame,
Burst every bond, and dissipate, and die:
Lest heaven in thunders perish, and below
The baseless earth forsake us, downward urged:
And loose, and lifeless, man's dissev'ring frame,
Mixt with the rushing wreck of earth, and skies,
Waste through all space profound; till nought remain,
Nought, in a moment, of all now surveyed,
But one blank VOID, one mass of seeds inert.

For once to act, when primal atoms fail,
Fail where they may, the doors of death are ope,
And the vast whole unbounded ruin whelms.

These subjects if, with trivial toil, thou scan,
Each, each illuming, midnight shall no more
Thy path obstruct; but Nature's utmost depths
Shine as the day: so things irradiate things.

CHAPTER VIII
NEO-PLATONISM: PLOTINUS

It has already become clear that in the Platonic-Aristotelian metaphysics there is a residue persistently recalcitrant to the idealistic type of explanation. Plato was partial to honorific ideas and so tended to leave neutral and dishonorific entities hanging loose from complete reality by having nothing for them to "participate in" for full-bodied being. Aristotle had pure matter left over as a conceptual limit—a limit that tended to become substantialized in proportion as he culminated his metaphysics in a pure form. This residue was obdurate and only proper motivation was needed to make it the source of evil. The loss of nerve that attended the twilight of Greek civic pride and communal responsibility furnished the needed motivation. We have already seen in Stoicism, Epicureanism, and Skepticism types of practical adjustment to these altered facts. But all of these inclined to ground themselves in pre-Platonic metaphysics. It remained only for the same impetus, made somewhat more poignant by religious admixtures, to be derived from the classic philosophers. This neo-Platonism did. Plotinus (ca. 204–70) first at Alexandria, where the Greek and oriental worlds met and mingled, and later at Rome, became the leading figure. Starting with the completely super-rational, he sought to explain all else by an overflow, as it were, from this and to evaluate it by means of its relative distance from the pure form, God. Matter is farthest away, and so becomes the source of evil. But it is not wholly evil, since it derived from God, as the emphasized theodicy made clear. Nevertheless, it is the part of wisdom to treat with contempt the body and whatever else partakes of matter and to climb again the steps back to the source of Being. Philosophy is a way of salvation from a world relatively evil to a realm absolutely good. Mysticism comes into its own in the final stages of the soul's climb—"the flight of the alone to the alone."

*Porphyry (232–301) wove the Aristotelian categories into
this Platonic tradition, and the Christian Boethius of Rome
(ca. 480–525) translated and interpreted works of Aristotle
and wrote at last from prison his celebrated work, "On the Con-
solations of Philosophy."*

. . .

PLOTINUS

These selections are from the translation by Thomas Taylor, arranged under
subheadings provided by the editor. Porphyry, the student of Plotinus, grouped
the master's work into six divisions, called *enneads* because each of the six books was
divided into nine chapters (the word *ennead* means "nine").—T. V. S.

THE ONE IN RELATION TO THE MANY[1]

V. . . . . *The Good* is not at all in want of intellectual perception.
For there is not any thing else beside itself which is the good of it;
since when that also which is different from *the good* intellectually
perceives it, it does this in consequence of being boniform, and possessing a similitude to *the good*. It likewise intellectually perceives
that which it sees, as good and desirable to itself; and in consequence of receiving as it were the imagination of good. And if it
is always thus affected, it is always this [i.e. it is always boniform].
For again, in the intellection of itself, it accidentally perceives *the
good*. For looking to *the good*, it intellectually sees it, and also sees
itself energizing. But the energy of all things is directed to *the good*.

VI. If, therefore, these things are rightly asserted, intelligence
will have no place whatever in *the good*. For the good which is
present with an intellective nature is different from *the good itself*.
Hence *the good* is unenergetic. For why is it necessary that energy
should energize? For in short, no energy whatever has again
energy. But if to other energies which are directed to another thing,
we attribute something else, it is however necessary, that the first
energy from which other energies are suspended, should be that
very thing which it is, and that nothing else should be added to it.
An energy, therefore, of this kind is not intellectual perception.
For it does not possess that which it intellectually perceives; since
it is the first energy. In the next place, neither does intelligence

[1] *Ennead* V. vi.

intellectually perceive, but that which possesses intelligence. Again, therefore, two things take place in that which perceives intellectually. But that which is first is by no means two. Farther still, the truth of this may be seen in a still greater degree by him who considers how this twofold nature subsists in every thing which is more clearly intellective. For we say, indeed, that beings as beings, that each thing itself [by itself,] and truly existing beings, are in the intelligible place; and this not merely because some things abide invariably the same in essence, but others, and these are such as are in the sensible region, continually flow and are not permanent. For perhaps there are some things in sensibles of a permanent nature. But we assert this of intelligibles, because they possess the perfection of existence. For it is necessary that the essence which is primarily so called, should not be the shadow of existence, but should have the fulness of being. Existence, however, is then full, when it receives the form of intellectual perception, and of life. Hence, in [real] being, to perceive intellectually, to live, and to exist, are consubsistent. If, therefore, it is being, it is also intellect, and if it is intellect it is being. And intellectual perception is simultaneous with existence. Hence, to perceive intellectually is many things, and not one thing. It is necessary, therefore, that with the nature which is not a thing of this kind, there should not be intellectual perception. Hence, among the several forms contained in true beings, there are man, and the intellectual perception of man; horse, and the intellectual perception of horse; the just, and the intellection of the just. Hence too, all things there are double, and the one is two. And again, two passes into one. But that which is the first of things is not either of these; nor does it consist of all the things which are two; nor is it, in short, two. It has been, however, elsewhere shown by us, how two derives its subsistence from *the one*. But since *the one* is beyond essence, it is also beyond intellectual perception. There will be no absurdity, therefore, in asserting that *the one* does not know itself. For being one it does not possess with itself that which it may learn. But neither is it necessary that it should know other things. For it imparts to them something better and greater than the knowledge of them; and this is the good of other things. But it rather imparts to them the ability, as much as possible, of coming into contact with it in the same thing.

THE ONE IN ITSELF[2]

III. What then will *the one* be; and what nature will it possess? Or may we not say that it is not at all wonderful, it should not be easy to tell what it is, since neither is it easy to tell what being is, or what form is. But our knowledge is fixed in forms. When, however, the soul directs its attention to that which is formless, then being unable to comprehend that which is not bounded, and as it were impressed with forms by a former of a various nature, it falls from the apprehension of it, and is afraid it will possess [nothing from the view]. Hence, it becomes weary in endeavours of this kind, and gladly descends from the survey frequently falling from all things, till it arrives at something sensible, and as it were rests in a solid substance; just as the sight also, when wearied with the perception of small objects, eagerly converts itself to such as are large. When, however, the soul wishes to perceive by itself, and sees itself alone, then in consequence of being one with the object of its perception, it does not think that it yet possesses that which it investigates, because it is not different from that which it investigates, because it is not different from that which it intellectually perceives. At the same time, it is requisite that he should act in this manner, who intends to philosophize about *the one*. Since, therefore, that which we investigate is one, and we direct our attention to the principle of all things, to *the good*, and the first, we ought not to be far removed from the natures which are about the first of things, nor fall from them to the last of all things, but proceeding to such as are first, we should elevate ourselves from sensibles which have an ultimate subsistence. The soul, likewise, should for this purpose be liberated from all vice, in consequence of hastening to *the* [vision of the] *good;* and should ascend to the principle which is in herself, and become one instead of many things, in order that she may survey the principle of all things, and *the one*. Hence it is requisite, that the soul of him who ascends to *the good* should then become intellect, and that he should commit his soul to, and establish it in intellect, in order, that what intellect sees, his soul may vigilantly receive, and may through intellect survey *the one;* not employing any one of the senses, nor receiving any thing from them, but with a pure intellect, and with the summit [and as it were,

---

[2] *Ennead* VI. ix.

flower] of intellect, beholding that which is most pure. When, therefore, he who applies himself to the survey of a thing of this kind,
imagines that there is either magnitude, or figure, or bulk about
this nature, he has not intellect for the leader of the vision; because
intellect is not naturally adapted to perceive things of this kind,
but such an energy is the energy of sense, and of opinion following
sense. But in order to perceive *the one*, it is necessary to receive
from intellect a declaration of what intellect is able to accomplish.
Intellect, however, is able to see either things prior to itself, or
things pertaining to itself, or things effected by itself. And the
things indeed contained in itself, are pure; but those prior to itself
are still purer and more simple; or rather this must be asserted of
that which is prior to it. Hence, that which is prior to it, is not
intellect, but something more excellent. For intellect is a *certain*
one among the number of being; but that is not a *certain* one, but
is prior to every thing. Nor is it being for being has, as it were, the
form of *the one*. But that is formless, and is even without intelligible form. For the nature of *the one* being generative of all things,
is not any one of them. Neither, therefore, is it a certain thing,
nor a quality, nor a quantity, nor intellect, nor soul, nor that which
is moved nor again that which stands still. Nor is it in place, or in
time; but is by itself uniform, or rather without form, being prior
to all form, to motion and to permanency. For these subsist about
being which also cause it to be multitudinous. Why, however, if it is
not moved, does it not stand still? Because it is necessary that one
or both of these should subsist about being. And that which stands
still, stands still through permanency, and is not the same with it.
Hence permanency is accidental to it, and it no longer remains
simple. For when we say that the one is the cause of all things, we
do not predicate anything as an accident to it, but rather as something which happens to us, because we possess something from it,
the one in the meantime subsisting in itself. It is necessary, however,
when speaking accurately of *the one*, neither to call it *that*, nor *this*.

EMANATION OF INTELLECT AND SOUL FROM THE ONE[3]

VI. How does intelligence see; what does it see; and, in short,
how does it subsist; and how is it generated from *the one*, so that it
may see? For now indeed the soul perceives the necessity of the

[3] *Ennead* V. i.

existence of these things. It desires, however, to understand this which is so much spoken of by the wise men of antiquity, viz. how from *the one* being such as we have said it is, each thing has its subsistence, whether it be multitude, or the duad, or number; and why *the one* did not abide in itself, but so great a multitude flowed from it, as is seen to have an existence, and which we think should be referred to *the one*. We must say, therefore, as follows, *invoking God himself, not with external speech, but with the soul itself, extending ourselves in prayer to him, since we shall then be able to pray to him properly, when we approach by ourselves alone to the alone.* It is necessary, therefore, that the beholder of him, being in himself as if in the interior part of a temple, and quietly abiding in an eminence beyond all things, should survey the statues as it were which are established outwardly, or rather that statue which first shines forth to the view, and after the following manner behold that which is naturally adapted to be beheld. With respect to everything that is moved, it is necessary there should be something to which it is moved. For if there is nothing of this kind, we should not admit that it is moved. But if any thing is generated posterior to that which the moveable nature tends, it is necessary that it should always be generated in consequence of that prior cause being converted to itself. Let, however, the generation which is in time be now removed from us who are discoursing about eternal beings. And if in the course of the discussion we attribute generation to things which exist eternally, let it be considered as indicative of cause and order. Hence, that which is from thence generated, must be said to be generated, the cause not being moved. For if something was generated in consequence of that cause being moved, the thing generated after the motion would be the third, and not the second from the cause. It is necessary, therefore, the cause being immoveable, that if any thing secondary subsists after it, this second nature should be produced, without the cause either verging to it, or consulting, or in short being moved. How, therefore, and what is it necessary to conceive about that abiding cause? We must conceive a surrounding splendour, proceeding indeed from this cause, but from it in a permanent state, like a light from the sun shining, and as it were running round it, and being generated from it, the cause itself always abiding in the same immoveable condition. All beings, likewise, as long as they remain, necessarily pro-

duce from their own essence, about themselves, and externally from
the power which is present with them, a nature whose hypostasis is
suspended from them, and which is as it were an image of the archetype from which it proceeded. Thus fire emits from itself indeed
heat, and snow not only retains cold within itself [but imparts it to
other things]. This, however, such things as are fragrant especially
testify. For as long as they exist, something proceeds from them, of
which whatever is near them partakes. All such things, likewise, as
are now perfect generate; but that which is always perfect, always
generates, and that which it produces is perpetual. It also generates
something less than itself. What, therefore, is it requisite to say of
that which is most perfect? Shall we say that nothing proceeds from
it; or rather that the greatest things posterior to it are its progeny?
But the greatest thing posterior to it, and the second, is intellect.
For intellect sees it, and is in want of it alone. But this most perfect nature is not in want of intellect. It is also necessary that the
thing generated from that which is better than intellect, should be
intellect. And intellect is superior to all things after the first, because other things are posterior to it. Thus for instance, soul is the
reason of intellect, and a certain energy of it, just as intellect of that
first God [who is beyond intellect]. But the reason of soul is indeed
obscure. For as it is the image of intellect, on this account it is
necessary that it should look to intellect. After the same manner
also, it is necessary that intellect should look to the highest God,
in order that it may be intellect. It sees him, however, not separated from him, but because it is after him, and there is nothing between; as neither is there any thing between soul and intellect. But
every thing desires its generator. This also it loves, and especially
when that which is generated and the generator are alone. When,
however, that which generates is the most excellent of things, the
thing begotten is necessarily present with it in such a manner, as
to be separated by *otherness* alone.

VII. But we say that intellect is the image of this most excellent nature. For it is necessary to speak more clearly. In the first
place, indeed, it is necessary that intellect should in a certain respect be generated, and preserve [in itself] much of its generator;
and also that it should have such a similitude to it, as light has to
the sun. Its generator, however, is not intellect. How therefore did
he generate intellect [so far as it is intellect]? May we not say, be-

cause intellect, by conversion, looks to him? But the vision itself
is intellect. For that which apprehends another thing, is either
sense or intellect. And sense indeed may be compared to a line,
but the other gnostic powers of the soul to a circle. A circle, however, of this kind is as it were partible. But this is not the case with
intellect. Or may we not say that this also is one? But the one
here is the power of all things. Hence intelligence surveys those
things of which it is the power, divided as it were from the power;
for otherwise it would not be intellect. For intellect now possesess
from itself a co-sensation as it were of the great extent of its power;
in which power, its essence, consists. Intellect, therefore, through
itself defines its own being, by a power derived from him [i.e. from
the first God,] and perceives that essence is as it were one of the
parts of and from him, and that it is corroborated by him, and perfected by and from him into essence. It sees, however, itself derived from thence, as something which is as it were partible from
that which is impartible; and not only itself, but life, and intellection, and all things, because the first God is nothing of all things.
For on this account all things are from him, because he is not de-
tained by a certain form. For he is one alone. And intellect, indeed, in the order of beings is all things. But he on this account is
none of the things which are in intellect; and all things which have a
subsistence among beings are derived from him. Hence also these
are essences. For they are now definite, and each possesses as it
were a form. Being, however, ought not to be surveyed in that
which is as it were indefinite, but as fixed by bound and permanency. But permanency in intelligibles is circumscription and form,
in which also they receive their hypostasis. This intellect, therefore, which deserves the appellation of the most pure intellect, and
which is of the genus of intelligibles, originates from no other source
than the first principle. And being now generated, it generates together with itself beings, all the beauty of ideas, and all the intelligible Gods. . . .

VIII. On this account all things are distributed by Plato in a
triple order about the king of all. For he says, "that all things are
about the king of all;" second things about that which is second,
and such as are third about that which ranks as the third. He also
says that this king is father of cause, denominating intellect cause.
For with Plato, intellect is the demiurgus. But he says that this

cause produced soul in that *Crater* [mentioned by him in the *Timaeus*]. The cause, however, being intellect, he says that the father is *the good*, and that which is beyond intellect, and beyond essence. In many places, also, he calls being and intellect idea; so that from Plato we may know that intellect and idea are from *the good*, but soul from intellect. . . . .

X. It has been shown, however, as far as it is possible to demonstrate about things of this kind, that it is requisite to think that beyond being there is *the one*, such as reason wishes to unfold; that next to this, being and intellect subsist; and that, in the third place, follows the nature of soul. . . . .

PRESENCE AND NATURE OF MATTER[4]

XV. . . . . Matter must be said to be of itself infinite, although having an arrangement opposite to reason. For as reason not being any thing else is reason, thus also it must be said, that matter being opposed to reason according to infinity, is infinite in such a way as not to be any thing else.

XVI. Is, therefore, matter the same with difference, or is it not the same? Perhaps it is not the same with difference simply considered, but with a part of difference which is opposed to beings properly so called, and which are productive principles. Hence, also, non-being is thus a certain being, and the same with privation, if privation is an opposition to the things which subsist in reason. Will, therefore, privation be corrupted by the accession of that of which it is the privation? By no means. For the receptacle of habit, is not habit, but privation. The receptacle, likewise, of bound, is not that which is terminated, nor bound, but the infinite, and this so far as it is infinite. How is it possible, therefore, that bound approaching should not destroy the nature of the infinite, especially since this infinite has not an accidental subsistence? Or may we not say that if this infinite was infinite in quantity, it would perish? Now, however, this is not the case, but on the contrary its being is preserved by bound. For bound brings that which the infinite is naturally adapted to be, into energy and perfection; just as that which is not yet sown [is brought to perfection] when it is sown, and as the female [when impregnated] by the male. For then the female nature is not destroyed, but possesses the female

[4] *Ennead* II. iv.

characteristic in a greater degree; since then it becomes more eminently that which it is. Is, therefore, matter evil when it partakes of good? Or shall we say it is evil on this account because it was in want of good? For it did not possess it. For that which is in want of any thing, and obtains what it wants, will perhaps become a medium between good and evil, if it is equally disposed towards both. But that which possesses nothing, as being in poverty, or rather being poverty itself, is necessarily evil. For this is not the want of wealth or of strength, but it is the want of wisdom, and the want of virtue, of beauty, strength, morphe, form, and quality. How, therefore, is it possible it should not be deformed? How is it possible it should not be perfectly base? How is it possible it should not be perfectly evil? The matter, however, which is in intelligibles is [real] being. For that which is prior to it is beyond being. But here [in the sensible region,] that which is prior to matter is being. Hence the matter which is here is not being, since it is different from it when compared with the beauty of being.

PURIFICATION THROUGH VIRTUE AND OTHERWISE[5]

I. Since evils are here, and revolve from necessity about this [terrestrial] place, but the soul wishes to fly from evils, it is requisite to fly from hence. What therefore is the flight? To become similar, says Plato, to God. But this will be effected, if we become just and holy, in conjunction with [intellectual] prudence, and in short if we are [truly] virtuous. If therefore we are assimilated through virtue, is it to one who possesses virtue? But to whom are we assimilated? To divinity. . . . . Divinity has virtues, though not such as the political. . . . .

III. Since, however, Plato indicates that this similitude to God pertains to a greater virtue [than that which is political], let us speak concerning it; in which discussion also, the essence of political virtue will become more manifest, and likewise the virtue which is essentially more excellent, which will in short be found to be different from that which is political. Plato, therefore, when he says that a similitude to God is a flight from terrestrial concerns, and when besides this he does not admit that the virtues belonging to a polity are *simply* virtues, but adds to them the epithet political, and elsewhere calls all the virtues purifications,

[5] *Ennead* II. ii.

evidently admits that the virtues are twofold, and that a similitude
to divinity is not effected according to political virtue. How, therefore, do we call these purifications? And being purified, are we especially assimilated to divinity? Shall we say, that since the soul is
in an evil condition when mingled with the body, becoming similarly passive and concurring in opinion with it in all things, it will be
good and possess virtue, if it neither consents with the body, but
energizes alone, (and this is to perceive intellectually and to be
wise,) nor is similarly passive with it, (and this is to be temperate,)
nor dreads a separation from the body, (and this is to possess fortitude,) but reason and intellect are the leaders (and this will be
justice). If any one, however, calls this disposition of the soul, according to which it perceives intellectually, and is thus impassive,
a resemblance of God, he will not err. For divinity is pure, and the
energy is of such a kind, that the being which imitates it will possess
wisdom. . . . .

V. We must, however, show how far purification proceeds. For
thus it will be evident to whom the similitude is made, and with
what God the soul becomes the same. But this is especially to
enquire how far it is possible to be purified from anger and desire,
and all the other perturbations, such as pain, and things of a kindred nature, and to separate the soul from the body. And perhaps,
indeed, to separate the soul from the body, is for the soul to collect
itself as it were, from different places, so as to become entirely impassive, and to make the necessary sensations of pleasures to be
only remedies and liberations from pain, in order that the soul may
not be disturbed [in its energies]. It likewise consists in taking
away pain, and if this is not possible, in bearing it mildly, and
diminishing its power, in consequence of [the rational part] not being co-passive with it. And besides this also, in taking away anger
to the utmost of our ability, and if possible, entirely; but if not, the
rational part must not at the same time be angry, but the anger
must be the passion of another part, and unaccompanied with deliberation. And this sudden impulse must be small and imbecile.
Fear, however, must be entirely removed; for the purified soul will
fear nothing. Here, also, the energy must be unattended with deliberation, except it be requisite to admonish. With respect to desire, it is evident that there must not be a desire of anything base.
And as to the desire of meats and drinks for the sake of a remission

of pain, the soul herself will be without it. This likewise will be the case with the venereal appetite. But if the soul is desirous of connection, it will be I think in the natural way, and this not unattended with deliberation. If, however, it should be an unadvised impulse, it will only be so far as it is accompanied with a precipitate imagination. But, in short, the [rational] soul herself will be purified from all these. She will also wish to render the irrational part pure, so that it may not be agitated. And if it is, that the agitation may not be vehement, but small, and immediately dissolved by proximity to the rational part. Just as if some one being near to a wise man, should partake of his wisdom by this proximity, or should become similar to him, or through reverence should not dare to do any thing which the good man is unwilling to do. Hence, there will be no contest. For reason being present will be sufficient, which the inferior part will reverence, so as even to be itself indignant, if it is at all moved, in consequence of not being quiet when its master is present; and it will on this account blame its own imbecility.

UP THE PILGRIM PATH—TO THE END[6]

IX. . . . . *He however who knows this, will know what I say,* and will be convinced that the soul has then another life. The soul also proceeding to, and having now arrived at the desired end, and participating of deity, will know that the supplier of true life is then present. She will likewise then require nothing farther; for on the contrary, it will be requisite to lay aside other things, to stop in this alone, and to become this alone, amputating every thing else with which she is surrounded. Hence, it is necessary to hasten our departure from hence, and to be indignant that we are bound in one part of our nature, in order that with the whole of our [true] selves, we may fold ourselves about divinity, and have no part void of contact with him. When this takes place therefore, the soul will both see divinity and herself, as far as it is lawful for her to see him. And she will see herself indeed illuminated, and full of intelligible light; or rather, she will perceive herself to be a pure light, unburthened, agile, and becoming to be a God, or rather being a God, and then shining forth as such to the view. But if she again becomes heavy, she then as it were wastes away.

[6] *Ennead* VI. ix.

X. How does it happen, therefore, that the soul does not abide there? Is it not because she has not yet wholly migrated from hence? But she will then, when her vision of deity possesses an uninterrupted continuity, and she is no longer impeded or disturbed in her intuition by the body. That however which sees divinity, is not the thing which is disturbed, but something else; when that which perceives him is at rest from the vision. But it is not then at rest according to a scientific energy, which consists in demonstrations, in credibilities, and a discursive process of the soul. For here vision, and that which sees, are no longer reason, but greater than and prior to reason. And in reason, indeed, they are as that is which is perceived. He therefore who sees himself, will then, when he sees, behold himself to be such a thing as this, or rather he will be present with himself thus disposed, and becoming simple, will perceive himself to be a thing of this kind. Perhaps, however, neither must it be said that he sees, but that he is the thing seen; if it is necessary to call these two things, i.e. the perceiver and the thing perceived. But both are one; though it is bold to assert this. Then, indeed, the soul neither sees, nor distinguishes by seeing, nor imagines that there are two things; but becomes as it were another thing, and not itself. Nor does that which pertains to itself contribute any thing there. But becoming wholly absorbed in deity, she is one, conjoining as it were centre with centre. For here concurring, they are one; but they are then two when they are separate. For thus also we now denominate that which is another. Hence this spectacle is a thing difficult to explain by words. For how can any one narrate that as something different from himself, which when he sees he does not behold as different, but as one with himself?

XI. This, therefore, is manifested by the mandate of the mysteries, which orders that they shall not be divulged to those who are uninitiated. For as that which is divine cannot be unfolded to the multitude, this mandate forbids the attempt to elucidate it to any one but him who is fortunately able to perceive it. Since, therefore [in this conjunction with deity] there were not two things, but the perceiver was one with the thing perceived, as not being [properly speaking] vision but union; whoever becomes one by mingling with deity, and afterwards recollects this union, will have with himself an image of it. But he was also himself one, having with respect to himself no difference, nor with respect to other things. For then

there was not any thing excited with him who had ascended
thither; neither anger, nor the desire of any thing else, nor reason,
nor a certain intellectual perception, nor, in short, was even he himself moved, if it be requisite also to assert this; but being as it were
in an ecstasy, or energizing enthusiastically, he became established
in quiet and solitary union, not at all deviating from his own essence, nor revolving about himself, but being entirely stable, and
becoming as it were stability itself. Neither was he then excited by
any thing beautiful; but running above the beautiful, he passed beyond even the choir of the virtues. Just as if some one having
entered into the interior of the adytum should leave behind all the
statues in the temple, which on his departure from the adytum
will first present themselves to his view, after the inward spectacle,
and the association that was there, which was not with a statue or
an image, but with the thing itself [which the images represent], and
which necessarily become the second objects of his perception. Perhaps, however, this was not a spectacle, but there was another mode
of vision, viz. ecstasy, and an expansion and accession of himself, a
desire of contact, rest, and a striving after conjunction, in order to
behold what the adytum contains. But nothing will be present with
him who beholds in any other way. The wise prophets, therefore,
obscurely signified by these imitations how this [highest] God is
seen. But the wise priest understanding the enigma, and having
entered into the adytum, obtains a true vision of what is there. If,
however, he has not entered, he will conceive this adytum to be a
certain invisible thing, and will have a *knowledge* of the fountain and
principle, as the principle of things. But when situated there, he
will *see* the principle, and will be conjoined with it, by a union of like
with like, neglecting nothing divine which the soul is able to possess.
Prior to the vision also it requires that which remains from the
vision. But that which remains to him who passes beyond all
things, is that which is prior to all things. For the nature of the
soul will never accede to that which is entirely non-being. But proceeding indeed downwards it will fall into evil; and thus into non-
being, yet not into that which is perfect nonentity. Running, however, in a contrary direction, it will arrive not at another thing, but
at itself. And thus not being in another thing, it is not on that account in nothing, but is in itself. *To be in itself alone, however, and
not in being, is to be in God.* For God also is something which is not

essence, but beyond essence. Hence the soul when in this condition associates with him. He, therefore, who perceives himself to associate with God, will have himself the similitude of him. And if he passes from himself as an image to the archetype, he will then have the end of his progression. But when he falls from the vision of God, if he again excites the virtue which is in himself, and perceives himself to be perfectly adorned; he will again be elevated through virtue, proceeding to intellect and wisdom, and afterwards to the principle of all things. *This, therefore, is the life of the Gods, and of divine and happy men, a liberation from all terrene concerns, a life unaccompanied with human pleasures, and a flight of the alone to the alone.*